Tails from the Classroom

Learning and teaching through animal-assisted interventions

Helen Lewis and Russell Grigg

Crown House Publishing Limited
www.crownhouse.co.uk

First published by

Crown House Publishing Limited
Crown Buildings, Bancyfelin, Carmarthen, Wales, SA33 5ND, UK
www.crownhouse.co.uk

and

Crown House Publishing Company LLC
PO Box 2223, Williston, VT 05495, USA
www.crownhousepublishing.com

Cover image © Ermolaev Alexandr - stock.adobe.com. Page 16, Figure 1.1: image available from https://www.gutenberg.org/files/43286/43286-h/43286-h.htm. Page 16, Figure 1.2: image available from http://www.thebookofdays.com/months/jan/17.htm. Page 18, Figure 1.3: image available from https://en.wikisource.org/wiki/Goody_Two-Shoes_(1888). Page 18, Figure 1.4: image available from https://en.wikisource.org/wiki/Black_Beauty#/media/File:Black_Beauty_(1877),_page_6.jpg. Page 19, Figure 1.5: image available from https://www.tate.org.uk/whats-on/tate-britain/exhibition/hogarth/hogarth-hogarths-modern-moral-series/hogarth-hogarths-4. Page 21, Figure 1.6: image from G. A. N. Lowndes (1937), The Silent Social Revolution, 1st edn. Oxford: Oxford University Press. Page 21, Figure 1.7: image from G. A. N. Lowndes (1937). Page 22, Figure 1.8: image from G. A. N. Lowndes (1937). Page 25, Figure 1.9 © Everett/Shutterstock. Page 44, Figure 2.2: photograph by Gillian Ball. Page 51: Figure 3.1 © Stanley Coren (2013), from 'Which emotions do dogs actually experience?' Available at: https://www.psychologytoday.com/gb/blog/canine-corner/201303/which-emotions-do-dogs-actually-experience from the blog series at: https://www.psychologytoday.com/ca/blog/canine-corner, used with permission. Page 60: extract from J. C. Muldoon, J. M. Williams and A. B. Lawrence (2016), 'Exploring children's perspectives on the welfare needs of pet animals', Anthrozoös, 29(3): 357-375. Page 61, Figure 3.2 © Paylessimages - stock.adobe.com. Page 69, book image © Avector - stock.adobe.com. Page 71, Figure 4.2: photograph by Hilary Warren and used with permission of Burns By Your Side. Page 76, Figure 4.3: photograph by Kim Jameson and used with permission of Burns By Your Side. Page 82, Figure 4.4: extract from an ethnographer and children's comics by Donna Carlyle. Page 96, Figure 5.1: photograph by Grace Vobe and used with permission of Burns By Your Side. Page 97, Figure 5.2: photograph by Alistair Corbett and used with permission of Burns By Your Side. Page 106, Figure 6.1: photograph by Yamni Nigam, Swansea University. Page 116, Figure 6.3: worksheet © Egypt Centre, Swansea University. Pages 117-118, Table 6.2 © Egypt Centre, Swansea University. Page 135, Figure 7.2: photograph by Laura Braun. Page 138, Figure 7.3: photograph by Sharon Smith. Page 182, Figure 9.3: photograph by Vanessa Thomas. Pages 184-185, Figure 9.4 © The Bishop of Llandaff High School. Page 189, Figure 9.5 © The Kennel Club Limited. Reproduced with their permission. Page 193, Figure 9.8: photograph © Africa Studio - stock.adobe.com. Pages 203-205, Appendix 1 © Grace Thomas. Pages 206-211, Appendix 2 © Burns By Your Side.

British Library Cataloguing-in-Publication Data

A catalogue entry for this book is available from the British Library.

Print ISBN 978-178583505-6
Mobi ISBN 978-178583515-5
ePub ISBN 978-178583516-2
ePDF ISBN 978-178583517-9

LCCN 2021942210

Printed and bound in the UK by
TJ Books, Padstow, Cornwall

For Grace and Sofie, Alice, Thomas, Ava and Ruby, the young people in my life. And to the many furry and feathered companions who over the years have helped to make my house a home – HL

To Tom Webb and Colin, who loved their animals – RG

Acknowledgements

We would like to say thank you to the following people and pets for their contributions to this book:

Ava, Ruby and Sarah Clements

Beverley Gardner, CEO, Trinitas Academy Trust, Kent

Brad and Mel Rundle, founders and directors of Therapy Animals Australia

Caitlin Jones and Nora the dog

Carol Lincoln

Dr Diahann Gallard, Liverpool John Moores University

Donna Carlyle and Ted the dog

Gillian Ball, Sarah Cornish, Natalie Carroll, Kelly Sevenoaks, Otis the dog, and pupils at Christ Church (Erith) Church of England Primary School, Kent

Grace Vobe and Hoola the dog

Hannah Sweetapple and the team at the Egypt Centre, Swansea University

Hayley Anthony, Jonesy the dog, and staff and pupils at Ysgol Bryn Teg, Llanelli

Dr Janet Goodall, associate professor at Swansea University School of Education (and her panda)

Jerri and Joe Kropp and the much-missed Wrigley the dog

Jo Bowers, associate dean at Cardiff Metropolitan University

Joanna Thomas, Georgie the dog, and staff and pupils at Bishop of Llandaff School, Cardiff

John Burns, Abbi Steanson, Natasha Rudge, Katie Gardener and the team, volunteers and dogs at Burns By Your Side, Kidwelly, including Carole and her dog Sally and Emma and her dog Beau

John-Tyler Binfet, associate professor at University of British Columbia, Canada

Jude Penny, University of Gloucestershire

Judith Stephenson, Ollie the dog, and staff and pupils at Barbara Priestman Academy, Sunderland

Julie Carson and the staff, pupils and dogs at Woodlands Academy Trust, Bexley and North Kent

June and Mac Allen and the much-missed Honey the dog

Kim Jameson, Willow, Robyn and the much-missed Toby the dog

Laura Braun and Year 5 and 6 pupils at Bury Church of England Primary, West Sussex

Lindsey Watkins and the staff and pupils at Millbrook Primary School, Newport, Gwent

Michael Kaufman and Miyako Kinosita, Green Chimneys, United States

Mike Gough, Claire Whatley, Huw Waythe, Peter Pudding the rabbit, and pupils at Deighton Primary School, Tredegar

Nick Oswald, executive head teacher at Great Ouseburn Community Primary School and Nun Monkton Foundation Primary School, and the late Hedgie hedgehog

Odette Nicholas, Jade the dog, Daisy and Chip the geese, and staff and pupils at Burry Port Community Primary School, Llanelli

Sarah Ellis

Thereza Rees, the much-missed Takoda the dog, and staff and pupils at Glyncollen Primary School, Swansea

Wendy Davies and staff and pupils at Ffrindiau Bach Tegryn nursery, Aberporth

Professor Yamni Nigam and the 'Love a Maggot' team at Swansea University

Thanks also to the team at Crown House Publishing – David Bowman, Beverley Randell, Rosalie Williams, Tom Fitton and particularly Emma Tuck for her meticulous eye for detail.

Contents

List of figures, tables and boxes

Figures

Tables

Boxes

Introduction

Clearly, animals know more than we think, and think a great deal more than we know. (Pepperberg, 2013: 214)

One of the Internet sensations of recent years is the remarkable story of Tyler and Beaker in Texas. The story began when 9-month-old Tyler spotted a little duckling called Beaker in the local pet store. Tyler's father bought Beaker there and then. And over the last four or so years the remarkable intimacy between Tyler and Beaker has been recorded in photographs and videos.[1] When Tyler cries, Beaker quacks and runs over to him. Tyler's first reported word was 'duck'.

One of the things that most children around the world have in common is their love of animals. Studies show that even when presented with attractive toys to play with, given the choice, young children opt to interact with live animals. Remarkably, Lobue et al. (2013) found that toddlers aged 18–36 months even prefer to interact with potentially harmful animals, such as a black tarantula and a California mountain kingsnake, rather than their favourite toys. For research purposes, these particular creatures were placed in a cage; the outcomes may have been very different if the children had encountered them in the backyard. Psychologists suggest that most children love animals for a combination of reasons. They are attracted by their appearance, noise, movement, visibility and unpredictability, but they also see animals as 'good listeners' and comforters. More fundamentally, humans are biologically disposed to care for others, especially those in a vulnerable state. Children naturally stretch out to touch, fondle, cuddle or play with kittens and puppies that are only a few weeks old.

Animals certainly play a prominent part in children's lives. Around one in two homes in the UK has a pet.[2] In another survey covering 4,300 children in the UK, 42% were reported to have more fun playing with their pets than their siblings or friends (Pets at Home, 2015). As soon as children open their eyes, they see

---

1 See https://youtu.be/5VcxRepz7TY.
2 See https://www.pdsa.org.uk/get-involved/our-campaigns/pdsa-animal-wellbeing-report/uk-pet-populations-of-dogs-cats-and-rabbits.

animal mobiles, toys, pictures, motifs and objects, and they soon hear animal-related fables, stories, songs and rhymes. On average, around a third of a baby's earliest vocabulary is animal words or sounds. Interestingly, one study of 900 English- and Chinese-speaking children found that even though babies in the United States were unlikely to have ducks living in their immediate families, as compared with children in Beijing, 'ducks' still featured in their top twenty words (Tardif et al., 2008).

Of course, there are animals who instil fear and anxiety among humans. More than one in three children (and adults) are reported to strongly dislike spiders and snakes (Muris et al., 1997). Some researchers suggest that over time humans have inherited a hardwired fear of such animals (New and German, 2014). In one recent study, children aged 4 were shown images of spiders and snakes on white backgrounds for five seconds. The children sat on their parents' laps, but to prevent parents from seeing the images and inadvertently influencing their children's reactions they were given opaque sunglasses. When the children saw pictures of the snakes and spiders, their pupils consistently dilated more than when they were shown control images of flowers and fish. The dilation of pupils is widely accepted as a sign of stress. It is difficult to overcome the irrational fear of certain creatures. In the children's book *I'm Trying to Love Spiders* (Barton, 2015), an arachnophobe tries to overcome her fear. In so doing, she learns about spiders' impressive web-spinning talents and their habit of consuming insects that are harmful to humans. Education clearly has a key role in helping children to manage their animal phobias.

The western attitude towards animals largely stems from the notion that, as 'inferior creatures', they are subservient to humans. After all, humans could tame animals and therefore were superior to them. Historically, legal and religious systems have permitted humans to use animals to meet their needs, even when this might result in the animal's pain and suffering. Sadly, there is a very long, dark history of the way humans have treated animals, even among those professing to be a nation of animal lovers. For example, it is not widely known that 750,000 pets were destroyed in Britain within one week in the summer of 1939. Pet owners took this decision on the advice of the newly formed National Air Raid Precautions Animals Committee, which urged householders to take their pets to the country for safety or, if they could not do so, 'it really is kindest to have them destroyed' (Campbell, 2013: xi).

Unfortunately, as Horowitz (2019) observes, in the last fifty or so years, despite scientific advances which show that animals feel pain, are capable of rational thinking and (in some cases) demonstrate self-awareness, such knowledge is not universally reflected in the laws of the land.[3] Neither is it reflected in practice. For every animal which enjoys human affection, there are myriads more victims of brutality at the hands of humans or machines. Each year, organisations who try to care for and protect animals around the world report unspeakable cases of neglect and cruelty. On average, the Royal Society for the Prevention of Cruelty to Animals (RSPCA) reports that someone rings their 24-hour cruelty line every thirty seconds. In 2019, it received more than 1.2 million telephone calls and each year typically investigates more than 185,000 cases of neglect and cruelty.[4] We hope that education can support the development of young people's understanding and compassion, the need for which features highly in this book.

Throughout this book we use animal-assisted interventions (AAI) as an umbrella term to cover various schemes and initiatives which feature animals for the broad purpose of improving human behaviour in an ethical way. Within the field there are different types of intervention. The American Veterinary Medical Association distinguishes between animal-assisted therapy (AAT), animal-assisted education (AAE), animal-assisted activities (AAA) and AAI resident animals. The differences mainly relate to who provides the intervention and the intended goals (Table I.1). In AAA sessions focusing on reading, children read to a dog mainly on a one-to-one basis, with the dog handler present to ensure safety for all parties while also occasionally offering supportive prompts. In AAE sessions, where there is always an educational goal, the teacher or education expert provides small groups of students with explicit reading strategies and discusses what they have read with them, while the role of the animal is to make the setting more informal and relaxed, thereby motivating the students. Animals can also be actively involved in the sessions, even distributing resources. The use of service animals, such as those which support people with disabilities or those handled by the police, are not considered to represent an AAI.

---

3   In 2007, however, the Animal Welfare Act became law in England (already passed in Wales). It places a legal obligation on owners and keepers of animals to care for them properly. In 2019, the case of a police dog called Finn, who was stabbed while pursuing a suspect, highlighted the need for changes in the law to protect service animals who were harmed, and led to the Animal Welfare (Service Animals) Bill.

4   See https://www.rspca.org.uk/whatwedo/latest/facts.

Table I.1. Different types of animal-assisted interventions

Intervention	Main provider	Goals
Animal-assisted therapy	Health services	Physical, social, emotional or cognitive
Animal-assisted education	Schools, colleges and other educational providers	Educational
Animal-assisted activities	Specially trained professionals or volunteers	Mainly motivational or recreational
AAI resident animals	Owners of particular facilities such as residential care homes	Social

Source: Adapted from https://www.avma.org/KB/Policies/
Pages/Animal-Assisted-Interventions-Definitions.aspx

Anthrozoology describes the study of human–animal interactions. As an academic field, it has experienced significant growth over the last twenty-five years. Scholarship has consistently revealed the strong emotional bonds that exist in human–animal relationships, as well as highlighting the broader health benefits humans derive from companion animals for therapeutic purposes.

One of the premises behind AAI is that stress is a significant variable in learning and that it can be mediated through interactions with animals (Sroufe, 2017). The emphasis is very much on fostering students' self-management skills through AAIs, such as learning to handle stress and self-motivation, as well as building self-confidence and positive attitudes. These social and emotional aspects of learning are discussed further in Chapters 2 and 3. Despite the growing body of literature on AAIs, the theoretical basis is often overlooked. Geist (2011) suggests there is a lack of a coherent, unified conceptual framework, which presents problems for professionals seeking a scientific evaluation of the effectiveness of AAIs and possible funding.

A less studied but equally valid line of enquiry is the impact such interactions have on animal welfare (Hosey and Melfi, 2018). Becky Bishop owned a dog therapy business in Washington state and took her dogs to visit hospices. She noticed that while people felt better after the visits, her dogs seemed depressed. After hearing about the Reading Education Assistance Dogs (READ) programme, in 2000 Bishop started her own Reading with Rover programme in her local library. She found not only that parents reported gains in their children's reading, but also that the dogs appeared much happier. On the basis of such stories, there is a need to conduct more systematic and rigorous research on the impact of AAIs on all participants, including the animal.

From an educationalist's perspective, it is possible to discern the application of various learning and developmental theories to AAIs. Biophilia (literally 'love of the living world') suggests that humans have an innate tendency to connect with nature and other forms of life (Wilson, 1990; Kruger and Serpell, 2006). In Chapter 3, we discuss the theory of attachment (Bowlby, 1953, 1969), which posits that learning requires a sense of emotional and physical security gained through 'attachment' to another person or, in the context of this book, an animal. Behaviourism emphasises learning through repetition and responding to external stimuli. Ivan Pavlov's famous experiments on dogs in the 1920s revealed how their behaviour could be conditioned by ringing bells to signal the arrival of food (see McSweeney and Bierley, 1984). The American psychologist John Watson (1930) argued that humans differed from other animals only in the behaviour they demonstrated, and such behaviour could be modified, whereas B. F. Skinner (1965) argued that animal and human behaviour was shaped through positive and negative reinforcement, such as giving rats food pellets or mild electric shocks. Constructivism sees learning as an active process of constructing meaning through interacting with others and their environment. When children interact with animals, they 'read' cues and begin to make sense of their surroundings. Jean Piaget's theory of cognition suggests that children see animals as peers (Piaget, 1929), while, in line with Jerome Bruner's theory, there are suggestions that 'play with pets might well have the "horizontal" and symbolic properties shown to be developmentally beneficial' (Melson, 2001: 11). It is possible to see the influence of these theories when observing AAIs.

'Learning by doing' is not so much a theory but a philosophy advocated by John Dewey (1938), who valued first-hand, real-life experience as a basis for learning. Similarly, David Kolb (1984) advocated experiential learning in which students engaged in 'concrete' experiences, observing and reflecting on these and then abstracting conceptual understanding from them. Through the direct acts of feeding and caring for animals, students acquire knowledge, skills and values that would not be possible through reading about animals or hearing what others have to say.

Motivation has attracted several theories which seek to describe why people behave the way they do. Abraham Maslow (1954) suggested that there is a hierarchy of needs, from basic ones (e.g. food, shelter, love) which must be met before an individual can fulfil his or her talents or potential (a state of self-actualisation). David McClelland (1988) theorised that each of us are motivated by the need for achievement (and the recognition this brings), affiliation (to be with others) and power (to control others). Carol Dweck's (1986) work on mindsets suggests that some students attribute success to innate talent (fixed) rather than effort and repeated practice (growth). These theorists are relevant to AAIs because motivation is often reported to be a key factor in their success, and is a recurrent theme in this book. Students are intrinsically motivated by their love of animals to interact with them, and learning is optimised when students enjoy the companionship of animals.

The book follows a straightforward structure. Chapter 1 provides a historical overview of human–animal interactions. It highlights how animals have played a central part in humans' social, spiritual and cultural development, featuring in rituals, ceremonies and customs. While human attitudes towards animals and their treatment of them has always attracted the interest of historians, a growing number of scholars are challenging the notion that only humans make history (e.g. Kean and Howell, 2018). For example, a recent exhibition at the Museum of London called 'Beasts of London' explored how animals such as elephants, horses, rats and pigeons have shaped the city and its beastly history. The curators were inspired by the museum's collection of animal artefacts. Chaline (2011) lists fifty animals – including horses, dogs, rats, beavers, fleas and falcons – that have dramatically changed the course of history.

Chapters 2, 3, 4 and 5 focus on particular dimensions of well-being. This is a complex, overarching concept relating to the quality of people's lives. The Children's Society definition of well-being is a useful starting point: 'It is about how well we are, and how our lives are going.'[5] And so one way of reading this book is to see it as a commentary on how children's love of animals can contribute to their all-round development or well-being: social (Chapter 2), emotional (Chapter 3), intellectual (Chapter 4) and physical (Chapter 5). These are naturally interrelated dimensions and should be viewed holistically. For example, when a child physically stretches out and smooths an animal, this action releases endorphins in the nervous system, which can reduce anxiety and form the basis of social attachment to animals (Levinson, 1962). It is only out of structural convenience that we examine the physical, social and emotional aspects in isolation.

Chapters 6 and 7 discuss how AAIs can contribute towards learning in different subject areas and across the curriculum. We have not explored the potential of AAIs in every subject; rather, examples are chosen to illustrate possible starting points for teachers in a range of subject and thematic contexts. In some cases, such as science, it should be fairly obvious that learning about animals can develop children's subject-specific knowledge (e.g. of habitats and life cycles) and skills (e.g. observation, questioning). But animals also feature strongly in less obvious areas, such as the arts, literature, and religious and moral codes.

Chapter 8 addresses the general ethical and practical challenges of managing animals in school. As with any learning experience, careful planning and organisation increase the likelihood of anticipated gains being realised. Finally, given that dogs are the most popular of pets and the growing body of literature surrounding their presence in educational settings, Chapter 9 focuses on maximising the learning potential associated with school dogs. Any intervention that involves animals raises questions about ethical and welfare considerations. As Serpell et al. (2010: 497) point out: 'the use of animals for animal-assisted activities and therapy imposes a unique set of stresses and strains on them that the "industry" has only recently begun to acknowledge'. The ethical standards underpinning AAIs have not been subjected to any systematic review. Moreover, there are concerns over a lack of standardised training for handlers and practitioners, the absence of regulations regarding working conditions, such as breaks and age restrictions, and the impact such interventions have on the animal's psychological and physiological condition.

....

5   See https://www.childrenssociety.org.uk/what-we-do/research/what-is-child-wellbeing; see also Rees et al. (2008).

However, researchers should always adhere to established ethical protocols, with university-based staff expected to follow the respective university's ethical procedures. Writers themselves also have to make ethical decisions over what to include in their publications based on their own personal convictions. For example, we have not referred to any of the research involving children and dolphins because we believe that the latter should not be kept in aquariums, notwithstanding questions over whether these animals were captured from the wild. Similarly, we have not referred to specific examples of school farms where animals enter the food chain.

Despite the growing interest in AAIs, a running theme throughout the book is the shortage of longitudinal studies to confirm whether the short-term gains which are widely reported are sustainable. However, while longitudinal research provides a stronger evidence base for the benefits or otherwise of AAIs, conducting such research is time-consuming and expensive. An over-reliance on small-scale case studies makes generalisations in a range of educational contexts more difficult. Many such studies rely on personal experiences which are prone to bias because those who are 'treated' successfully are naturally inclined to share their stories, raising doubts in the wider scientific community in which hard empirical evidence is sought.

This is not to say that we should dismiss such anecdotes. For example, when 9-year-old Jefro's autism disrupted the family Christmas, his mum found support through Pawsitive Squad CIC, a non-profit organisation dedicated to helping families of autistic children through the use of dogs (Montague, 2019). The provision of a puppy proved a lifeline in teaching Jefro to handle his stress and anxiety. While they lack the universality that researchers may crave, anecdotes are often more impactful than substantial data. Individual stories leave more of an impression on people than a mass of figures. They are immediate and appeal to the emotions, rather than more abstract and remote statistics which take time to gather, digest and analyse. Nonetheless, more systematic and large-scale studies in diverse settings, which draw on multiple disciplines, will help to enhance our understanding of how, when, where and why animals influence human thinking, emotions and behaviour. Such research will also place AAIs on a more rigorous scientific footing than at present.

Stepping aside from academic questions about research methodology and ethics, it is not surprising that almost all the evidence presents a positive picture of interventions. There is a deep-seated attraction to animals embedded in the human psyche. Arguably, there is no need for scientific research to confirm that the mere act of gazing at animals is beneficial to people of all ages. And just in case you had any doubts, scientists have proven that staring at fish lowers people's blood pressure and reduces heart rate (Knapton, 2015). Perhaps this is why fish tanks are to be found in dental waiting rooms and doctor's surgeries.

Chapter 1
Tales from the past: human-animal relationships in history

We are not animals. We are not a product of what has happened to us in our past. We have the power of choice. (Covey, 2013: 305)

The special relationship between humans and animals, particularly dogs, has a very long history. Deep in Chauvet Cave in southern France archaeologists have found two sets of prints preserved in the soft clay. One set belongs to a child aged between 8 and 10 and the other is the paw prints of a wolf or large dog. Archaeologists think the child was carrying a torch and had stopped during the walk, probably to clean a torch and look at the wall paintings or bear skulls. This is the first recorded dog walk in history and it is estimated to have happened around 26,000 years ago (Harvey, 2019).

This chapter sketches the development of human-animal interactions to provide historical context to the themes discussed in subsequent chapters. While the term 'animal-assisted interventions' is a modern one, the basic idea of using animals to improve aspects of human life is very old. Through the ages, animals have provided us with sources of food, clothing, security, entertainment, companionship, wealth and status. They have been worshipped and abused, though not in equal measure. Animals were the main victims of the first agricultural revolution (c.10,000 BC), when humans began the long process of settling and farming the land. Sheep, donkeys, chickens and other animals supplied food (meat, milk and eggs), raw materials (wool and skins) and muscle power. As Harari (2011) points out, the domestication of chickens and cattle was based on brutal practices which included premature slaughtering, mutilation and castration.

Dogs were the first animals to be domesticated by humans. They were used for hunting and fighting, effectively acting as an alarm system against intruders. Over generations, dogs' keen sense of smell coupled with humans' bow-and-arrow weaponry represented cutting-edge biotechnology to support the development of both species (Fagan, 2009). But dogs were not simply valued for their hunting skills. Our earliest ancestors also appreciated their companionship. In northern Israel, for example, archaeologists discovered a 12,000-year-old tomb containing the skeleton of a 50-year-old woman whose left hand rests on the remains of a puppy (Davis, 1978). One interpretation suggests there was a strong emotional connection between the two, although the puppy may, of course, have been an offering to the gods.

Domestication meant that, over time, humans created dog breeds to suit their purposes. For hunting, bloodhounds are exceptionally good at tracking scents, while collies are intelligent and skilled at herding animals. Other breeds are suited to protecting people and property or demonstrate extraordinary physical stamina. Then there are dogs which have a gentle nature and are suitable as playmates for young children. The evolutionary biologist Mark Pagel (2012) argues that the process of domestication, which he likens to residing in a protective bubble, has changed the temperament and genetic make-up of animals. Domesticated dogs, cats, rats, goats, pigs, sheep and horses all have smaller brains than their prehistoric ancestors. We know that wolves outperform dogs when set searching tasks. Pagel suggests that over the millennia, domestic animals have jettisoned genes they no longer need because humans now do much of the thinking for them. Dogs have become less pack like, while sheep and cows have become calm and relaxed around humans.

An alternative interpretation of these early relationships suggests that it was not humans who domesticated wolves but the other way around. Gradually, some wolves started to live with groups of human hunters and gatherers in a mutually helpful way and, over a long period of time, evolved into dogs. Such a symbiotic relationship even led to a reduction in humans' sense of smell 'because our association with dogs had rendered it unnecessary' (Groves, 2012). Whatever the timing and nature of the human–dog relationship all those millennia ago, the basic principle that this has been a reciprocal one holds true.

In prehistoric societies, it was widely believed that all living creatures and natural objects were imbued with a spirit that animated the body, but which could exist without it. Nineteenth-century anthropologists called this belief system 'animism' (from the Latin *anima*, meaning 'breath, spirit, life') and it remains a world view of many indigenous peoples. If animals were treated cruelly, their spirits could return to haunt the living, inflict pain and bring about personal or collective misfortune, such as illness or crop failure. The food that people ate and the clothes they wore were, naturally, drawn from animals whose spirits lived on despite the loss of their bodies. When animals were sacrificed to the gods, it was based on the belief that their spirits could convey a positive account of how they were treated, at least up to that point. Animal sacrifice, of course, continues as a prevalent practice around the world. In 2011, for example, the Kyrgyzstan parliament sacrificed seven sheep to drive evil spirits out of the building (Parfitt, 2011).

Ancient civilisations such as Egypt, China, Greece and Rome kept animals for companionship and amusement. They introduced the first menageries, wildlife parks, safaris and zoological gardens as places where animals were collected and displayed to entertain humans. These early zoos also symbolised the status and power of their owners (Carr and Cohen, 2011). We do not know whether pet-keeping in private homes preceded the domestication of animals, but certainly in distant times the owning of pets was something of a luxury. In wealthy households, animals were often pampered. The dogs owned by the Chinese emperors were said to have human wet nurses when pups and, in adulthood, their own servants (Magrane, 2016). Alexander the Great named one of his conquered cities after his favourite dog, Peritas (meaning January). Well-to-do Roman families even paid for tombstones to commemorate their beloved dogs. One grief-struck dog owner declared that he wept with tears for the loss of his dog Patricus: 'never again shall thou give me a thousand kisses. Never canst thou be contentedly in my lap' (Abbott, 1912: 187–188).

For thousands of years, humans have used animals for therapeutic purposes. Although the Egyptians sacrificed dogs, they also believed that people's sores could be healed by a dog's saliva. The Greeks held the same view and trained dogs to lick wounds at their temple to Asclepius, the god of medicine and healing. Serpell (2010: 22) cites examples of surviving inscriptions which testify to the belief that miracles happened: 'Thuson of Hermione, a blind boy, had his eyes licked in the daytime by one of the dogs about the temple, and departed cured.' He suggests that this represents one of the earliest examples of AAIs in history. Similar practices continued through the ages. The first documented example of the therapeutic use of animals in western Europe occurred in ninth-century Geel, Belgium, where animals were part of the *thérapies naturelles* provided for people with disabilities by members of the community.

Animals have also found a role in the care of the mentally ill. In 1796, the wealthy philanthropist William Tuke established the York Retreat, which was markedly different from the usual institutions for the insane. Tuke had been moved by the inhumane treatment of a fellow Quaker who died at what was then the York Asylum. Tuke's new arrangements included provision for gardens and domestic animals (e.g. rabbits, hawks, poultry). Patients wore their own clothing and had the opportunity to work at crafts, read books, write and wander the grounds, spending time interacting with animals. Samuel Tuke (1996 [1813]: 96), the founder's grandson and mental health reformer, reported that the animals pro-vided 'the means of innocent pleasure', while the interchanges 'tend to awaken the social and benevolent feelings'. In the nineteenth century, the use of pet animals in asylums became more widespread and received support from the British Charity Commissioners.

Animals have had a long association with the world's major religions. In ancient Egypt it was forbidden to kill cats. They were mummified in such huge numbers that in the early twentieth century archaeologists sold the remains in bucket loads to be ground up as fertiliser (Clutton-Brock, 1981). In Christianity, God told Adam and Eve to 'Multiply and fill the earth and subdue it; you are masters of the fish and birds and all the animals' (Genesis 1:28). This mandate of human domination over animals set the course throughout much of Western Christendom's history, although it should also be noted that the Bible com-mands Christians to afford animals sufficient rest, food and protection (Exodus 23:4-5). In Hinduism, many animals are venerated, particularly the cow, tiger, elephant and mouse, because of the belief that God resides in all living things. Judaism also teaches that animals are part of God's creation and should be treated with compassion, given that God made a covenant with animals. In Islam, the Muslim aversion to dogs and pigs along with the Arab affinity for horses, hawks and camels are well-known stereotypes.[1] Buddhists believe that animals are sentient creatures with the potential for enlightenment and so treat them with respect, especially given that humans could be reborn as animals.

While religious belief and tradition has shaped the ways in which humans look upon animals, it is the legal system which has governed the parameters of their interaction. Particular species of animals have been protected by law as far back

---

1 In reality, there are many different attitudes among Muslims to dogs and other animals. See Foltz (2014).

as ancient Greece, when, for example, it was illegal to kill storks and grass snakes because they were the most effective means of keeping vipers and rodents under control. And societies have long held strict regulations governing the sale and slaughter of animals.

Under ancient Persian law, animals themselves were regarded as responsible for their actions. Hence, if a mad dog bit a person or sheep, it was punished along the same lines as if it had attempted to commit premeditated murder. The punishment took the form of progressive mutilation, beginning with the loss of the ears and ending with the amputation of the tail, the extent of the punishment depending on the number of victims. Similarly, in western countries from the thirteenth to the eighteenth centuries, animals could be placed on trial for alleged crimes. In his fascinating account, *The Criminal Prosecution and Capital Punishment of Animals*, Evans points out that some of the animals were attended to by a defence attorney and the verdict decided by a judge in the face of a prosecutor and witnesses. In 1457, a sow in France was found guilty of murdering a 5-year-old boy and sentenced to be 'hanged by the hind feet to a gallows-tree'. Her six blood-stained sucklings were included in the original indictment as accomplices. However, they were acquitted due to a lack of any proof that they had assisted in 'mangling the deceased' (Evans, 1906: 225). In old Germanic law, it was possible for someone accused of a crime to bring before the court animals as witnesses. Hence, in the case of night burglary, where other witnesses were not available, an injured householder could bring in his cat, dog or rooster as a silent witness of the crime, while under French law a man accused of murder in his own house could swear his innocence in the presence of his cat, dog or cockerel (Hyde, 1916).

Evans lists caterpillars, flies, locusts, leeches, snails, slugs, worms, weevils, rats, mice, moles, turtle doves, pigs, bulls, cows, cocks, dogs, asses, mules, mares and goats as culprits brought before the courts. While this might make the modern-day person chuckle at the thought of caterpillars and the like being cross-examined, there was a serious side to this. Medieval and early modern thinking was shaped by superstition and the hard life-and-death realities of a successful harvest. So, the courts took seriously Captain J. B. Pestalozzi, who in 1659 brought a complaint against 'certain caterpillars on account of the devastations committed by them' in five areas of Italy. He demanded 'that these hurtful creatures be summoned by the proper sheriff'. A summons was immediately issued and five copies posted on trees in the surrounding forests

(Evans, 1906: 149–150). The illiterate caterpillars were duly charged with 'trespassing upon the fields, gardens and orchards and doing great damage therein, instead of remaining in their habitat, the forest'. Most significant for the modern reader are the judge's comments about the rights of caterpillars 'to life, liberty, and the pursuit of happiness', provided the exercise of this right 'does not destroy or impair the happiness of man, to whom all lower animals are subject'. It is noteworthy that the rights of living creatures were being discussed in the courtrooms of western Europe 400 years ago.

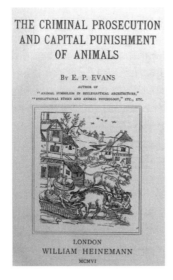

Figure 1.1. Frontispiece of *The Criminal Prosecution and Capital Punishment of Animals*

Source: https://www.gutenberg.org/files/43286/43286-h/43286-h.htm

Figure 1.2. A court scene showing the trial of a sow in 1457

Source: *Chambers' Book of Days* (1869): http://www.thebookofdays.com/months/jan/17.htm

It has long been recognised that education has a key role to play in preventing the abuse of animals. The English poet and philosopher John Locke (1693) suggested that young girls be given 'dogs, squirrels, or such things' to look after as a means of encouraging them to develop empathy for others and a sense of responsibility. Locke thought that through caring for animals, children would learn to care for others. Similarly, the seventeenth-century English political philosopher Thomas Hobbes advocated giving children opportunities to care for animals, albeit so they could curb their own beastlike tendencies (see Myers, 1998).

The notion of children taking responsibility in the care of animals became a theme in children's literature in the eighteenth and nineteenth centuries. In 1765, the anonymous fable *Goody Two-Shoes* was published as the very first major work of children's fiction in English (Figure 1.3). It featured the heroine Margery Meanwell, who devoted her life to the care of maltreated animals, and whose actions popularised the phrase 'goody two-shoes' to describe a do-gooder or overly virtuous individual.

But it is Anna Sewell's hugely successful *Black Beauty: The Autobiography of a Horse* (1877) that represents the peak of this moralising trend of kindness towards animals. In Chapter 13, the reader is left in no doubt that 'there is no religion without love, and people may talk as much as they like about their religion, but if it does not teach them to be good and kind to man and beast, it is all a sham'. The Victorian moral and social mores are well illustrated in one scene when Black Beauty stumbles and throws his rider, Reuben Smith, to the ground. Smith is portrayed as a gentle and caring groom but with one major failing, alcohol, which was widely seen by respectable society as the main source of moral corruption among the poor. On the night in question, the 'madly drunk' Smith demands that Black Beauty rides at full speed in the dark, whereby the poor horse catches a stone, splits his hoof and throws Smith to the ground:

The moon had just risen above the hedge, and by its light I could see Smith lying a few yards beyond me. He did not rise, he made one slight effort to do so, and then, there was a heavy groan. I could have groaned too, for I was suffering intense pain both from my foot and knees; but horses are used to bear their pain in silence.

As for Smith's wife and six small children, they are consigned to the much-dreaded workhouse. Beauty tears his knee, ending his life as an admired carriage show horse.

Figure 1.3. The cover of the 1888 edition of *Goody Two-Shoes*

Source: https://en.wikisource.org/wiki/Goody_Two-Shoes_(1888)

Figure 1.4. A scene from *Black Beauty*, 1st edn (Sewell, 1877: 121)

Source: https://en.wikisource.org/wiki/Black_Beauty#/media/File:Black_Beauty_(1877),_page_6.jpg

Unfortunately, regular reports from the RSPCA (established in 1824) highlight extraordinary cases of abuse against animals. In 1906, one typical inspector's report from north Wales referred to humans beating donkeys, kicking horses, mutilating dogs, plucking feathers from a live pigeon and placing hot cinders under a horse's tail.[2] In 1911, the Protection of Animals Act was passed to try to prevent such outright cruelty to animals, although this has persisted.

Cats, of all domesticated animals, have had a torrid history since they were once revered and honoured by the ancient Egyptians. For a thousand or so years, they have been associated with the devil and persecuted as a result. They were massacred whenever a plague broke out, most notably during the Black Death (1348) and Great Plague of London (1665), which ironically made the outbreaks worse in that there was one less control over the rodent population. In France during the 1730s, printers' apprentices became so jealous of their masters' cats,

2   *Rhyl Record* (10 February 1906).

who they believed were fed better, that they arranged for their mass slaughter in 'the Great Cat Massacre'.

The English artist William Hogarth highlighted the plight of dogs, horses, cats and other animals in his series of engravings known as the *Four Stages of Cruelty*, published in 1751 (Figure 1.5). The fictional Tom Nero begins his path of cruelty by torturing a dog, 'progressing' to beating his horse, and then to robbery and murder. His 'reward' is to be hung on the gallows, after which his body is dissected by surgeons. Hogarth was dismayed by the cruelty to animals he saw on the streets of London, and his prints – which appeared on cheap paper – were targeted at the lower classes often held responsible for such despicable acts. The simple moral message was that the path from childish thug to convicted criminal was a short one.

Figure 1.5. Hogarth's *Second Stage of Cruelty*, 1751. Nero beats his horse while four lawyers look on unperturbed

Source: https://www.tate.org.uk/whats-on/tate-britain/exhibition/hogarth/hogarth-hogarths-modern-moral-series/hogarth-hogarths-4

While legislation was one solution to animal cruelty, education was another. With the development of compulsory elementary schooling in the late nineteenth century, the potential of using animals in schools attracted the interest of educational reformers. In 1869, the philanthropist Angela Burdett-Coutts, who was passionate about animal welfare, wrote to *The Times* calling for 'systematic teaching' in schools about 'the principles of humanity towards animals and a knowledge of their structure, treatment, and value to man'.[3] This was a plea in the context of growing concern about the ill-treatment of animals.

3   *The Times* (14 September 1869).

Animals had featured in educational books for many years, first as a means of helping children learn to read and later as a form of moral instruction. One of the earliest reading books, the seventeenth-century Latin primer *Orbis sensualium pictus* ('The World of Things', 1658) contains phrases such as the 'Duck quacketh' and the 'Bear grumbleth'. The idea was that children would learn the alphabet by mimicking animal noises. In the eighteenth century, a market developed for children's books which offered an ideal means of conveying moral and religious truths. One of the most popular was Sarah Trimmer's *Fabulous Histories* (1786), which tells the story of how a family of baby robins and human children learn to live side by side in harmony (Shaw, 2015).

In the 1890s, the Church of England Society for Promoting Kindness to Animals (established 1893) lobbied the Education Department to include time in the curriculum for children to learn about the nature and requirements of familiar animals. Arthur Acland, secretary of the Education Department, responded by pointing out that new instructions to schools would direct them to talk about animals in 'object lessons', in which the emphasis was to be on highlighting the importance of being kind to animals. He suggested that schools might host 'caged birds, fish in aquariums or doves in the playground'.[4] Perhaps because of logistical reasons or fear of inciting too much excitement among the children, teachers preferred pictures of animals or even stuffed versions rather than the animals themselves (Figure 1.6).

Many teachers also misunderstood the purpose of these lessons, which was to stimulate children's curiosity about animal life - not 'a lecture but a lesson full of questions so directed as to make the children discover as much as possible for themselves'.[5]

---

4 *Evening Express* (26 March 1895).
5 Report of the Committee of Council on Education, Parliamentary Papers (PP) PP 1894-1895, Vol. XXVII.I, Mr Williams' General Report, p. 9; see also Report of the Committee of Council on Education, PP 1895-1896, Vol. XXVI.I. A. G. Legards' General Report, p. 15.

Figure 1.6. An object lesson on 'the dog', 1908

Source: Lowndes (1937: 36). Jews' Free School, Whitechapel. London Metropolitan Archives

During the first half of the twentieth century, as the curriculum broadened, schools became more creative with their teaching approaches. In the more progressive schools, nature study and local walk-arounds became popular, which enabled children to gain more first-hand experience of wildlife through visits to farms and zoos. In some schools, children ran pet competitions (Figure 1.7) and learned to look after animals such as chickens (Figure 1.8).

Figure 1.7. A pet club competition, 1906

Source: Lowndes (1937: 141). Cited source: Miss L. E. Walters, late HMI

Figure 1.8. A 'young farmer's club', 1930s

Source: Lowndes (1937: 141). Cited source: Kent Local Education Authority

In the nineteenth century, interest in animal intelligence grew in the wider context of what makes us human and distinct from non-human animals. Most famously, in 1868 Charles Darwin published his two-volume *The Variation of Animals and Plants Under Domestication*, based on his extensive studies of domestic animals, wild fowl, goldfish, bees, cultivated plants, ornamental trees, fruits, flowers and the like. Darwin was informed not only through his own meticulous observations but by spending time with those who worked every day with animals. He socialised, for example, with 'pigeon fanciers' in the local 'gin palace', or drinking house, gaining information about differences among pigeons. His daughter Henrietta also developed an interest in pigeons, recalling 'the Pouter pigeon was good-natured but not clever, and I remember a hen Jacobin which I considered rather feeble-minded' (Bodio, 2009). Followers of Darwin concluded that even the humblest of animals were capable of rational thought and that human and non-human animals only differed by degrees of intelligence rather than differences in kind.

The debate over animal thinking and intelligence was highlighted in the early 1900s by the story of 'Clever Hans', a horse in Berlin who became something of a celebrity. He was owned by a mathematics teacher, Wilhelm von Osten, who claimed to have taught Hans how to do simple sums, tell the time and understand German, among other accomplishments. The wonder of Hans was duly paraded around the country before an independent investigation led by the psychologist Carl Stumpf and his assistant Oskar Pfungst. They found that when

Hans could see his interrogator, he answered nine out of ten questions correctly. However, when the horse was blindfolded, his success rate dipped to less than one in ten correct answers. In short, the investigators concluded that von Osten conveyed signals to the horse just by looking at him. Hans did not have mathematical abilities and could not read German. Rather, he could pick up cues from his owner in the form of small body movements which told him when he had tapped his hoof the right number of times. Since then, scientists refer to the 'Clever Hans effect' to stress the importance of separating the owner from the animal if the animal's true intelligence is to be observed.

However, Robert Sheldrake (2011), a biologist and writer about animal intelligence, suggests that we should not generalise too much from this experience. He points out that the Clever Hans effect is a very specific one. It depends on body language, which forms an important element in communication between horses (as with many other species). Significantly, Sheldrake points out that there are many animals who are capable of responding to human beings even though they cannot see them. He has built up a database of hundreds of stories in which pets know precisely when their owners are about to return home, even though they cannot see them and despite the fact that the owners arrive back at different times of the day. He shows that this is not because of the animals' acute sense of smell or knowledge of household routines. Rather, Sheldrake argues that they have a kind of sixth sense, extrasensory perception or telepathic understanding which enables them to anticipate our behaviour.[6]

Humans have long taken advantage of animals' well-developed sensory abilities. This is particularly the case during times of war and in other dangerous situations. In the ancient world, elephants and horses carried soldiers into battle and transported life-saving supplies. During the First World War, around 16 million animals helped with transport and communication as well as offering companionship to keep up soldiers' morale. Air squadrons had their own mascots, such as fox cubs. Glow worms helped soldiers to read maps and canaries were used to detect poisonous gas, while cats and dogs were trained to hunt rats in the trenches. Horses, mules, donkeys and camels carried food, water, ammunition and medical supplies to men at the front. Dogs were employed in

6   You can see a remarkable film showing one of Sheldrake's experiments in action when Pam Smart's dog Jaytee waits for her to return home at: https://www.sheldrake.org/books-by-rupert-sheldrake/dogs-that-know-when-their-owners-are-coming-home.

search and rescue missions during the Blitz of the Second World War as well as to detect mines. The Soviets claimed that their dog Zucha found at least 200 mines in eighteen days.[7] Animals continue to be used by modern-day armed forces. Both the American and Russian navies, for example, use marine mammals in military operations. In 2019, Norwegian fishermen reported the sight of a beluga whale strapped with a GoPro-style camera with 'St. Petersburg equipment' embossed on the harness clips (Ismay, 2019).

Animals do not give their consent for war, of course, but throughout history men have also been press-ganged or conscripted into conflicts. There are countless accounts of heroism among individual animals. When a Norwegian trawler was torpedoed during the Second World War the survivors owed their lives to Daisy, their mongrel mascot. She swam from one crew member to another in the freezing water, licking their faces and keeping their spirits up (Price, 2004). More recently, Treo, a black Labrador, saved many lives by finding improvised explosive devices hidden by the Taliban. He is among those honoured at the Animals in War Memorial unveiled in 2004 in Hyde Park, London. Collectively, animals have also sacrificed their lives in huge numbers. During the First World War, of 16,544 pigeons parachuted into occupied countries fewer than 2,000 returned. The Germans had their own 'squadrons of hawks' posted across the borders. However, one plucky pigeon which returned to its base carried fifteen sketch maps and 5,000 words of text, relaying valuable information about the enemy's position and movements (Gardiner, 2006).

The beginnings of the use of AAIs to meet the psychological needs of individuals can be traced to an American professor of psychology, Boris Levinson. He was born in Lithuania in 1907 and with his Jewish family emigrated to a farming community on the outskirts of New York in 1923. Levinson was a deeply spiritual man who saw the value of animals in enriching the quality of people's lives. He believed that pets could bring people closer to nature, provide companionship and help to 'rehumanize society' (Levinson and Mallon, 1997, viii). As a trained child psychiatrist, Levinson sought new ways to heal those who were emotionally troubled. He found that when, by accident, he brought his dog Jingles to a session with a disturbed child the response was very positive. Levinson gathered further case studies to show that children who had communication difficulties were put at ease and made efforts to interact with Jingles. In 1961, he then

---

7   Sources vary, with some claiming he detected 2,000 mines. See Kistler (2011: 26).

presented his findings to the American Psychological Association. Unfortunately, the academic audience treated Levinson's 'preposterous' paper with scorn and derision, one asking what commission he had paid the dog (Levinson, 1962).

Despite the cynicism, Levinson's idea had unexpected support when posthumous evidence was published on the life of Sigmund Freud, the most respected figure in the field. Biographers revealed that Freud had also seen the therapeutic value of dogs. His status in the psychological community was such that the matter could not be ignored or deplored. Freud often had his chow, Jofi, in his office for companionship and he noticed how patients, particularly children and adolescents, began to talk more openly about their problems to the dog (Figure 1.9).

During psychoanalysis, patients enter the 'resistance phase' when they are nearing a point of uncovering the source of their problems. At this moment, patients can become hostile as they struggle to defend themselves from the psychological pain that revealing the repressed trauma might cause. It seemed to Freud that the presence of the dog lifted this burden and patients were less resistant to talking.

Figure 1.9. Freud and his dog, Jofi, 1937

Source: shutterstock.com

Freud speculated as to why this was so. He observed that when patients stretched out on a couch to relax, they were asked to simply say whatever came into their mind. Whenever they spoke about painful or embarrassing moments in their lives, the dog would lie calmly and quietly nearby, conveying a sense of safety and comfort. Freud's observations validated Levinson's work, and the first edition of his groundbreaking *Pet-Oriented Child Psychotherapy* appeared in 1969.

Since the mid-1970s, interest in AAIs has increased significantly. The earliest programmes introduced enabled animals to visit or co-reside in hospitals, long-term care facilities, rehabilitation facilities, public schools and community care settings (Johnson et al., 2002). In the United States, Therapy Dogs International was founded in 1976 as a voluntary group offering trained dogs and their handlers to whichever organisation felt their need. Pet Partners (formerly Delta Society) was established in 1977 as the first comprehensive, standardised training in animal-assisted activities aimed at volunteers and professionals within the healthcare services. A third organisation, Intermountain Therapy Animals, specialise in providing support for physical, occupational and speech needs, as well psychotherapies and special education.

The earliest reading programmes that started to use dogs began in the United States more than twenty years ago. In 1999, Sandi Martin, a manager of a hospital unit, observed how well children with burns responded to the visits of dogs from Intermountain Therapy Animals. In Martin's experience, many of these children had poor self-esteem, lacked focus and did not look forward to the usual activities planned by the hospital. However, the presence of dogs signalled a remarkable turnaround in their confidence levels and attitudes. Martin, who was an avid reader, pondered whether dogs could also have the same impact on children who struggled with reading.

Working with four Intermountain Therapy dogs, her own rescued dog (Olivia) and a cat, Martin reached an agreement with city library staff to trial a Dog Day Afternoons programme on Saturdays with six children. One of the first to attend was a 7-year-old boy who looked down at his shoes and quietly told her that he didn't read very well, to which Martin replied: 'Olivia doesn't either, but she loves to listen' (Abel, 2017). Another child did not want to participate but was encouraged to do so by her grandmother. Her improvement was such that after a few years she won a school essay competition with the winning title: 'Why Would You Want to Read to a Dog?' A third child was a Bosnian refugee. When Martin asked whether he would like to pet one of the dogs, he explained that he could not because as a devout Muslim he was taught not to touch dogs.[8] Martin suggested that he read to the dog instead. Over the following weeks, the boy did this, gaining confidence and fluency in reading to (but not petting) the same dog. As with the other children, there were noticeable improvements. Later in the year when the children were asked to write an essay on what they wanted to be when they were older, the boy explained that he wanted to be a veterinarian.

8 Contrary to popular belief, it is not forbidden by Islamic law to touch a dog or any other animal. However, if the saliva of a dog touches a Muslim or any part of their clothing, they are required to wash the body part and the item of clothing touched by the animal's mouth or snout. See: https://www.animalsinislam.com/islam-animal-rights/dogs.

Spurred on by such success stories, Martin next worked with elementary schools, targeting low-attaining readers. The READ programme involved a child reading an animal-related book once a week for twenty minutes to a therapy dog. After reading ten books, the children received a 'pawtographed' book to keep, which had been 'signed' by the therapy dog. The positive feedback soon led to the widespread adoption of similar schemes within schools across several states (Fisher and Cozens, 2014). These included Sit, Stay, Read! in Alabama, Dogs Educating and Assisting Readers in Maryland, Reading with Rover in Washington and Read to the Dogs in Oregon (Kirnan et al., 2016). READ and similar schemes can now be found in many countries, including the United Kingdom, Italy, Finland, South Africa, Slovenia and Spain. The scope of their work is impressive. Aside from schools, therapy dogs can be found in hospices, hospitals, waiting rooms, grieving programmes, boys' and girls' clubs, juvenile detention facilities, prisons, women and children's domestic violence shelters, special education units, and residential treatment centres for children and adolescents.

The movement of animals into educational and healthcare settings completes their all-round presence in the lives of children. Animals play a central role in children's social and cultural worlds. From the moment children are born they are surrounded by animal mobiles and cuddly toys, while most children grow up with a household pet. And throughout their childhood they encounter wild animals in visits to parks, the countryside and zoos. Most children are captivated by animal heroes and villains in books, comics, cartoons and films, while children's virtual pets are a growing multi-billion-pound industry. While such technological sophistication is a far cry from the child's prehistoric dog walk recorded in Chauvet Cave, at the heart of these developments through time are the social and emotional connections between children and animals discussed in the next chapters.

Summary

▓ Since prehistoric times, animals have featured prominently in all aspects of people's lives – at work, home, worship, travelling and pleasure.

- Dogs were the first animals to be domesticated by humans. They were used for hunting and fighting, effectively acting as an alarm system against intruders.

- The history of human–animal relationships is based on the notion of the former's dominion over the latter. This has often resulted in the exploitation and brutal treatment of animals.

- Humans have long recognised animals' sensory abilities and sought ways to make the most of these, particularly during war and other dangerous times.

- The earliest AAI programmes were introduced in the 1960s and 1970s, enabling animals to visit or co-reside in hospitals, long-term care facilities, rehabilitation facilities, public schools and community care settings.

- The first AAIs in school contexts targeted the use of dogs to support students in developing their confidence, language and literacy skills.

Chapter 2
Tales of friendship: animals and their impact on children's social development and behaviour

Animals are such agreeable friends – they ask no questions, they pass no criticisms. (Eliot, 1857: 33)

In 1915, a young British soldier, Henry Friston, found himself on the battlefields of Gallipoli, charged with rescuing casualties from the war zone. During the fighting, Henry was knocked into a shallow crater by a shell blast and was hit on the head by a hard object. This object turned out to be a tortoise, which Henry decided to rescue. Hidden in the Number Two Gun Turret of HMS *Implacable*, Ali Pasha the tortoise returned home with Henry. They spent the rest of their lives together, and Ali Pasha became a celebrity, even appearing on the television programme *Blue Peter* (Foreman, 2015). The story has been retold for children by Michael Foreman as *The Tortoise and the Soldier: A Story of Courage and Friendship in World War I* (2015). Friendships, then, can form between the unlikeliest of individuals and last a lifetime. They provide a source of companionship, comfort and protection; unsurprisingly, a lack of friends can be a source of anxiety and depression (Meadows, 2018).

Forming friendships involves utilising a range of social skills. Social development is the process by which a child learns to interact with others around them, which begins at birth. It is through interactions within secure relationships that babies and young children receive the feedback and recognition that helps them to be aware of their own special characteristics (DfES, 2007). As children develop their own sense of individuality, they gain skills in communicating with different people in a range of contexts. This involves learning how to convey feelings, speak clearly, listen, take turns, resolve difficulties in an appropriate manner and show empathy. In fact, social development can impact on many other forms of development. For instance, our ability to interact in a healthy way with the people around us can affect everything from learning new words as a toddler to being able to resist peer pressure as a high school student and successfully navigate the challenges of adulthood.

Good communication lies at the heart of successful social relationships, and research suggests that babies are primed to communicate from their earliest days (David et al., 2003). An ability to interact with other children allows for more opportunities to practise and learn speech and language skills. Such communication may take place through eye contact, gesture, body language and voice. However, there are children who find it difficult to interact with others, perhaps because they feel inferior or are socially anxious, fearful or shy. This is significant because social anxiety, fear or shyness can prevent children from achieving their full potential or enjoying social situations (Patwardhan et al., 2015).

Skills such as turn-taking and sharing are important in any social relationship, but for some these are difficult skills to acquire (Dowling, 2010). Children with poor social skills, for example, may find it hard to maintain eye contact, use appropriate body language, show an interest in others, respond to different tones of voice or facial cues, or demonstrate empathy. Poor social skills are seen among children with a variety of developmental difficulties such as language disorders and problems with hearing, eyesight, attention or coordination. Children with a diagnosis of an autistic spectrum disorder (ASD) may have three specific areas in which they find communicating and interacting with others difficult (Table 2.1).

Table 2.1. Three areas in which children with an autistic spectrum disorder may have difficulties

Communication and language	Social and emotional understanding	Flexibility of thought and behaviour
For example:	For example:	For example:
▪ Difficulties with the social use of language.	▪ Find it difficult to empathise with others or to form friendships.	▪ Prefer to follow predictable and known routines.

Communication and language	Social and emotional understanding	Flexibility of thought and behaviour
▪ May make inappropriate facial expressions or gestures. ▪ May interpret comments literally – for instance, may not understand jokes. ▪ Do not use language in the context of role play, pretend play, etc.	▪ Struggle to follow social conventions such as making eye contact when speaking. ▪ May not seek comfort when distressed.	▪ Often have a restricted range of interests, although those they do have may become a fixation. ▪ May find thinking creatively a challenge.

Source: Adapted from Cambridgeshire Community Services (2018: 3-4)

How could animals help with social skills?

Animals are considered by many to act as 'social others', just as people do. This means animals can provide engaging and meaningful opportunities for children to develop important social skills since 'children's interactions with animals demonstrate responsiveness to the same set of features that are hallmarks of social interaction' (Myers, 1996: 32). Dogs, for example, have been well documented as having a positive effect on social encounters. Research by McNicholas and Collis (2000) indicated that the presence of a dog can act as an icebreaker in situations requiring social interaction. In their study, in which a researcher with a dog waited to see whether strangers would strike up a conversation with them, the dog was a catalyst in generating an exchange. This was true regardless of the person's gender, type of dog or whether or not the person with the dog was dressed neatly or untidily. The researchers concluded that the presence of an animal may act as a conversation-starter and a stimulus for sharing experiences.

Animals can also be a useful 'social lubricant' for individuals with disabilities, with the animal providing a normalising effect (Wells, 2009). For instance, the presence of a service dog increased the social greetings given to a child in a wheelchair, both at school and in public places such as shopping malls (Mader et al., 1989).

The nature of such interactions can vary, and it is possible that different species of animals create different opportunities and conditions for this to happen. For example, Myers (1996) noted that young children's responses to dogs, ferrets, snakes and insects varied, although all offered opportunities for moment-to-moment communication. Hunt et al. (1992) examined the impact of rabbits and turtles on interactions with strangers. They explored the role of an animal in evoking conversations between adults and children in a park. They set up an experiment with a young woman sitting in a grassy area in a park. She had with her either a rabbit, a turtle, a TV set or a bottle of bubble mixture. The researchers observed how many unfamiliar adults and children approached her in each situation and analysed the types of discussion that followed. Both adults and children approached her most readily when she sat with the animals than with the TV set. Adults on their own approached the rabbit more than the turtle, whereas adults with children approached the rabbit and the turtle equally. Children were also interested in approaching when the bubbles were used, but the resulting conversation was different to when animals were present. The bubbles tended to elicit exclamations, whereas interactions when the animals were present involved exclamations, questions, teaching and personal statements. The researchers concluded that a clear focus for attention, such as bubbles, induce interest, but may not result in a social interchange because of the effort required in creating such interaction. However, the presence of the animal created an opportunity to communicate 'without effort, an obvious need, or a special request' (Hunt et al., 1992: 255).

Animals can also impact positively on the social environment. Dr Aubrey Fine, an American researcher and pioneer of AAIs, tells of how animals can cause a kind of rippling effect in an environment because their presence acts as an agent of change. He recalls working with a girl who was selectively mute, who did not speak to adults or peers when at school. Working with Puppy, a therapy dog, acted as a catalyst to encourage her to speak. During early sessions with Fine, she decided to talk to Puppy, giving her simple commands. She wanted Puppy to visit her in school, and so this prompted her to talk to the teacher – to introduce Puppy and to explain about her needs. While Fine suggests this girl would probably have started speaking in time, he has no doubt that this was accelerated through 'the cold nose [and] warm heart of a golden retriever' (see Chandler and Otting, 2018: 7).

Crawford and Pomerinke (2003) report a similar tale when they share the story of Matthew, a 3-year-old with autism who had not had any social interaction with others until Jeb, a big crossbreed dog, came into his life. On his first meeting with the dog, Matthew seemed non-responsive. However, when Jeb dropped his ball into Matthew's lap things changed. Matthew took the ball, looked at Jeb and gave it back to him. This may seem a small exchange, but it was the first time Matthew had made eye contact or had any interaction with another living creature. Chandler (2017) describes these interactions as a kind of 'social dance' that occurs between animal and child. Animals enter a social relationship with humans, which Chandler calls human–animal relational theory (HART).

Looking after animals can support the development of relationships between the animal caregivers themselves. Pederson (2009) suggests that looking after animals together creates a situation of special shared experiences, alongside the development of specialist knowledge, which can promote group bonding. This is one of the principles underpinning provision at Green Chimneys School for Little Folk, first opened in 1948 by Samuel B. Ross Jr, an animal-loving educator and philanthropist. Ross (2011) pioneered the idea that children could gain confidence and become socially adept by caring for animals. What began as a small boarding school for eleven students is now a fully accredited day and residential facility with two campuses in New York state. There are currently 243 students and at least as many animals (Schiffman, 2019). Ross explains that relationships can be strengthened among children through fostering shared interests in animals. As bonds between the children develop, the focus on the animal may become less essential (see Chandler and Otting, 2018).

Individuals with specific learning needs can also benefit from interaction with animals. For instance, children with attention deficit hyperactivity disorder (ADHD) may not make friends easily, misread social cues, have difficulty taking turns and find it difficult to manage their own behaviour. Schuck et al. (2018) carried out a randomised controlled trial (RCT) with eighty-eight 7–9-year-old children, all of whom had a diagnosis of ADHD, presenting with inattention and hyperactivity/impulsivity. All of the children in the study received social skills training and their parents attended parent behavioural training classes. In addition, one group of children worked with therapy dogs (following the Canine Assisted Intervention (CAI) model), while the other group of children had free playtime without dogs. Parents of children in both groups noted a reduction in ADHD symptom severity over the course of the twelve-week project. However, the CAI group made progress more quickly (with significant differences after eight weeks) and presented with slightly better social skills, especially relating to social initiation, than the non-CAI group. The researchers concluded that the dogs might provide a catalyst for improved attention, thereby supporting interaction.

Individuals with ASD often struggle to engage with peers and may experience feelings of social isolation as a result. O'Haire et al. (2013a) found that children with ASD talked to people more, looked at human faces more frequently and made more tactile contact with people when they were in the presence of guinea pigs than when they were in a room with toys (another social stimulus). They also made more social approaches to peers when in the presence of animals. This was despite the fact that the children actually touched the toys more than the animals, and spent more time looking at the toys than the animals, suggesting that animals contribute something unique to social situations. This is possibly because the presence of the animals has been shown to decrease the stress hormone cortisol in children with ASD (see Viau et al., 2010).

Behaviour

Another key aspect of getting on with others relates to how we behave in social situations. Teachers often rate more extreme behaviours as among the biggest concerns in the profession in terms of the effect on their well-being (Fox, 2018). However, in reality it is low-level challenging behaviours, such as the child who constantly calls out during the carpet time or the group of children who can't stop whispering in assembly, that are experienced most regularly (Ofsted, 2014).

Young children rapidly learn to behave in certain ways. Some behaviour, such as joyfulness and involvement, can support learning and social relationships.

Generally speaking, children who feel valued and who observe and experience respectful and caring relationships learn to behave in respectful and caring ways with other children and adults. Empathy is an important aspect of social relationships, and involves children developing the capacity to understand and respond to the feelings of others (e.g. Eisenberg and Strayer, 1987). Empathy is associated with prosocial behaviour such as helping (Castano, 2012).

However, other behaviours such as attention-seeking, withdrawal or aggression can be detrimental to both learning and social relationships. Learning to behave well can be difficult for some children because behaviour is shaped by a number of factors, some of which are illustrated in Figure 2.1.

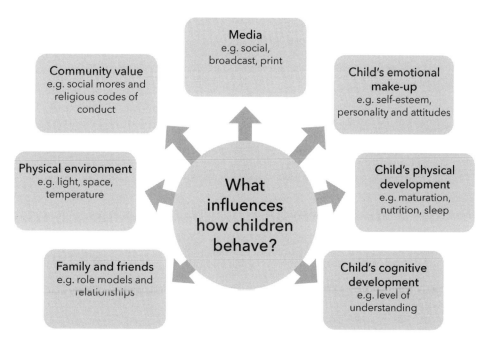

Figure 2.1. Factors impacting on behaviour

For some children, there is a developmental reason underlying their behavioural patterns. Schaefer (2015) suggests that the following are among the most commonly seen diagnoses that may impact on a child's behaviour:

- Attention deficit hyperactivity disorder – a chronic condition characterised by persistent inattention, hyperactivity and sometimes impulsivity.

- Oppositional defiant disorder (ODD) – patterns of irritable or angry moods, or argumentative/defiant behaviour, lasting at least six months.

- Autistic spectrum disorder – a developmental disorder characterised by restricted or repetitive patterns of thought and behaviour which contribute to difficulties in social interaction and communication.

- Anxiety disorder – intense and excessive feelings of anxiety and fear.

- Depression – intense feelings of despondency and dejection.

- Bipolar disorder – psychiatric illness characterised by both manic and depressive episodes.

- Learning disorders – difficulties in processing information which make it hard for someone to learn a new skill and apply it.

- Conduct disorders – difficulties in following rules and behaving in ways that are socially acceptable.

Each of these need careful, specific and considerate management. ODD, for instance, often features angry outbursts, typically directed at people in authority such as parents or teachers. Creating a structured learning environment with clear expectations, a focus on positive, prosocial and non-defiant behaviour, and the use of rewards – coupled with a calm attitude – may work effectively in supporting children with ODD (Davies, 2016). Conduct disorders involve behaviour one would consider cruel, both to other people, often peers, as well as to animals. This can include physical violence and even criminal activity. Treatment is often cognitive-behavioural therapy or peer group therapy. Autism is actually a broad range of disorders that can affect children in a variety of ways, including behaviourally, socially and cognitively. They are considered as having a neurological basis, and, unlike other behavioural disorders, the symptoms may begin as early as infancy.

How could animals help with children's behaviour?

Animals cannot provide a cure-all for behavioural issues. However, evidence suggests that, combined with careful adult support, they may help children learn to manage their behaviour more successfully (Purewal et al., 2017). Providing clear and consistent expectations, alongside structured frameworks to teach young people alternatives to unacceptable responses, and creating a classroom community where children feel a sense of belonging can make a difference. AAIs can provide frameworks, alternatives and supportive experiences to help children learn to behave appropriately.

Interactions with animals may support the development of empathy in young children (Wice et al., 2020). For example, children undertaking a programme of activities aimed at developing their ability to treat animals humanely showed higher levels of empathy than children not involved in the programme (Poresky, 1990). However, the quality and quantity of interaction is important. Just having a pet in the home or classroom and caring for its basic needs is unlikely to be enough. Wice et al. (2020) suggest that it is when children engage with animals as close companions that empathy and other prosocial behaviours are most likely to develop.

We cannot assume that just sitting children alongside a dog or other animal will magically lead to improvements in their social skills. Children need to learn appropriate behaviour in order to interact appropriately with animals. Adults should model a calm, quiet and gentle manner in the presence of an animal. Friedrich (2019) highlights the important role adults play as a safe haven when implementing AAI programmes and the need to target improving children's social communication skills. Fine suggests that even the smallest animal can have a large impact on children's behaviour. He tells of one boy who struggled to control his highly impulsive behaviour, and what happened when he brought his gerbil, Sasha, into the class:

He looked at me and said, 'Can I hold her?'... I said, 'Sure.' I said, 'But there's some rules. I'm going to put her in your hands and you have to promise that you're going to be gentle.' So there was this boy and Sasha, in her own gentle way, first sniffed his palms, and he smiled. Then she gradually went on his tummy. He looked at me with the greatest smile on his face and he said, 'I told you I won't move.' This was one of the first times I noticed how in control of his behavior he was. (see Chandler and Otting, 2018: 5)

Animals may also impact positively on more serious and extreme behaviours. The relationship between cruelty to animals in childhood and cruelty to humans in adulthood has been shown in a number of studies (e.g. Miller, 2001; Wright and Hensley, 2003). Therefore, teaching children to behave respectfully around animals may be a first step in decreasing violent and aggressive tendencies in adulthood. For example, in South Carolina, Healing Species is a violence prevention programme. It uses rescued dogs to teach messages about anti-violence to elementary and middle school students. The programme provides children with new ways to deal with confrontational situations. The presence of the dog allows the children to observe and practise behaviours such as being gentle. As a result, Sprinkle (2008) saw significant changes in children's displays of violent and aggressive behaviours.

Children can also develop responsibility through dealing with animals. Animals require a great deal of care and attention. Sometimes taking on this responsibility can mean that children and young people are distracted from antisocial activities, as in the case of Luis Tejada. Luis grew up in Washington Heights, New York, in the 1990s. As a teenager he fell into the wrong circle and became angry, violent and mistrustful of adults. But he was also a secret lover of animals, looking after the neighbourhood stray dogs. Luis was sent to Green Chimneys and fell in love with the horses, developing a special connection with one ex-racehorse called Bonz: 'They rescued him just like they rescued me,' recalled Luis, who is now 31 and working successfully in a nursing home in Pennsylvania (Schiffman, 2019).

A further benefit of interacting with animals is that as they respond to people on the basis of their actions – children get immediate feedback on their behaviour. For example, animal play therapist Tracie Faa-Thompson (see Chandler and Otting, 2018, ch. 3) frequently works with horses and children in therapy contexts. If a child's behaviour frightens the horse then the child will get an instant response, as the horse will often back away, ending the interaction. This feedback can have a significant impact on the child and can provide an opportunity for children to see situations from another perspective.

This can also help children to recognise and regulate their own body language. For example, Jack, a 12-year-old boy with a diagnosis of autism, found dealing with social situations very challenging. Then Jack met Dixie, a Shetland pony. Horses should be approached slowly and calmly, and you need to be sensitive to subtle cues like movements of the tail and the position of the ears to know whether or not you can safely draw near. Being with horses required Jack to learn the body language of horses, and he gradually transferred this to looking at similar body cues in people (Schiffman, 2019).

Animals, particularly those under stress, can also display behaviour that is of concern, and children can learn to recognise and empathise with this. Efrat Maayan (Chandler and Otting, 2018, ch. 7) works at a centre in Israel which treats addictions of various kinds in adults and children. One animal at the centre, a green parrot called Donna, became depressed and started plucking out her own feathers after her mate died. Children noted this and talked about how Donna was feeling and why she was behaving in this manner. This provided a gateway into discussing their own challenging behaviours such as self-harm. Similarly, Nancy Parish-Plass talks about Nezeq, an unpredictable cockatiel. The bird's behaviour helped a boy to recognise his own behavioural issues and opened up a way of talking about them:

Whenever anyone tried to talk to him about his behavior, he would say, 'I never get angry. I don't even know what you're talking about.' One day, he was talking to me about Nezeq, and he said, 'I know you love Nezeq very much, even though sometimes he can be a little bit biting and scary, but I think I can sometimes be like Nezeq too. I think I'm a very nice boy. I can be cute. But sometimes people say I can get very, very angry. So, I think I'm like Nezeq.' (see Chandler and Otting, 2018: 128)

Following this conversation, the boy was able to start talking directly about his own behaviour and began to explore ways to manage it. Chandler (2017) notes that interacting with animals often challenged her clients to recognise the impact of their own behaviours and attitudes.

Animals can also motivate children and young people to behave appropriately. Eight-year-old Xander, who has ADHD and dyslexia, would throw tantrums and often simply walk out of class. Most mornings, the school would call his mother to ask her to pick up her son. Then he started studying at Green Chimneys. One of his jobs there is to care for the goats, and he acknowledges the impact that this has had on his anger: 'The goats help one another ... They also really help me when I'm angry, because they are so peaceful and calm. If I feel sad, Snowflake comes and sits next to me' (Schiffman, 2019).

However, it is important to remain aware that in some cases the presence of an animal can lead to an increase in stereotypical behaviours such as hand-flapping among children with ASD, possibly due to excitement (Pavlides, 2008). The presence of an animal can, for some individuals, also be a sensory overload. Knowing the children very well and carefully observing interactions is essential to ensure all are benefiting. Different animals will suit different individuals, so it is important to know them well too. For example, my (HL) own dogs interact with people very differently. My large dog, Carlo, is enthusiastic and very confident in his interactional style, and people who are familiar with dogs tend to enjoy this. Many of my students who are missing their own dogs while they are away at university love to spend time with him. He will roll over for tummy tickles and if they sit on the floor he will try to get on their laps – not always easy as he is a 38-kg dog! My smaller dog, Scarlet, is less outgoing with her responses and has a more reserved interactional style. When I take her to work, my students who are less confident with dogs, but who do want to interact with an animal, tend to engage well with her. She is smaller, quieter and tends to sit calmly by their side which helps them to gain confidence.

Tails from the classroom

It is story time at Ffrindiau Bach Tegryn in Aberporth, west Wales, a Welsh-medium, part-time nursery for 2–4-year-olds. In a familiar scene, the children gather excitedly on the carpet. While some are chatting and fidgeting, Honey Allen is sitting nicely, ready for the story to begin. She models good listening skills and focuses on Wendy, the nursery manager, who praises her effort: 'Well done, Honey, you are sitting very well.' Immediately there is a ripple effect around the carpet as all the children sit up attentively, just like Honey. This kind of routine takes place in hundreds of settings every day. What is perhaps unusual is that Honey is not a 3-year-old child but a 12-year-old golden retriever with a fondness for sausages and liver cake.

Honey has been visiting the nursery regularly for over a year and her positive relationships with the children help them to become increasingly confident and independent. One child has been identified as being on the autistic spectrum, and while he finds forming relationships with peers and adults difficult, he is keen to interact with Honey. On a recent visit, June (Honey's owner) observed him going to where Honey's treats are kept, selecting a piece of cheese and bringing it over to give to Honey. This was a calm, confident independent interaction – a big step forward for this child.

Honey also provides a stimulus for gaining the children's attention and as a 'hook' for learning. For example, the children often invite Honey into different areas in the enhanced provision area. When this happens, the children engage and communicate with her creatively – for example, when recently 'taking her shopping' in the role play area. This meant the chance to explore a real-life context – talking about food and money, and exploring the language and routines involved in going to the shops.

Thinking about Honey has provided all of the children with the opportunity to talk about their own and others' behaviour, and its consequences. The children learn to adjust their behaviour to different situations – for example, they know not to run or shout when Honey is nearby because they don't want to scare her. Wendy has seen a marked improvement in the behaviour of two boys who were reluctant to settle and interact with their peers, and who previously showed little self-control in the classroom environment. The difference when Honey visits is noticeable; they are much calmer and will move alongside other children to pat Honey gently. This interaction often leads to more consistent periods of calm activity with peers.

Table 2.2 illustrates some practical ways in which Honey's presence has contributed to the development of the children's social skills.

Table 2.2. Honey the dog's potential for developing social skills
in young children

Type of social skill	Honey's influence
Expressing emotions	Children are encouraged to talk about how they feel when Honey comes to visit. They look for signs that Honey is relaxed and happy, and talk about the things that make her – and them – feel that way.
Communication	Honey provides a context for purposeful talk. Children are keen to ask June questions about Honey and tell their parents about the visit when they go home. Parents themselves are enthusiastic about the initiative and come to talk to Wendy and her team about Honey – fostering positive communication channels between home and setting.
Listening	Children are encouraged to listen carefully to instructions about Honey's needs, such as when she is able to have a treat.
Working together	Children at the nursery must learn to take turns to give Honey a treat. They take account of one another's ideas about how to organise their activity – for example, they suggested their own rota for turn-taking relating to holding Honey's lead.
Caring	Honey brings her own bag with her, which includes her toothbrush, toothpaste and wipes. Through modelling the use of these, the children can see how June helps Honey to have good personal hygiene. Children recognise when Honey is hot or tired and think about her needs. When Honey had major surgery, the children learned how this might have made her feel and how to be gentle around her.

Type of social skill	Honey's influence
Non-verbal skills	Honey has helped the children to learn about non-verbal communication. The children are taught how to approach a dog, basic canine body language signals and how they must never touch an unknown dog. This is very important from a safety perspective.

Caitlin Jones, a teacher in Pembrokeshire, Wales, shares another example of how teachers can use animals to support their management of behaviour. As a newly qualified teacher, Caitlin found that she was constantly reflecting on and developing her strategies to organise and manage her classroom provision. As part of the Burns By Your Side (BBYS) scheme (see Chapter 4), she began bringing her whippet, Nora, into school to read with some of her pupils. Almost by accident, Nora quickly became an integral part of Caitlin's behaviour management strategies. For example, on the days when Nora is in school, Caitlin has noticed that the children increasingly enter the classroom very quietly and calmly. One pupil, Joe, who has complex needs, found interacting with peers very difficult and frequently displayed some challenging behaviours as a result. However, Joe was keen to interact with Nora, and when Nora is present Joe is noticeably calmer and increasingly willing to interact with peers. Caitlin has noticed that if Nora sits quietly on the carpet to listen to a story, Joe will often also come to the carpet area and sit quietly, something that he has found difficult to do in the past. Nora provides the motivation for Joe to behave appropriately and helps him to self-regulate his behaviour without needing constant reminders from Caitlin herself.

Otis the labradoodle (a Labrador/poodle cross) works at Christ Church (Erith) Church of England Primary School in Kent (Figure 2.2). Head teacher Gillian Ball prepared carefully in advance of deciding to get a school dog, visiting other schools with dogs in order to identify issues such as appropriate outside space and risk assessment (see Chapter 8). Otis' role in school is varied, from listening to reluctant readers to working with children with anxiety and behavioural issues. He also attends all whole-school activities such as open days, staff meetings and sports days (he has won the staff race at sports day for the past two years!). Class teacher Sarah Cornish has noted the particular impact Otis has on the children's oracy and communication, with Otis providing purpose and focus for the conversations between children in her class:

Otis is a shared interest within the classroom and his presence encourages all pupils to talk to one another and share their excitement for him to join our lessons. You can hear the children discussing among themselves how to best look after Otis - for example, giving him a bit of space and questioning if he needs water. Otis has a positive impact on communication and relationships.

Otis also has an impact on children's behaviour throughout the school. For instance, the children have developed a better understanding of how their behaviour impacts on others, as they now understand that they need to be sensitive to his needs. They are aware that Otis does not like loud noises, so they need to be calm around him and this enables them to monitor their own behaviour. Pupils who usually react impulsively or who are loud and/or erratic have shown that they can alter this behaviour in order to make sure they are kind and thoughtful towards Otis. Kelly Sevenoaks, the school's special educational needs coordinator, believes that Otis' calm and loving temperament is part of the reason why children with specific behavioural and emotional needs benefit from spending time with him. He is non-judgemental, calm and quiet and this has far-reaching benefits for the children.

Figure 2.2. Otis, resident at Christ Church (Erith) Church of England Primary School in Kent

Source: Gillian Ball

Natalie Carroll, the school's vice principal, also notes that the promise of spending time with Otis has proven to be a motivating reward for positive behaviour for many children, not just those he works with on a regular basis. His presence is also beneficial for staff well-being and parental engagement: he often attends staff meetings, and after a busy school day many staff enjoy the opportunity to spend some time with him in order to unwind and relax.

The potential impact of animals on children's social development and behaviour is also evident with older learners. Barbara Priestman Academy, part of the Ascent Academies Trust, is a special needs school in Sunderland. It caters for 152 students aged 11-19 who have a diagnosis of ASD and/or complex needs. Ollie is a 2-year-old sprockerpoo (a springer spaniel/cocker spaniel/poodle cross) who has been visiting the school since he was 5 months old. He has achieved the Association of Pet Dog Trainers Good Companion Award at Jubilee level.

Judith Stephenson, lead practitioner for teaching and learning in the school, explains why Ollie is so important to learners in terms of helping with their social development and behaviour:

Ollie supported one pupil, Alfie, in the lead-up to his exams, when Alfie was finding it particularly difficult to cope and behave appropriately. Alfie recognised that Ollie's behaviour reflected his, so when he was behaving boisterously, Ollie was very playful. Conversely, when he was quiet and upset, Ollie was calmly next to him, waiting for him to reach out and stroke him. Through working with Ollie, Alfie has been able to better recognise how he is feeling, but also to reflect on the effect of his behaviour on both himself and others.

You can read more about Ollie in the next chapter.

Summary

- Interactions with animals can benefit social and behavioural development.
- Animals of many different species can provide opportunities for learners to communicate with one another, with other people and with the animal itself.

- This communication may serve a number of purposes, from talking about the animal's needs to talking to and about the animal.

- Recognising the needs of the animal and gaining feedback directly from the animal may also help children to behave calmly and to self-regulate their behaviours.

- Encouraging learners to take responsibility for animals may support the development of prosocial behaviour and increased empathy.

Chapter 3

Tales with feelings: animals and their impact on children's emotional development

Because horses so easily reflect back our state of mind [...] they serve as 'divine mirrors'. They return to us our emotional truth; what we feel is what they see. (Hamilton, 2011: 91)

Animals make people feel special irrespective of their wealth, gender, age, physical condition or social standing. The Queen's famous fondness for Pembroke Welsh corgis began aged just 7, in 1933, when the royal family chose their first pet dog. As a breed, Pembroke corgis traditionally had docked tails.[1] 'The Duke' was chosen because he had the longest tail. In the words of the Queen Mother, this meant they could 'see whether he is pleased or not'.[2] In a Netflix documentary on the royal family, the social anthropologist Kate Fox suggested that the reserved nature of the Queen and her position means that she rarely has the opportunity to express her feelings: 'Her inner brat doesn't get let out very often, does it?' (quoted in Heimbrod, 2019). One royal biographer summed up the Queen's relationship with dogs as 'a special feeling, and even an empathy for them' (Pimlott, 2012: 28). In the 1930s, her affection for dogs led to the emergence of a new genre of literature called 'royal caninism'.

At the other end of the social scale, the emotional bond between dogs and homeless people is illustrated through a recent multimedia project by the New York charity My Dog is My Home. Researchers noticed how the mood of

---

1 In England and Wales, tail docking in all but a few exceptions has been illegal since 2006. See https://www.thekennelclub.org.uk/our-resources/media-centre/issue-statements/tail-docking/.
2 He was named The Duke because of his apparent loftiness around other puppies. In 2015, the Queen decided not to breed corgis any longer over fears that she may trip over and hurt herself, but it was also reported that she didn't want to leave any behind on her death. Her last corgi died in 2018 (*The Telegraph*, 2018).

homeless people who suffered, or continue to suffer, from mental illness, inadequate healthcare or violence changed once they started to talk about their dogs. They explained how their pets made them feel loved and safe. The study concluded that 'In these stories, the humans care for dogs, but the dogs also care for the humans' (Eckart, 2017; see also Lindgren et al., 2019).

Of course, not everyone shares such feelings of affection. In the case of the Queen's corgis, many might share Prince William's complaint about their noise: 'I don't know how she copes with it,' while his brother, Harry, said that he had been barked at for thirty-three years (Coren, 2018). Moreover, we all know pets who are perfect companions with their owners but bad tempered and ill-disposed to others. As Sheldrake (2011: 74) reminds us: 'pets are not magical, they are good, bad, or indifferent, like people'. Animals do not automatically provide unconditional love, and just like people they can be selective with their affections. Every year, thousands of pets are abandoned, particularly after Christmas, because they do not fulfil the expectations (usually unrealistic) of their owners. Nevertheless, the fact that around one in two households in the UK own a pet dog illustrates the widespread emotional attachment to animals, particularly to dogs.

In many households, pets are widely regarded as members of the family. Children and young people often seem to have a special affinity to animals, whom they look upon as close friends, playmates and confidants. There is even a suggestion that relationships with pets can be stronger than those with siblings (Cassels et al., 2017). One Scottish survey of over 1,000 7–12-year-olds reports that the majority of children are strongly attached to their pets, although attachment scores differ depending on pet type and child gender (Hawkins and Williams, 2017). The researchers concluded that encouraging children to care for pets may bring a range of positive outcomes in terms of reducing aggression and general better well-being for children and improved treatment for pets. While children participating in AAIs would typically have less time with animals in school than at home with their pets, this chapter focuses on what we know about the emotions associated with AAIs in educational settings.

The question of whether animals and humans share the same basic emotions and feelings has been a long-running debate and continues to attract interest (see Thagard, 2017). The Roman writer Cicero thought that while animals share similar behaviours with humans, they have no feelings other than pleasure, to which they direct all their inclinations. Plutarch, on the other hand, adopted the opposite view (see Newmyer, 2011). He loved animals and argued that they were (emotionally) intelligent creatures. In 1932, visitors at Chester Zoo were intrigued by the sight of a rhesus monkey who started to gnaw at a length of rope. After tying one end to a branch, he formed a noose with the other. Then he put it over his head and jumped. The apparent suicide of this monkey caused much debate over the monkey's emotional state (Barkham, 2014) – did he jump because he was depressed? While distress among animals isn't difficult to spot, scientists are still trying to understand their emotions: can geese laugh? Are some dog breeds more optimistic than others? Can animals really show love, fear, anger and compassion for others? Those who believe that they can are quick to point to the everyday observations of pets who are very happy to be fed, the excitement of dogs about to go for a walk or the fear animals experience during firework displays. Most pet owners are in no doubt that when a cat purrs or a dog wags its tail, they are happy. The scientific community, on the other hand, is more cautious and divided.

Sceptics point out that we should not confuse behaviour with emotions, and that there is no guarantee that animals experience the same emotions as we do. Rather, they suggest that animals behave in certain ways simply because of their neural connections. They cannot tell us whether they are happy or sad, and we should not infer emotions from their actions. Their behaviour is a matter of responding to rewards or reacting to threats. Michael Steinberg (2005: 35) concludes that we should not be fooled into thinking that our dogs love us; rather, they are genetically programmed to exploit our foibles. Moreover, he argues, they cannot show empathy because they lack conscious thinking or a theory of mind. Put simply, this means they cannot sense thoughts, beliefs and emotions in the same way as humans.

However, others argue that animals are capable of feeling a range of complex emotions. Peter Wohlleben is one writer who takes issue with scientists who dismiss animal emotions. In his fascinating book *The Inner Life of Animals* (2016), Wohlleben explores a range of topics such as whether animals can lie, show gratitude and kindness, act in a fair manner, feel embarrassment, and experience grief and joy. Wohlleben suggests that very basic signs of consciousness, if defined as thinking and reflecting on experience, have been found in tiny insects such as fruit flies. They can filter out different smells and focus attention on specific things – just like humans.

Experiments with goldfish show that they can experience pain and fear. In one study (Nordgreen et al., 2009), two groups of goldfish were equipped with miniature jackets containing a tiny flexible foil heater. One group was given a painkilling injection of morphine and the other (control group) an inactive saline solution. While both groups showed similar 'escape responses' when the heat was turned up, there were clear differences when the fish returned to their normal home tanks two hours later. The control group which had not been given morphine displayed more signs of fearful behaviour, such as 'hovering' and flicking their tails. The researchers argued that the behavioural differences could not be attributed to reflexes only. Fish feel pain, and this conclusion has support from organisations such as the RSPCA (Dobson, 2009). Wohlleben and others support the view that animals share the same basic brain structures as humans and that these structures generate emotions. Some animals even share the hormone oxytocin, which in humans evokes feelings of love and affection for others.

The environmentalist Carl Safina is in no doubt that dogs and other animals have emotions. In his highly engaging book *Beyond Words: How Animals Think and Feel* (2018), he describes how a humpback whale sweeps a seal onto its back and out of the water, away from killer whales. And how do you explain incidents such as an elephant risking her own life by wading into a river to save her handler, other than because she thought he was in trouble?[3] These are only remarkable stories because humans have recorded them. The likelihood is that animals have been showing such feelings over millennia.

Of course, animals and humans differ in how they express emotions and feelings. There is some debate over whether animals have the same range and maturity of emotions experienced by humans, and whether they are capable of holding mixed emotions at the same time (Barkham, 2014). Current thinking suggests that the emotional maturity of dogs is at the level of a toddler (12–18 months) and this applies to both cognitive and affective domains (see Figure 3.1). Thus, we should not expect animals such as dogs to exhibit the range of emotions that human adults do, just as we would not expect the same maturity from young children. Nonetheless, we should respect the fact that animals are

---

3   See https://www.youtube.com/watch?v=uVceZEfAsTc. The video, which has been viewed more than 14 million times, was captured by Save Elephant Foundation, founded by Sangdeaun Lek Chailert, who has devoted her life to rescuing Asian elephants.

sentient beings who have ups and downs in their lives, just as we do (Bekoff, 2007).

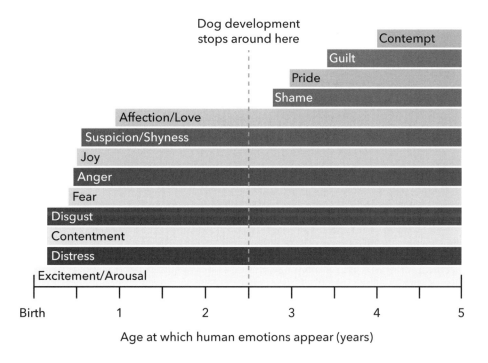

Figure 3.1. The development of emotions in children and dogs

Source: Coren (2013)

In humans, emotions such as shame, pride and guilt do not typically appear until children are at least 3 or 4 years of age (Coren, 2013). While dogs can express basic emotions such as joy, fear, anger, disgust and even love, they reach their stage of maturity by the age of 4-6 months and, according to current research, there is no indication that they can display more complex emotions. Dogs will not feel pride at winning competitions or shame at wearing ridiculous costumes bestowed upon them by their dotty owners. Similarly, there are many online pictures and videos of 'guilty' looking dogs who have chewed or eaten (or worse) items belonging to their owners. In reality, the dogs are unlikely to feel guilt about their past behaviour, but they may feel anxious and show signs of appeasement that we misinterpret as shame (McLaughlin, 2016).

Neither was it thought that animals possess more complex emotional responses, such as holding a grudge. However, recent observations at the University of Washington have led scientists to rethink this. When they started to trap crows for research purposes, they found that the birds seemed to exact revenge by swooping against them whenever they left their office, regardless of what clothes they were wearing. Even when they wore masks to disguise their faces when trapping the birds, it didn't make much difference. Whenever they later walked around campus, the birds once again wouldn't leave them alone. The researchers hypothesise that crows learn to recognise threatening humans from both parents and others in their flock (Gannon, 2012). Similarly, octopuses have been found to express their dislike of individual researchers by squirting them with water on the back of their necks as they walked past their tanks (Godfrey-Smith, 2017).

The question of whether animals are able to show self-awareness has interested researchers for many years. Primatologist Gordon Gallup devised a simple test to examine whether chimpanzees were able to recognise themselves. Gallup placed a full-length mirror outside the chimps' cages, arguing that 'If self-awareness is the ability to become the object of your own attention, then mirrors can be used to measure and objectify this capacity. In front of a mirror, you are the object of your own attention. When you look at yourself in a mirror you are an audience to your own behavior' (Gallup et al., 2011: 80). At first, the chimps tried to attack their image in the mirror. However, within a few days, they seemed to use the mirror to examine their own reflections, paying particular attention to parts of their bodies that they could not normally see, such as up their nostrils. To examine whether they were aware of the image being of themselves, Gallup then placed red dots on the chimps' heads. When they saw the red dots in the reflection, the chimps touched these spots on their own heads, which the researchers interpreted as passing the test of self-awareness. Whether this represents a genuine measure of such awareness has been questioned in the literature. However, elephants, dolphins and a magpie remain among the few species of animals to pass it. Yet dogs, arguably our closest animal companions, have not been successful in passing the test.

Nonetheless, this may be a fault of the test design, rather than the dogs' limited self-awareness. Alexandra Horowitz, a leading researcher in the field, argues that the mirror test is not relevant to dogs since they rely less on visual cues than on olfactory ones. She designed a test based on scent rather than sight, arguing that this is the primary sense in which dogs make sense of the world around them (Horowitz, 2017). Dogs were given different canisters of urine to smell. Some contained their own urine, some an unfamiliar dog's urine, while others held some of the dog's own urine along with another scent. Finally, some canisters contained no urine, just the unfamiliar scent. By observing how long the dogs investigated each canister for, Horowitz noted that dogs could distinguish the olfactory 'image' of themselves when modified. The dogs were least interested in their own urine, somewhat interested in another dog's urine and most interested in their own urine that had the additional scent added. Such behaviour implies that the dogs were able to recognise the odour as being of or from 'themselves'.

Box 3.1. The mirror test

The consensus is that animals have human-like personality traits which means that they can appear to demonstrate grudge-like behaviour. However, generally speaking, because animals do not judge us by such things as our intelligence, income, job or physical appearance, people from all backgrounds and ages get very attached to them. In some cases, individuals become so emotionally close that they are willing to risk their own lives, and those of others, if it means saving their animals. One study reported that four in ten respondents would allow someone they did not know to die if it meant preserving their animal's life. When asked to justify this, the pet owners put it down to their love and bond for the animal (Topolski et al., 2013).

Perhaps this is not as surprising as it sounds. There have been lots of surveys which show that pets are perceived to play a positive role in their owners' emotional health. For example, a survey of 2,000 US citizens, aged between 50 and 80, found that about 90% of pet owners said that their animals helped them to feel appreciated and enjoy life more, while more than half of the respondents said that their emotional needs were addressed by their pets to some extent. Unsurprisingly, the most positive responses came from elderly people living alone (Headley, 2019). Indeed, during the 2020 coronavirus pandemic, the companionship of a pet was seen by many as crucial to combat feelings of loneliness and bouts of anxiety (Whitehead, 2020).

Central to such discussion is the concept of attachment. This has been defined as 'an enduring relationship with a specific person that is characterized by soothing, comfort, pleasure, and safety. It also includes feelings of intense distress when faced with the loss, or threat of loss, of this person' (Ludy-Dobson and Perry, 2010: 30-31). Attachment is a major concept in child development studies, with widespread recognition that infants seek proximity, physical contact and emotional closeness with their main caregivers. The theory of attachment was first proposed by the child psychiatrist John Bowlby. He questioned the prevailing view that children's emotional problems were due to what was happening in their minds and bodies. Instead, he highlighted the importance of bonding with the main caregiver, family relationships and exploring the childhood experiences of parents (Bowlby, 1949, 1953). According to Bowlby (1969), infants who do not form close attachments are unable to regulate stressful experiences and face a 'fight-or-flight' choice. When children lack the ability to regulate their emotions, they can remain in a fight-or-flight mode for most of the day, which causes socio-emotional and behavioural distress (Geist, 2011).

One of the assumptions of attachment theory is that by interacting with significant others (called attachment figures), an individual begins to form conscious and unconscious mental representations of self and relationship partners. These models shape how children feel and act around others. These interactions matter, particularly during times of need, offering a sense of security and boosting self-worth and positive mental health. However, when attachment figures are not available or prove unsupportive, then children feel undermined and develop negative models of self and others, increasing the likelihood of later emotional problems and maladjustment in adult life (Mikulincer and Shaver, 2007). Supporters of attachment theory argue that parents should be ready to respond to their children's emotional distress – for example, if children cry when a dog barks, they should provide reassurance, talk to them and distract their attention to occupy their minds. The broader goal is to support children's own self-regulation so they can control their feelings (Miller and Commons, 2010).

Attachment theory has also been applied to explain the bond that develops between a human and an animal. This human–animal bond is defined as a 'reciprocal and persistent' relationship that benefits both parties involved (Hosey and Melfi, 2012: 14). There are studies which suggest that such a bond exists in multiple species, including dogs, horses and various other farm and zoo animals. What seems to matter is the particular personalities and temperaments of both the animal and human. Chimpanzees, for example, have been shown to respond differently to someone who acts in a shy or bold manner (Hebb, 1949). It is also the case that human–animal bonds are highly individualised. Some elephants will only respond to the commands of their particular handlers, or mahouts, which is thought to reflect the trusting relationship they have established. All of this is important because it contributes to a safe and productive working environment for elephants and their handlers (Rossman et al., 2017).

Most of the research, however, has focused on companion animals (i.e. pets) and their relationships with adults, rather than school-based programmes and the attachment between children and animals. Given the relatively short time children spend reading to dogs, more research is needed to establish whether such relationships are comparable. Davison (2015) reports that children in her study experienced feelings of loss when their participation in a reading-to-dogs programme came to an end. The dog represents a safe haven and dependable source of comfort, particularly during times of emotional distress. When a dog puts its paw or muzzle on you, or when it licks you, it sends a message of comfort and interest, 'sorta like your psychiatrist in fur' (Kwong, 2008: 16). Such physical contact mirrors the cuddling and prolonged skin-to-skin contact and extended mutual gazing that is characteristic of the infant–caregiver relationship. Often, dogs can sense when their owners are feeling low. They can act as a stabilising influence, with children gaining a sense of 'felt security' knowing that the dog is always there for them. This gives children confidence to try again and keep going, drawing comfort from the dog's unconditional love. People generally feel good about themselves when they are alongside companion dogs, and feelings of loneliness and anxiety decrease (Bennett et al., 2015). The argument for animals as attachment figures takes on added significance for those individuals who may find it difficult to accept social support from humans.

However, there is a long-running debate over whether animals can truly fulfil the role of an attachment figure in the complete sense of a protective caregiver (Rynearson, 1978; Ainsworth, 1991; Hazan and Zeifman, 1994; Rockett and Carr, 2014; Meehan et al., 2017). It should be noted that some studies report a pet owner's sense of relief rather than anxiety when separated from the animal – for example, they may feel there has been a lifting of responsibility to care for the animal (Kwong, 2008). Moreover, it is also the case that two individuals can feel a strong attachment to their dogs but feel differently in terms of emotional security: one might feel very content and the other anxious about the pet's conditional love and loyalty (Zilcha-Mano et al., 2011b). In weighing up the arguments, Carr and Rockett (2017) suggest that animals could play a role similar to that in sibling relationships.

How could animals help?

One of the major findings from various research projects is that dogs are able to read human emotions by interpreting signs such as facial gestures, which they also use to locate hidden food (Buttelmann and Tomasello, 2013). In 2016, researchers discovered that Portuguese and British dogs were able to combine pictures and sounds to assess the emotional state of human voices. As Natalia De Souza Albuquerque explained: 'What we found is that when dogs were hearing positive sounds they would look longer to positive faces, both human and dog. And when they were listening to negative sounds they would look longer to negative, angry faces' (cited by Stock, 2016). The researchers believe that dogs possess an innate ability to read an individual's tone of voice and facial expressions, for example, and this is a possible explanation as to why their relationship with humans has been so successful throughout history.

There is little doubt that animals play an important role in providing emotional support for humans. There is growing evidence to show that children with significant emotional disturbances particularly benefit from AAIs. Hergovich et al. (2002), for example, showed that when a dog was placed in a first-grade class (6-7-year-olds) over a three-month period, the children made significant improvements in three key measures of empathy, when compared to children in a no-dog control class:

1   Children in the dog class were more able to show 'field independence' (a perceptual task related to empathy).

2   They displayed more positive attitudes towards animals.

3   They exercised greater control over their emotions (e.g. they were less aggressive), as reported by teachers.

The researchers concluded that the presence of the dog helped the children to show more sensitivity to the feelings of others because they were better able to segregate the self and non-self.

More recent studies confirm the correlation between the presence of dogs in educational settings and the improved emotional well-being of students. For example, in Germany, Beetz (2013) examined the effects of a dog's presence for one day per week on third-grade students' socio-emotional experiences, in comparison with a control class. She found that the dog-class students reported a stronger improvement with regard to positive attitudes towards school and positive emotions related to learning over the course of a year. This is significant because positive attitudes and feelings are prerequisites to effective learning.

One area for further research is the extent to which AAIs support children who have experienced bereavement. One estimate is that around one in twenty-nine children in the UK suffer the loss of a parent or sibling.[4] In other words, the likelihood is that if you are a teacher this will affect one member of your class. Children respond to bereavement in different ways. Anxiety, significant depression and disruptive behaviours are common, which can lead to low self-esteem, academic underachievement and poor social functioning (Sandler et al., 1988; Kranzler, 1990). At its worst, depression can result in suicide, which according to the World Health Organization is the second leading cause of death among 15–29-year-olds.[5] Unfortunately, there are reports that depression is on the rise among children and young people. In the United States, for example, the rate of major depressive episodes among adolescents (aged 12–17) has increased from 8.1% in 2009 to 13.2% in 2017 (Twenge et al., 2019a), while their feelings of loneliness are also on the rise (Twenge et al., 2019b). Girls are more vulnerable than boys, with one out of every five teenage girls experiencing major depression. Increasing use of social media and a decline in sleep duration have been suggested as possible causes.

Supporting students who are experiencing major depressive disorders and grief can be very challenging for teachers. The American Psychiatric Association

4   See http://www.childrensgriefawarenessweek.com.
5   See https://www.who.int/news-room/fact-sheets/detail/depression.

defines depression as 'a common and serious medical illness that negatively affects how you feel, the way you think and how you act'.[6] It can lead to a variety of emotional problems. Grief can coexist with depression and can trigger a major depressive episode. However, grief due to a significant loss is also normal and can, ultimately, be very healing.

There are research studies which indicate that animals play an important role in helping people come to terms with bereavement – for example, acting as a consoling grief partner (Mallon, 1992). In one randomised controlled study, the effects of animal-assisted support were tested with forty 12-year-old female children (Murry and Todd Allen, 2012). They volunteered to participate in one of two treatments: animal-assisted support or control support. All participants had experienced the death of a parent in the preceding year. When offered animals for their support group, the children chose reptiles (bearded dragons), which is unusual, as most studies focus on cats and dogs. The reptile-assisted support group had the opportunity to discuss death and grief while also learning how to care for animals and how they expressed emotions and grief. In contrast, children in the control group were able to discuss death and grief but had no direct contact with bearded dragons.

Primary caregivers were asked to complete the Child Behavior Checklist-Parent version (CBCL-P) before and after the sixteen-week support group programme. This comprehensive checklist consists of 113 questions scored on a three-point Likert scale (0 = absent, 1 = occurs sometimes, 2 = occurs often). The questions cover a range of topics, such as rule-breaking behaviour, attention problems, anxiety and social problems. For example, the respondents are asked to rate how often the child:

- Can't sit still, is restless or hyperactive.
- Clings to adults or is too dependent.
- Complains of loneliness.
- Cries a lot.
- Is cruel to animals.
- Destroys his/her own things.

6   See https://www.psychiatry.org/patients-families/depression/what-is-depression.

- Doesn't eat well.

- Doesn't get along with other kids.

- Breaks rules at home, school, or elsewhere. (Achenbach, 1991)

The researchers examined the differences between the two groups of participants. Because of the magnitude of experiencing a parental death, the researchers did not expect a reduction in anxiety and depression within the short time frame of their study (sixteen weeks). The reptile-assisted group played with the reptiles while the other group used traditional talk therapy. Each group of four or five participants was supported by a trained counsellor of the same level of experience. The reptile-assisted group discussed loss and grief with reference to the bearded dragons, speculating on how reptiles coped with loss (e.g. a bitten-off tail). The children were trained in how to handle, feed and care for the animals, while also learning how to interpret their moods (e.g. posturing for defence, head tilting and bobbing indicating a desire for food or a warning of aggression). The control group discussed how individuals differ in expressions of grief, stages of grieving, the display of perceived emotions of guilt or loss and conjecture as to how other children coped with loss.

Murry and Todd Allen (2012) found that the reptile-assisted group improved significantly in areas such as somatic (physical) behaviour, social skills, thinking (e.g. focusing on important tasks) and attentiveness, while showing reduced aggression and delinquency, as compared with the control group. While participants did not improve on the withdrawal or anxious/depressed measures, this was something that the researchers anticipated given the significance of the trauma experienced by the girls and the short duration of the project. However, other studies have indicated that anxiety and depression can be reduced through animal-assisted therapy (Barker and Dawson, 1998; Souter and Miller, 2007). Overall, the researchers concluded that the findings validated the use of animal-assisted support. What this research did not cover, however, was the children's self-perceptions of their feelings, anxieties and social relationships. In a recent systematic review focusing on studies of mental health treatments among adolescents, researchers reported that AAIs confer benefits such as reducing anxiety, anger and disruptive behaviours within treatment sessions. They also had a positive impact on primary diagnoses (Jones et al., 2019).

Anecdotal evidence is an important source to illustrate the potential animals have to lift people's mood. Muldoon et al. (2016: 362) cite the following conversation among 11-year-old girls to illustrate the emotional appeal of dogs:

Siobhan: [Talking about dogs] It's not like a cat. You can speak to them and have your own relationship with them, like them being your friend as well.

Janine (the researcher): They feel like that, do they, they feel like a friend?

Siobhan: Yeah.

Janine: A cat doesn't feel the same do you think?

Emily: No.

Siobhan: When you say anything to it they just walk off.

Emily: A dog is more of an animal who senses when you're upset or you're feeling down. It'll come and comfort you.

Siobhan: My dog does that, every time he sees me with my head down, he comes over and licks me.

Emily: They understand you.

An increasing number of dogs and animals are working on university campuses around the world, primarily to support student mental health. For example, the University of British Columbia has fifty-five dog therapy teams working on campus to reduce stress and homesickness and to increase campus affinity (Binfet and Struik, 2018), while Swansea University in the UK invites in dog therapy teams on a termly basis to support student well-being. A number of studies report the benefits of such approaches. For example, Gallard and Taylor (2017) found that AAI had a beneficial effect on undergraduate university students. In a study of twenty-five students, who attended tutorials with no animals or with either a dog or a guinea pig, all the students who took part reported that they felt less anxious when in the presence of the animals. Students said things like: 'It was calming to have a distraction and something else to focus on while my tutor looked through my work' (Gallard and Taylor, 2017: 44). They also reported feeling more relaxed after interactions with the animals. For one student, being able to spend time in the company of animals reminded her of her family home, where there were many companion animals. She missed them and said she felt 'a normality' return to her life. However, it is important to note that the students in the study were self-selecting, and several members of the faculty team did not think that the intervention had value.

Tails from the classroom

Evidence from practitioners shows that the presence of animals in educational settings such as schools can bring emotional benefits to students, particularly those with emotional difficulties. Children at Deighton Primary School in south Wales value spending time with Peter Pudding the school rabbit. For pupils Maddi, Amy-Leigh and Keegan, spending time with Peter gives them the chance to cool down when they feel anxious or stressed, and lets them relax during the busy school day. He also provides them with moments of joyfulness – such as when he hid under the sofa and they had to try to encourage him out with his favourite foods. They say that being with Peter feels calming, and when Keegan holds the rabbit he gets a similar feeling to when he 'cwtches [hugs] my mam'. This opportunity to develop self-regulatory behaviour is very important, as research suggests that this can have a positive impact on mental health and well-being (e.g. Beauchaine and McNulty, 2013). Claire Whatley, a higher level teaching assistant in the school, feels that looking after Peter gives children the chance to develop nurturing behaviours. For Keegan, taking on a role as a 'Peter Prefect', meaning he takes responsibility for looking after Peter during the week, has boosted his self-esteem.

Figure 3.2. Rabbits can provide appealing companionship

Source: Paylessimages – stock.adobe.com

Judith Stephenson, lead practitioner for teaching and learning at the Barbara Priestman Academy, has found that this is the case with students diagnosed with ASD. Such students can find the world emotionally challenging. Those who are teenagers also have to contend with the hormonal changes of puberty and the effect this has on their feelings. Their moods can swing suddenly and are often difficult to explain or attribute to a particular cause. As a result, they find it frustrating not to be able to put into words why they feel the way they do, let alone control and understand their feelings. Judith finds that it is essential to explicitly teach her students about emotions and how to regulate them. She uses a range of strategies to help students recognise how they are feeling. However, she admits that there are occasions when none of these strategies work and students are unable or unwilling to communicate. In such situations, she finds that the presence of sprockerpoo Ollie can be invaluable. For example, a Year 11 student, Alfie, had anxiety issues but wouldn't talk to the school's therapists. Often such therapeutic support is carried out in a clinical setting, which can be very off-putting for students, so Ollie goes to the students in whatever environment they find comfortable. Judith explains:

They will often take him to a room in school that is set out like a home, with beanbags and kitchen facilities. They can sit with him on the beanbags or talk to him while making a cup of tea; they will even just talk to him while walking him around the school grounds. Ollie has enabled a number of our students to begin to recognise the effect their emotions have on others where previous work around this emotional intelligence has failed.

Judith and her colleagues use Zones of Regulation (states of mind) with several students who find it difficult to regulate their actions. This is geared towards helping students gain skills in consciously regulating their actions, which in turn leads to increased control and the ability to solve problems more effectively. Using an approach based on cognitive psychology, students are helped to recognise when they are in one of four zones, each represented by a different colour. They are also taught and practise how to use strategies or tools to stay in a zone or move from one to another. By exploring various calming techniques, cognitive strategies and sensory support, they build up a toolbox of methods so they can move between zones. Students are also taught to interpret others' facial expressions, read their body language and recognise a broader range of emotions. They learn about perspective and how others may view and react to their behaviour. As a result, they begin to develop insight into events that trigger their less regulated states, and into when and how to use tools and problem-solving skills.

Despite such efforts, some students do not respond as well as might be expected and make limited progress using Zones of Regulation. Bryn is an example of such a student. However, when he started to spend time with Ollie, the teachers noticed a change in his mood. They arranged for Bryn to take Ollie for walks and encouraged him to share his feelings with Ollie. Bryn has experienced a very traumatic childhood, so he would sit and draw or make things out of salt dough and use them to talk through scenarios relating to his past. Ollie would sit calmly and allow Bryn the time and space he needed to talk without pressuring him. As the sessions with Ollie progressed, staff started to appreciate, through incidental comments, that Bryn could recognise how Ollie was feeling by the way he behaved. Although he couldn't recognise the zone he was in himself, he was able to recognise what zone the dog was in, and through discussing Ollie's feelings he eventually became able to relate those feelings and behaviours to himself. Bryn communicates quite loudly, and this was something he was unable to moderate no matter how many strategies staff had tried to put in place. When working with Ollie he was able to do this naturally – although he is still trying to transfer this skill to the classroom!

Occasionally, children and young people experience a crisis in their lives. In one such case (student C), staff found that Ollie really helped by simply lying down alongside him and waiting for the student to make the first move. Judith explains that the teacher doesn't need to say anything; rather, she takes up the role of observer in noticing the student's emotional reactions. Student C craves sensory input during these times, but he isn't able to let staff support him; however, he will use the dog to self-regulate, stroking and sniffing his fur. Interestingly, student C is also able to support other students and will encourage them to use the dog when they are upset. Judith reports that he was overheard asking one student, 'Haven't you heard about the research that says stroking a dog releases endorphins, which calm you down and can help regulate you?' For Judith, the power of seeing students recognising when another person needs support is 'fantastic, as empathy is something many autistic students struggle with'.

Another case from the school illustrates the contribution dogs can make in helping students to overcome feelings of embarrassment. Student D is someone who when feeling anxious seeks sensory input in the form of pacing. As he has become older, he has become more aware that this looks different and in school struggles at times to fulfil this need because he feels embarrassed. Ollie was brought in to offer support, so now when student D is having a particularly bad day he takes Ollie for a run in the field within the forest school. He is told that Ollie needs a run, so therefore he has a legitimate reason to run himself without feeling self-conscious.

For a student who struggled to form a normal attachment with a primary caregiver in early childhood (i.e. who has attachment disorder), Ollie has been able to support him through just 'hearing' his story. Ollie was the runt of the litter and was rejected by his first family before being chosen by the school trust's behaviour support manager. The students are able to relate to Ollie's story and see that something positive can emerge from a negative experience. Through working with Ollie on a regular basis, the children gain confidence that he will always be there when he is supposed to be, which helps to allay their anxieties. As one member of staff commented:

There's a lovely, comforting feeling to having a dog in school. Ollie seems to know what is expected of him; there's a playful side but he seems to recognise when to go to students and when to back off. Therapeutically with Ollie, students have no social pressures, no need to process anything and the dog puts no demands or expectations on them, which is really beneficial to so many of our students.

There are countless psychologists, veterinarians, doctors, teachers and pet owners who testify to the contribution animals can make in the treatment of patients and children who need emotional healing (Box 3.2). As Spadafori (2005: H5) puts it, 'No one who has ever watched one [therapy dog] work can doubt the difference they make.'

When I worked with children who had fears, I would talk to them about Wrigley's fear of thunder. It seemed to help children to know that even this great big dog had things he feared and had ways to cope with them. Rather than come to me for comfort, he would find the mom if there was one in the room, and stay close to her. Smart dog.

When I worked with two sisters, aged 6 and 4, learning to cope with their parents' divorce and the fact that they never got to be with both parents at the same time, I brought Wrigley in front of the two girls and, as we all petted him, I told them Wrigley never got to see his mom or his dad. The 6-year-old said, 'He doesn't?' And when I told her it was true, she said, 'I'll bet he feels like I do. I bet he thinks that's unfair.' After which her younger sister asked me if Wrigley's mom was a dog.

Box 3.2. The experience of one psychologist, Joe Kropp,
and his therapy dog, Wrigley

Boris Levinson (1962: 59) summed up the reciprocal feelings that often characterise child–animal interactions: 'A pet is an island of sanity in what appears to be an insane world ... one can rely upon the fact that one's pet will always remain a faithful, intimate, non-competitive friend – regardless of the good or ill fortune life brings us.'

Summary

- AAIs make a wide-ranging contribution to children's emotional development.

- Many scientists accept that animals have emotions but not in the same range or depth as humans.

- The theory of attachment was first proposed by the child psychologist John Bowlby, who suggested that it is important for infants' long-term development to form a close attachment with their primary caregiver.

- Some animals can represent an important attachment figure in children's lives.
- Our attachment to dogs is not surprising given their ability to interpret emotional signals from humans and adapt their behaviour accordingly.
- Animals themselves can gain from a close attachment to humans, including more humane treatment.

Chapter 4

Literary tales: animals and their impact on children's language, literacy and communication skills

---

The eyes of an animal have the capacity of a great language. (Buber, 2008: 144)

Fourteen-year-old Billy Casper was a student who had very little interest in school. He found lessons uninspiring and made little academic progress. He was bullied at school as a misfit and was so poor he had to wear his brother's cast-off clothes. He was brought up by a single mother who dismissed him as 'a hopeless case'. He had a bleak life and a bleaker future. Billy is the main character in Barry Hines' novel *A Kestrel for a Knave*, popularised in Ken Loach's award-winning film *Kes*, released in 1969. In fact, Billy's only hope rests with a kestrel chick that he finds on a nearby farm and lovingly rears and trains. It inspires him to find out more about falconry and so he visits the local library and then pilfers a book about training birds from a second-hand bookshop.

Later, in a poignant scene, Billy has the opportunity to share his passion in front of the class during an English lesson on 'fact and fiction'. Billy's knowledge leaves his classmates in awe. He talks about the technical meaning of terms such as 'jesses' and expertly answers their questions in an animated, authoritative manner. Mr Farthing is the only teacher who takes an interest in Billy's life. He not only draws him out using his interest but also visits Billy at home to learn more about his kestrel. Gazing at the bird, Billy says, 'I feel as though she's doin' me a favour just lettin' me sit here' (Hines, 1968: 118).[1]

---

1 Some research suggests that simply gazing at animals, even pictures of puppies, increases focus and makes us more productive (Nittono et al., 2012).

Here is a powerful example, albeit a fictional one, of how creatures can motivate and inspire students to read, speak with confidence and communicate to others. The beauty of the story is in the simplicity of the message: the hawk soars and symbolises hope and freedom, to be treasured when those around are seeking to crush it. This chapter focuses on how AAIs can benefit children's development in language, literacy and communication, with a particular focus on reading.

It is important not to underestimate how challenging it can be to become a fluent reader. As leading expert in reading Maryanne Wolf (2008, 2018) points out, we were never born to read, and mastery of reading is the most remarkable of human inventions. To read effectively, children need to master five components (Figure 4.1).

Considering Figure 4.1, it is important not to lose sight of the basic point that animals cannot 'teach' these fundamentals of reading. Pedagogy – which combines observation, judgement and intervention – is only found in humans. The nearest thing to this in the animal kingdom has been found in chimpanzees, who, for example, teach nut cracking, a skill that takes ten years to master (Premack and Premack, 2002).[2] Rather, what animals can do is to put children at ease and contribute towards an environment in which they are more willing to read, make mistakes, talk about how they feel, read aloud, self-correct and grow in confidence.

Reading is a complex business. Typically, in the UK and many other countries, we expect children to have acquired the fundamentals of reading by the age of 7, forgetting that reading is not something which comes naturally to us. Biologically speaking, we have no process specifically assigned to help us read, whereas children have a rich neural network designed to support the acquisition of oral language (Wolf, 2008). From infancy, children hear the sounds and structure of language, which activates parts of the brain. There is an instinctive tendency to speak, as we observe in the babbling of infants, whereas there is no such instinct to read or write.

Children need to develop these reading skills using a brain that has actually evolved for other purposes, such as speaking, vision and attention (Dehaene, 2009). As Steven Pinker (1997: ix) points out, children are 'wired' for language

---

2   However, this is a growing area of study, with some researchers discovering how animals teach their young (Morell, 2015).

Phonemic awareness – learning that words consist of smaller segments of sound (phonemes) which can change the meaning of words (e.g. hat, mat, pat).

Phonics – learning that the letters of the alphabet represent phonemes, which can be blended together to form words.

Fluency – the skill of reading quickly, accurately and with expression.

Vocabulary – both those words which appear in print and those spoken about texts.

Comprehension – cognitive understanding and retention of information that is being read.

Figure 4.1. Five components of reading

but 'print is an optional accessory that must be painstakingly bolted on'. The key bridging point in the development of reading is when children acquire both the accuracy and speed which no longer calls for huge conscious effort – what academics call automaticity. They are then able to concentrate on deeper levels of comprehension and thought.

Given this biological and evolutionary context, it is remarkable how much progress has been made in the development of widespread literacy. Or, to put it another way, how illiteracy among young people has been largely eradicated. For example, whereas in the 1970s around one in four of the world's young people (aged 15-24) lacked basic literacy skills, the figure is now less than 10%.[3] And in what the World Bank calls 'upper middle income' countries, which include the likes of Lebanon, Libya, Jordan, Sri Lanka, Thailand and Tonga, literacy levels are at 100%, alongside European countries.

However, such progress should not disguise significant challenges. It is estimated that around 15% of the world's population cannot read, while there are many young people who may have a command of the basic skills but do not enjoy reading.[4] Surveys regularly show that there is normally 'a decline by 9' with the percentage of children *wanting* to read for fun falling away by their ninth birthday.[5] The importance of getting it right in the early years and primary education is borne out by the fact that those students who struggle with reading at a young age are never likely to achieve full literacy (Ecklund and Lamon, 2008).

It is therefore not surprising that there is global interest in the factors that affect reading. Programmes such as READ are highly structured interventions which follow the same typical pattern:

1   The child first sits on the floor and plays with the dog for a few minutes.

2   The child reads to the dog for up to thirty minutes.

---

3   According to the World Bank, the global literacy level for young people aged between 15 and 24 has risen from 77% (1975) to 91% (2016): https://data.worldbank.org/indicator/SE.ADT.1524.LT.ZS. However, there have been changes in the methodology of measuring literacy rates which have tended to inflate figures (see UNESCO, 2017). Adult literacy rates are at or near 100% in most countries in Central Asia, Europe and northern America, and eastern and south-eastern Asia.

4   See https://data.worldbank.org/indicator/se.adt.litr.zs.

5   For example, see Scholastic's biennial *Kids and Family Reading Report*, based on surveys in the United States: https://www.scholastic.com/readingreport/home.html.

3   The dog handler sits in and gently helps the child with any mispronounced words.

4   Afterwards, the child plays with the dog.

To develop trust and a secure relationship, the same dog meets with the child on each occasion. The exact timing of the sessions is agreed upon with the dog handler, school or library. The intervention by the dog handler is kept to a minimum and occurs only to support reading accuracy and comprehension. To avoid embarrassment, the child is told that the dog hasn't heard that word before and asked if they can explain it. The emphasis is on the dog, who doesn't understand, rather than the child, who moves from being a passive reader to becoming an active teacher. This is good practice and is indicative of wider research which endorses the value of students acting as teachers (Hattie, 2012). Of course, this kind of interaction could take place with animals other than dogs. In two south Wales primary schools, Millbrook and Deighton, children read to rabbits and the schools report similar benefits for the children.

However, the 'trainability' of dogs means that the interactions that take place can have additional elements. BBYS is a scheme aimed at children who could benefit from improved reading and communication skills.[6] It is designed to help children in a variety of educational settings gain confidence by reading to a dog. Using specially trained volunteers and their companion dogs, the dogs come to a school or library to hear the children read. BBYS carefully considers legal, ethical and risk factors, and ensures that the welfare needs of the dog are paramount. Only after rigorous training and assessment by BBYS are the

Figure 4.2. Flynn and his book

Source: Burns By Your Side

dogs allowed into a school. As part of the training, BBYS dogs are taught simple

---

6   See https://burnspet.co.uk/burns-by-your-side.

tricks – for example, one BBYS dog, Flynn, can fetch specific books for the reading session, which delights the children.

In the Dogs Helping Kids scheme, dogs are trained to look at the book, focus on the pages, do tricks to show gratitude and 'tell' the child when the session is about to end.[7] Some dogs are even trained to 'read' flashcards. One word is taught at a time, with each word printed in a large, clear font. Using clicker training, the dog responds to a cue word before the flashcard word is introduced. For example, the word 'down' is taught and when the dog responds reliably, it is then associated with a flashcard of the said word, without other distractions. This allows the dog to link the action with the particular flashcard word. With constant repetition, the dog learns to go down when shown only the flashcard. Other words can then be learned, such as 'roll over', 'beg', 'wag' and 'paw'.

Davison (2015) suggests that through 'playful reading' to dogs, children develop a more relaxed attitude towards books as they benefit from a close, non-critical and informal relationship. As the dog appears to listen and show interest in the child reading, this increases the child's confidence and time spent on the reading task. Playfulness, more generally, has been shown to be an important means of learning, particularly in the early years (UNICEF, 2018).

It is important for teachers to reflect on the age-appropriateness of a particular AAI for the children and young people concerned. Davison (2015) argues that reading-to-dog schemes are best suited to younger children because of their apparent natural affinity with animals. She adds that teenagers 'outgrow' such friendships as they enter adolescence, although we would argue that this conclusion is too general. People of all ages are motivated to interact with animals. And, as seen throughout this book, AAIs have proven to be effective in supporting the overall well-being of children and young people in primary, secondary and tertiary education.

---

7   Unfortunately, the COVID-19 pandemic has prompted the closure of the scheme in August 2020.

How could animals help?

Unfortunately, much of the evidence claiming improvements in students' language and literacy skills associated with AAIs is anecdotal. Typical of this, the Kennel Club cites the example of a 9-year-old boy whose life has been 'transformed' after he began reading to dogs as part of the Dogs Helping Kids scheme. Finn, diagnosed with dyslexic traits, was a reluctant reader, which affected his confidence and progress. But when Finn started to read to Dexter, a shih tzu/poodle cross, and Kym, a Cavalier King Charles Spaniel/poodle cross, his mother and school staff noticed that he gained confidence and was more positive about reading. This left one teacher to conclude: 'He is a bit of an expert on reading to a dog in the eyes of his peers and has been heard telling other children about Dexter. His progress is lovely to have seen. It has been a total transformation; he's a completely different child' (Kennel Club, 2013).

Within months, Finn moved on from reading a page a night to a whole chapter. Although he found it difficult to explain his love of reading to dogs, clearly the experience offered him the opportunity to relax and enjoy reading. He added: 'I get to do tricks with them after I've read to them. I love Kym and Dexter.'

Of the more rigorous studies, academic gains have been reported in students' reading and writing skills, as well as in their attitude to and enthusiasm for reading, particularly among students with special educational needs and those who struggle with reading. Jalongo et al. (2004) found students advanced by two to four grade levels in reading proficiency. Kirnan et al. (2016) partly reinforced these findings, but only in kindergarten, where the children in the reading-to-dogs group achieved higher end-of-year reading scores than a control cohort. Researchers in Germany randomly assigned twelve second graders (6–7-year-olds, six boys and six girls) to read from a book in the presence of a dog. They were then asked to read to a friendly and encouraging young female college student. The children read more confidently and competently in the sessions with the dog, with significantly better recognition of words, punctuation and line marks (Wohlfarth et al., 2013).

In another study, Lewis and Nicholas (2018) explored the impact of reading to dogs on children's engagement with reading and vocabulary. They worked with twenty-seven 5–10-year-olds in six primary schools in Wales. The children were identified by teachers as lacking confidence, motivation or expected skills in reading. Highly trained dogs and their owners visited and worked with the children on an individual basis. Children read to the dogs weekly for approximately fifteen minutes at a time over a four-month period. Pre- and post-intervention data were gathered using the British Ability Scales II (Elliot et al., 1997), and semi-structured interviews were conducted with the participants at the start and end of the project. Initially, one-third of all pupils did not enjoy reading and nearly half did not choose to read in their free time. At the end of the project, pupils who had not read with the dogs showed no change in their enjoyment of reading, while all pupils involved in the project showed an increase in self-reported enjoyment of reading. Reasons included: 'it was fun', the dogs were 'good listeners' and the presence of the dog helped them to feel 'less worried' about reading. Some reported that they now chose to read in their spare time, often to their own pets.

Teachers in all of the schools reported that nearly every child responded positively to the scheme and looked forward to sessions, and noted specific improvements in oracy, reading and social skills. Pupils who read to the dogs made significantly greater progress in vocabulary tests than those pupils who did not. In one school, the teacher reported that 'reading with the dogs gives the children a boost - they are all making far greater and quicker progress with their reading than we would normally expect to see'. Many parents also commented on noticing their children enjoying reading more and being more willing to pick up a book at home than they were before the project. The impact went beyond reading. One teacher reported:

Our two children with a diagnosis of autism are willing to read with the dog, while they refuse to read in class. One has moved from being non-communicative to speaking in very simple sentences when with the dog. This is helping her to integrate with other children, and being the special person who reads to the dog has clearly made her feel special.

In another school, the intervention motivated independent use of the writing area; pupils wrote letters to Jade the dog and wanted to write their own books to read to her during their sessions. However, further research is needed to ascertain whether these improvements are sustained over time, as this study did not revisit the children after the intervention ended.

Motivation and attitudes

Motivation, or inner drive, plays a key role in reading competence (Pressley and Harris, 2006; Morgan and Fuchs, 2007). Studies of motivation show that it is more complex than it might at first appear because it is affected by a combination of things, such as effort, desire, curiosity and enjoyment of learning. Moreover, the type of motivation that makes the most difference is when we are driven by the joy of reading and the pleasure this brings – for example, in learning new things (Usher, 2012). This intrinsic motivation trumps the use of external rewards such as prizes, praise, certificates, seeking to achieve good test scores or some other public recognition. But in order to boost poorly motivated readers, schools need to think creatively about how children are introduced to reading. And this is where reading to animals offers considerable promise, particularly for those children who find reading a struggle. This can affect their confidence and they soon enter a destructive cycle in which their reading does not improve.

There is growing evidence that reading-to-animals programmes have a positive impact on motivating children to read (Beetz et al., 2012). One recent study compared the reading skills of two groups of second grade (7–8-year-olds) public school students over a six-week period. One group read to a therapy dog for thirty minutes once a week, while a control group followed a standard classroom curriculum. The researchers assessed the children's attitudes towards reading at the start and end of the intervention, as well as assessing progress in their reading skills (Linder et al., 2017). The children were selected on the basis of their performance in a standardised test. Those who scored 'average' results participated in the study. The findings indicated that the reading skill results did not change significantly in either group, and neither did attitudes about recreational reading outside of school. However, the children who read aloud to dogs developed a much more positive attitude towards reading. Put another way, they were better motivated to read.

In explaining why there was no noticeable improvement in academic reading skills, the researchers suggest that this might be because of the short duration of the scheme, the frequency of the sessions or the pre-existing reading levels. The last point relates to the view that if students with below-average attainment had been selected, the impact may have been greater. It is the case that low-attaining readers often demonstrate high levels of anxiety, and typical class-room behaviours such as reading aloud can trigger negative responses related to peer ridicule and teacher judgement. READ and similar programmes main-tain that the positive experience of reading to dogs helps to counteract these destructive feelings which inhibit reading mastery in the classroom. There are small-scale studies (e.g. Smith, 2010; Emmert, 2013) which indicate that both home-schooled students and those who attended mainstream classes improved their academic reading levels when reading to dogs, as compared to control groups who did not.

In another study, Lewis (2018) measured children's attitudes to learning using the Myself As a Learner Scale (MALS) (Burden, 2000). This is a short, effective measure of pupils' perceptions of their own abilities and approaches to learn-ing. The study involved bringing trained dogs into primary school classrooms to read with children (3–11-year-olds) on a regular basis over an academic year. The dogs and the handlers were trained and assessed by an external organisa-tion, and health and safety arrangements and appropriate insurances were established prior to the study commencing. All of the handlers were female and were aged between 40 and 72, and the dogs included a range of breeds and ages and both males and females.

The dogs and their handlers worked with twenty-seven learners aged 5 to 10. Their scores on the MALS were measured at the start and end of the project and compared with a group of chil-dren who did not read to dogs. After a year, the children who read to dogs showed positive changes in attitudes towards reading, and their views of themselves as learners showed small but significant posi-tive improvements.

Why did pupils' views of their learn-ing capabilities change? This could be attributed to them seeing the dog as a non-critical friend, whose very presence may calm and relax reluctant and anxious readers.

Figure 4.3. Dogs make for a patient and relaxing audience

Source: Burns By Your Side

Dew (2000: 199) suggests that the dog brings a non-verbal but collaborative language to the classroom since the dog 'never expresses himself or his wisdom verbally, but he can speak volumes nonverbally'. The children also told the researcher that they felt they were special when they went to read to the dog, and it is possible that this provided a boost to their self-esteem. Other children wanted to talk to them about the dogs and this also provided them with a sense of value in their school community.

However, it is difficult to generalise findings from the various reading-to-dogs programmes because they differ in several important areas: the age of the students who participated, the length of the reading time, the location (e.g. school, library, bookshop, childcare centre), the breeds of dogs used, the method of selecting participants and their ability levels. Moreover, most of the evidence is of a local, small-scale nature, involving a handful of students. Methodologically, it is worth noting the challenges facing researchers in managing variables. In research terms, a variable simply refers to a person, place, thing or phenomenon that you are trying to measure in some way – in this case, the presence of an animal (i.e. a dog). The canine can be regarded as an independent variable in the sense that it is stable and unaffected by the other variables. In other words, it is the presumed cause of any effects on dependent variables (e.g. reading comprehension or motivation).

We know that motivated readers are more likely to read more and feel more comfortable about reading than unmotivated readers, and there is evidence that correlates motivation with reading achievement (Takaloo and Ahmadi, 2017). Poorly motivated students are less likely to understand what they read compared to those who are well motivated. While this may sound like common sense, clarity is needed over the mechanisms by which human–animal interactions are motivating, how this can be measured and, most significantly, how to improve intrinsic motivation and self-efficacy for reading.

There have been various attempts to identify specific constructs, aspects or dimensions of motivation linked to reading. Wigfield and Guthrie (1995) first proposed several constructs that mediate individuals' reading achievement. These can be summarised as follows:

- *Ability and efficacy beliefs* – how students evaluate their competence in reading; the extent to which students like challenging books, think of themselves as good readers, avoid words that are too difficult; student beliefs in whether they can succeed in the task.

- *Subjective task values* – the incentives students have to carry out the task; how much they like the task; the perceived importance and usefulness of the task.

- *Achievement goals* – these may be ego-orientated (e.g. 'Will I look smart?', 'Can I read better than others?') or task-orientated, which focus on mastering skills within the tasks (e.g. 'How can I complete this task?').

- *Intrinsic motivation* – how curious students are to engage in reading for its own sake rather than extrinsic reasons; how engrossed students are in the moment of reading; the extent to which students sustain such feelings of satisfaction outside of the immediate context (continuing motivation).

These theoretical concepts, seen through the eyes of young readers, can be reduced to two questions: (1) Can I succeed in this reading? and (2) Do I want to succeed? On the basis of these constructs, Wigfield and Guthrie devised a Motivations for Reading Questionnaire to measure motivation across eleven dimensions (Table 4.1).

Table 4.1. Dimensions of motivation to read

Dimension	Description
Efficacy	Belief that one can be successful at reading.
Challenge	Willingness to take on difficult reading material.
Work avoidance	Desire to avoid reading activity.
Curiosity	Desire to read topics of interest.
Involvement	Enjoyment received from reading.
Importance	Value placed on reading.

Dimension	Description
Recognition	Pleasure of receiving a tangible form of recognition for success in reading.
Grades	Desire for positive school evaluations by teacher.
Competition	Desire to outperform others in reading.
Social	Sharing meaning gained from reading with others.
Compliance	Reading to meet others' expectations.

Source: Adapted from https://www.rand.org/education-and-labor/projects/assessments/tool/1995/motivations-for-reading-questionnaire-mrq.html

Taking these dimensions together, there is emerging evidence that AAIs motivate students to read. In one recent study of an early years setting in England, researchers suggested that the READ programme not only increased children's motivation to read but also fostered their reading for enjoyment and increased attainment (Noble and Holt, 2018). As is the case with most of these studies, however, the small number of participants over a short period of time prohibits generalisations.

The reason why motivation matters so much is because those students who struggle to read often have low self-esteem and tend to withdraw from classroom activities, partly because of embarrassment at not being fluent at reading. Well-motivated readers tend to value reading for the pleasure it brings, and spend time choosing their own books and talking about them.

Reading skills

In a systematic review of the literature on reading to dogs, Hall et al. (2016) conclude that there are several benefits, which include the creation of a positive learning environment to support improved reading performance. However, they acknowledge that such inferences are based on low-quality evidence. One study found that children who participated in a programme which allowed them to read to a therapy dog at the local library saw an increase in their fluency levels by 12% (Siejka, 2016). Other library-based studies report gains in reading accuracy, time spent reading and specific comprehension skills, such as the ability to explain, describe, analyse and infer (Fisher and Cozens, 2014). More generally, these studies from the United States highlight the benefits in terms of the reading environment, with students saying that they felt comfortable, happy and supported while reading to dogs (Lane and Zavada, 2013). It seems that the presence of a dog also breaks the monotony of reading, which for some children (including more able readers) is seen as a chore. The novelty factor is an important one in terms of explaining why some children (and their parents) opt into reading-to-dogs schemes (Davison, 2015).

There is clearly a need for more robust research which includes increased use of RCTs across a longer period of time. In the few cases where RCTs have been used the findings are positive. In one study, academics focused on 102 children (aged 7-13 years) who had been identified as poor readers. They assessed the effect of the presence of a dog on reading rate, accuracy and comprehension during a ten-week reading programme (Le Roux et al., 2014). The 'dog group' scored higher on the reading tests than the other three groups. In another study using an RCT methodology, a team of researchers compared the reading performance of two groups of second-grade students: one paired with a dog that they would read to each week (always in the presence of the dog's handler) and the other paired with a human volunteer (Lenihan et al., 2016). Although there were no statistically significant differences in the reading skills of both groups at the end of the project, one interesting finding was that the drop-out rate was greater in the control group. The suggestion being that reading to dogs may increase retention in reading programmes, although such research is limited very much by its small-scale (only nine students participated in each group, eighteen in total). Another conclusion worth noting is that the timing of such schemes is significant. The researchers speculate that if they were held over the summer vacation this might help to address the decline in reading habits and skills that typically occurs.

Another study looked at students from kindergarten (aged 5-6) to grade 4 (aged 9-10 years, based on 169 participants), some of whom were taught in 'traditional classrooms' and others in special education classrooms (Kirnan et al., 2016). These scholars found that it was only in kindergarten that the children in the reading-to-dogs group achieved higher end-of-year reading scores than a control cohort. However, in all the year groups they found that there were improvements in reading and writing skills as well as attitude to and enthusiasm for reading. The greatest gains were seen in the special education classes and among poor readers.

Oracy skills

As Chapter 3 highlights, AAIs can prove effective in supporting students' oracy skills as part of their wider social development. Using therapy dogs in reading programmes in school environments has the potential to reduce stress and allow students to read and talk more openly in a non-threatening climate (Lenihan et al., 2016). Therapy dogs that have been incorporated into reading programmes improve children's attention, focus and oral fluency skills (Levinson et al., 2017). More generally, providing children with opportunities to talk about how they might care for animals can build their confidence in speaking. Children with speech and language difficulties have benefited from interacting with therapy animals. One researcher interviewed trained animal-assisted therapists about their experiences of supporting children with mental health and neurobiological difficulties. One participant recalled the satisfaction of reassuring parents of a child with language difficulties that their child is able to communicate clearly: 'The therapist can tell [the parents] forever that [their children are] speaking and they understand them, but when they tell the dog to sit, and he sits, there's that immediate confirmation' (Ries, 2013: 38). But until more longitudinal studies of AAIs are published in peer-reviewed journals, in which the methodology, analysis and findings are subjected to rigorous critique, then the positive soundings for the wider language gains associated with such programmes should be treated with a little caution (Beetz and McCardle, 2017).

Writing skills

Although most studies focus on the impact of AAIs in terms of motivation to read, there have also been reported gains in writing (Kirnan et al., 2016). Interacting with animals presents children with many opportunities to develop writing skills, such as creating a poster or writing a blog about animal care, keeping a diary or sending thank-you cards. Researchers in Canada noted that elementary school pupils benefited from the opportunities to write reflectively in journals about their reading to dogs (Friesen and Delisle, 2012). Children can record their feelings about animals in various written and other forms. In one project, children produced a comic strip based on a selection of fifty photographs taken on GoPro cameras worn by themselves and strapped to Dave the dog (Carlyle, 2019). Examples show the comic strip as an emergent process with the appearance of

Figure 4.4. An extract from an ethnographer and children's comics

Source: Donna Carlyle

Dave marked with words such as 'relaxed', 'happy' and 'safe'. The children voted to rename Dave as 'Tails' and agreed the title 'The Terrific Tale of Tails! An Amazing School Dog'.

Tails from the classroom

There are many case studies of teachers and others involved in education which testify to the reading gains associated with AAI programmes (see Box 4.1). One innovative scheme based in the Maryland region of the United States aims to engage young children (from the age of 4) in good reading habits using their local library on two Saturday mornings each month. The Tail Waggin' Tutors programme involves young readers choosing books that they think their canine friends will enjoy. Loveridge (2017) discusses the impact of the programme on individual students. Seven-year-old Zac and his 5-year-old brother Tyler's love of reading is attributed directly to their participation in the programme. Both started at the age of 4 and have been motivated to bring along their own books from home, as well as choose from the library collection, to read aloud to their dog friends. While anecdotes like these do not carry the weight of social scientific research, nonetheless they matter to those boys and their parents. The very act of choosing books and taking them to the library indicates that these boys want to read.

One lay pressed up against Hools and read sweetly and smiled continuously (unbeknown to me, he has anger issues, which truly shocked me as he is so sweet and gentle around Hoola). The other sat cross-legged, reading brilliantly, using different voices for the different characters. Hools was stretched out by his side until a really exciting bit of the story when she sat up and rested her head across his thigh so that she could see the book. He was delighted and read his heart out - it was joyous to see.

Box 4.1. Grace Vobe's observation of students reading to her therapy dog, Hoola

For two years, BBYS volunteer Carole and her rescued golden retriever Sally made weekly visits to Myrddin Special Needs Unit in south Wales. The school caters for thirty pupils aged 3-11 years with profound and severe learning difficulties, some of whom are on the ASD continuum. As such, many of the children have a range of additional learning needs relating to their communication skills.

Sally works with all the children on a rota basis, with the nature of the activities depending on a child's individual needs. Some children may just look at or touch Sally, while others groom or read to her. One pupil, 10-year-old Lucas, previously found that Sally seemed to enjoy listening to him read the first chapter of Tolkien's *The Hobbit*. Some of the children carry out simple training routines with Sally, in which they are required to listen to simple instructions and repeat them so that Sally can earn a treat, thus supporting and developing their communication skills. Giving simple commands to Sally provides a meaningful and motivating context in which to communicate. Children who are otherwise reluctant to interact with other people will interact with Sally. This communication may take subtle forms, such as making eye contact with her, but it marks a big step forward for them. One of the unit's teachers, Llinos Thomas, notes that discussion of Sally and her imminent arrival can serve as an incentive for the children to communicate with the teaching staff.

Another BBYS volunteer, Emma, and her cockapoo (cocker spaniel/poodle cross), Beau, make weekly visits to St Florence Church in Wales School, Tenby. They read with selected children in Years 3 and 4 who have low self-esteem and find it hard to enjoy reading. Head teacher Julie Davies is positive about the impact Beau is having, noting that the whole school is very enthusiastic about the dog's visits, and that the children's confidence and enthusiasm for reading has improved. Indeed, Julie has seen Beau's impact first hand: 'I have observed Beau listen to the children read on many occasions, and I always have a lump in my throat when I see him move closer or place his paw next to the child to reassure them.' The children agree, with one pupil stating that she feels 'very excited' when Beau arrives and that he really helps her learn to read (Lewis, 2017).

Sarah Ellis is an experienced dog trainer who worked as the project coordinator for BBYS. She has seen the benefits of the approach on many occasions. For example, one primary-aged learner, 'Megan', worked with Sarah and her dog Saffron because of her 'severe communication problems', which were impacting on her progress across the curriculum. Although Megan was reticent to speak and communicate during the normal school day, Sarah observed her engaging in sustained conversations with Saffron during the one-to-one sessions. In time, this impacted positively on her willingness to talk to peers and staff in the school. Sarah also noted that Megan demonstrated a clear and improved desire to read, bringing the books that she shared with Saffron to school every day in order to share them with her friends. This had been unheard of prior to her working with the dog.

Julie Carson, head of the Woodland Academy Trust in the London Borough of Bexley, and north Kent, has a dog in each of her four primary schools - Betsy, Treacle, Elsie and Willow. She reports similar findings in terms of the children's motivation to read with the dog and also their confidence as readers. For example, Julie says that children who receive specific interventions related to speech and language are more confident in their work when they are working with the dogs - perhaps because the dog does not make judgements or perhaps their presence is calming and the children feel less anxious. For one of the children, who was an elective mute, the impact of working with the dog was significant. The child would not communicate orally with adults or peers during school. After spending daily sessions with one of the dogs for three weeks, the child elected to talk to an adult about her experiences.

While much evidence comes from interventions involving dogs, animals of all shapes and sizes can have a positive impact on pupils. Nick Oswald, executive head teacher at Great Ouseburn Community Primary School, brought Hedgie, an African pygmy hedgehog, into school as part of a topic on animal care. Hedgie proved a particular support for one child who struggled with independent writing. With some adult direction, he began to talk to Hedgie about his ideas. He would stroke Hedgie's spines as he told him what he planned to write about and how he was feeling. Nick noticed that the pupil soon began to gain the confidence to write independently.

Such stories are testimony in a small way to the impact animals can have on students' language development. Animals should never be regarded as a substitute for adults in the teaching of literacy and communication skills, but they can prove a supportive and enriching intervention.

Summary

- The importance of learning to read well should never be underestimated. Poor literacy has wide-ranging implications, including a negative impact on health and hygiene, economic growth, social participation, increased accidents and job absenteeism.

- We know that learning to read requires explicit instruction, opportunities to practise and early intervention when students are struggling to master fundamental decoding skills. They also need to know what words and phrases mean, and so corrective feedback is important alongside role models of high-quality reading.

- Schemes such as READ or BBYS can act as supplements (and not substitutes) to aid those students who need a boost in self-confidence and motivation.

- Specially trained dogs represent reassuring, uncritical audiences who will not mind if mistakes are made. When students make reading errors, they can be addressed in other contexts at other times. The intervention allows more capable readers to experiment with intonation and 'voices', knowing that the dog will respond positively – helping to build fluency and further developing comprehension in readers.

Chapter 5

Tales of adventure: animals and their impact on children's physical well-being and development

Intimacy with a beloved pet or special animal makes millions of people feel as though they win the lottery every day. (Becker and Morton, 2002: ix)

In Japan, many children's first encounter with nature is collecting insects. It is very much a tradition for children, particularly boys, to spend time finding stag beetles and other insects (*mushi*). The insects have become a prominent part of children's cultural world, appearing as toys in television programmes, as electronic games and on snack wrappers, for example. Department stores even have their own insect corners where they sell collecting equipment. For generations, Japanese children have spent time in the outdoors catching insects such as cicadas from spring to autumn. This can form part of what the Japanese call *Shinrin-yoku* which literally translates as 'forest bath' (*Shinrin* means forest and *yoku* means bath). The idea is that families take time out to 'soak' in the natural world, and studies over four decades highlight the health benefits in reducing stress, depression, fatigue, anxiety and confusion (Brelsford et al., 2017). These physiological gains are facilitated by the attitude of repect towards nature shown by many Japanese people.

And yet in Japan, and around the world, there are growing concerns that children's outdoor physical activity is declining (Itoi et al., 2015). Many factors contribute to what some commentators call a global crisis in children's physical activity (Aston, 2018; Children's Hospital of Eastern Ontario Research Institute, 2018). These include the attraction of screen time, a fast-food diet, the decline in children travelling by foot rather than car, parents' risk-averse attitudes towards children's adventurous outdoor activity and fewer public spaces for play. In sum, more and more children follow a sedentary lifestyle (Farooq et al., 2018).

In this broader context, AAIs have an important role to play in contributing to children's physical well-being. This is defined as 'the ability to be fully engaged, on a regular basis, in all developmentally appropriate activities' (Cole, 2006: 1). If children are to become healthy citizens, then they need to acquire sufficient knowledge of healthy lifestyles, regularly practise large and fine motor skills, develop spatial awareness, and build up the necessary energy and stamina to participate in sustained activity. This chapter considers the physical and physiological benefits of children interacting with animals, and of more challenging roles such as taking responsibility in caring for animals. It should be noted that most of the research in this area focuses on psychological rather than physical benefits, which remains an area for further study.

The extent to which children are engaged in physical activity is subject to a range of influences. These include internal factors (e.g. physical attributes), dispositional variables (e.g. attitude, perceived competence, motivation), school characteristics (e.g. teacher expertise, sports programmes, curriculum opportunities) and wider social influences (e.g. parental support, access to facilities). Among unmotivated students in physical education lessons, there are particular barriers, such as changing, sweating, anticipated feelings of humiliation and a lack of stylish clothing (Kretschmann, 2014). What works well in overcoming many of these challenges is introducing interventions that focus on developing a 'mastery' motivational climate, enjoyment, achievable goals and feelings of competence. In this context, this chapter explores the potential of AAIs to motivate students to become more physically active.

How could animals help?

It has long been known that when humans interact with animals there are potential physical health benefits across a range of measures and conditions. For example, while people with dementia often lose weight, studies show that those with dementia in several nursing homes successfully gained weight after fish tanks were installed in the dining rooms (Edwards and Beck, 2002, 2013). Although a few residents lost weight, on average, the body weight of the residents increased by two pounds over the ten-week trial period. A more recent literature review of nineteen research studies which explored the effects of interacting with fish in aquariums on human health and well-being found a range of potential benefits, including a reduction in stress and increased relaxation (Clements et al., 2019).

However, one of the limitations of such research is that not all participants reported such benefits. This may be because much depends on the strength of attachment between a human and companion animal, or it might reflect differences in the amount of care afforded to the fish. When the main responsibility for feeding fish and cleaning the aquarium falls on one individual, he or she may perceive more benefits than when such responsibilities are shared. Another possible explanation is the influence of the different socio-demographic characteristics (e.g. age, ethnicity, gender, level of education) of the individual. Furthermore, there are studies which show no significant effects from keeping or watching fish. When aquariums were installed in the hospital rooms of patients awaiting a heart transplant, researchers found no significant reductions in anxiety or depression after eleven days (Cole and Gawlinski, 2000). Another study which explored the pain threshold of participants who watched fish continuously for thirty minutes found that this was significantly higher five, ten, twenty and thirty minutes after viewing, compared to the initial values, and remained elevated for ten minutes after viewing ended (Sanchez et al., 2015). In short, research on the health effects of interacting with fish is inconclusive and, in places, contradictory.

One of the major methodological problems is the small sample size which makes generalisations impossible. It is also the case that there are few specific studies, based on a rigorous methodology, which focus on the health benefits of child–animal interactions. This is largely due to the particular ethics relating to medical research with children. One of the key ethical principles is that 'research involving children should only be carried out if it cannot feasibly be carried out on adults' (Medical Research Council, 2004: 13). This does not mean such research is off limits. Without the participation of children, it is impossible to answer questions posed in relation to the effects of AAIs on their health as we cannot base this on the findings on adults. Children are not small adults; they have their own physical, emotional and psychological needs.

The World Health Organization identifies childhood obesity as one of the most serious public health challenges of this century. Small-scale studies show that AAIs increase children's physical activity, subject to a range of influences, including for those clinically diagnosed as obese. In one study (Wohlfarth et al., 2013), researchers explored whether obese children (aged 8–12 years) would profit more from a dog's presence, when compared to the presence of a friendly person, while performing various movement games. All the children had several opportunities to interact with the white hunting dog and the friendly person before the experiment, so that neither were strangers. The children were randomly assigned to wear accelerometry-based motion sensors in two groups in a crossover trial. They followed similar programmes on agility, speed play and ball skills. For example, in one exercise the dog ran an agility course and the children were instructed to try to run faster than the dog. A follow-up agility course involved children trying to beat the dog's time while carrying small figures with a spoon or water with a sponge. The exercises were repeated with the non-dog group, who tried to run faster than the friendly person. During the sessions of about twenty minutes, the dog was only active twice for ten minutes in total, while for the rest of the time the children did things for the dog. An experimenter observed and recorded the child–dog interactions.

The results showed that the presence of a therapy dog has the potential to increase physical activity in obese children. Those children who exercised in the presence of a dog were less passive (i.e. did less sitting, standing or lying down) than the control group. They also spent more time engaged in slow walking and showed more active behaviour, which means physical activity without making steps (e.g. sitting and moving the upper body). The most significant finding, however, was that the children walked faster over a longer period of time in the presence of the dog. The researchers concluded that the presence of a dog also acted as a trigger for the children's implicit motives.

Case study research has also shown the benefits of AAIs to support the physical development of children with a range of special educational needs. Tepfer et al. (2017) focused on the experiences of a 10-year-old boy with cerebral palsy. Such children often get less physical exercise than those who do not have cerebral palsy. They are also physically weaker, less fit and have lower cardiovascular endurance compared to typically developing children. The researchers tested pre- and post-intervention, which lasted eight weeks and consisted of adapted physical activities performed with the family dog, a Pomeranian, once a week for an hour in a laboratory setting. These activities included, for example, brushing the dog with the hand, 'sit-stands', fetching and standing on a wobble board. They were supplemented with at-home daily interactions with the family dog.

The findings showed that the carefully planned intervention helped the boy to develop motor skills and become more physically active, and contributed to the general improvement in his quality of life. What was unusual about this small piece of research was that the dog was not a trained therapy dog, but a family pet. This is not an isolated case. Researchers report wide-ranging gains for children with cerebral palsy who have engaged in various AAIs. These include: 'Gross motor functioning, re-establishing muscle symmetry, improving trunk stability, postural control, balance, gait, range of motion, functional skills, strength, co-ordination, and muscle tone' (Joseph et al., 2016: 52).

The most popular intervention for children with cerebral palsy is equine-assisted therapy, in which children, with or without motor difficulties, perform activities on and alongside a horse (Bizub et al., 2003). There are two types of equine-assisted therapy: in hippotherapy, a physical or occupational therapist controls the horse to influence the child's posture, balance, coordination, strength and so on, while the child interacts with the horse and responds to the movement of the horse. In therapeutic horseback riding, the child actively controls the horse as a form of exercise, led by a trained riding instructor. Joseph et al. (2016: 55) report:

Movement generated by horses walking, allows riders to experience 3-dimensional motions, forward/backward, left/right, upward/downward … the movement of horses, transmitted to the riders, is similar to the pattern of movement which occurs in the pelvis of walking humans, and generates the same feelings of motion effects, as though the riders were walking themselves.

Sterba et al. (2002) found that recreational horseback riding improves the gross motor function in children with spastic diplegia, spastic quadriplegia and spastic hemiplegia types of cerebral palsy. By participating in one hour of therapy per week over an eighteen-week period, children improved their gross motor functions of walking, running and jumping by around 8%, confirmed by more recent studies (see Joseph et al., 2016). There is a growing body of evidence which suggests that through such interventions children improve their flexibility of movement, posture, balance and mobility (Snider et al., 2007; de Milander et al., 2016), while even small acts such as brushing or stroking a horse (and other animals) lower cortisol levels, which is indicative of reduced stress (Beetz et al., 2011).

In another study, children with pervasive developmental disorders (i.e. those who experience a delay in the development of socialisation and communication skills) were exposed to a toy, a stuffed doll and a live dog. Children who became involved with the dog were more interactive with their environment, more playful and more focused (Martin and Farnum, 2002). This can have health benefits. For example, the Pet Health Council runs a Petsercise programme which encourages people and their pets to get fit and healthy together.[1] A recent study (Saunders et al., 2017) also shows that the immune systems of children (particularly between the ages of 5 and 8) of pet-owning families are more stable than those of children from non-pet-owning families – the result being that pet-owning children are better able to fend off illness.

However, there is a need for caution. While most small-scale studies show that AAIs can have a positive impact on children's health and physical well-being, in many cases we are less clear over exactly how this occurs (Wohlfarth et al., 2013). Moreover, there are many gaps in the scientific research – for example, we do not know what the desirable frequency and duration of equine-assisted interventions is. For these and other reasons, health professionals are not convinced about the benefits of these therapies (Joseph et al., 2016).

When children are in the presence of animals, the tactile experience can generate mutually positive feelings. Patting, stroking and massaging, along with mutual gazing, are all signs of connectedness which serve to strengthen children's sensory and perceptual awareness as well as a shared sense of well-being. When researchers explored insecurely attached boys' (aged 7-12 years) responses to a real dog, a toy dog and a friendly person during a socially stressful situation, they found that the levels of children's salivary cortisol (a measure of stress) were significantly lower in the real dog condition than in the other two conditions (Beetz et al., 2011). The researchers observed that the more the children stroked the dog, the less pronounced their stress reaction was. When Beetz et al. (2012) reviewed sixty-nine research studies on human–animal interactions, they found that there was clear evidence for improvements in physical and physiological health, among other benefits. They highlight the activation of oxytocin as one of the key underlying common factors.

---

1 See http://www.pethealthcouncil.co.uk/petercise/news.html.

In her study, Carlyle (2019) likened children's touching of Dave the dog to 'piano fingers' as they lightly pressed his body as if it were a musical keyboard. Continuing the metaphor she adds: 'The hand patting also became reminiscent of gently tapping notions, like percussion and beating on a bongo drum' (Carlyle, 2019: 205). Carlyle suggests that through touch the children became calmer, and when Dave rested his head on her she felt grounded and connected to everything around her.

Over many years, it has been demonstrated that AAIs result in statistically significant health benefits, with improvements in blood pressure, heart rate and salivary immunoglobulin A levels, and in depression, anxiety, perceived quality of health and loneliness (see e.g. Friedmann et al., 1983; Morrison, 2007). More recent research highlights further health benefits including pain management and wider neurological rehabilitation (Muñoz Lasa et al., 2015).

Being with animals can have positive physiological effects on an individual's heart rate and blood pressure. One of the earliest studies showed that pet ownership improved cardiovascular health and demonstrated it to be a significant predictor of survival in patients one year after a heart attack (Friedmann et al., 1980). Researchers have since targeted various groups: frail, elderly nursing home patients have benefited from lower blood pressure by holding and petting visiting cats (Stasi et al., 2004), and city stockbrokers who were diagnosed with stress and prescribed drugs were randomised into two groups, one which cared for pets and one which did not (Allen et al., 2001). In one study in which reptiles were used to support girls who had suffered parental bereavement, researchers found that the children experienced fewer headaches, ate better and vomited less often (Murry and Todd Allen, 2012). Other studies have shown that pet owners experience fewer minor health problems (Flynn, 2008).

Talking to pets has proven to be physiologically good for humans. When researchers have observed pet owners greeting and touching their dogs, they found that their blood pressure dropped (Thomas et al., 1984). At first it was unclear whether this was due to the talking or the touching, so the researchers introduced tropical fish into their experiments on the premise that these creatures were the least likely to be stroked or petted. They also thought that it was unlikely that the tropical fish were spoken to with any great frequency. In the experiment, individuals were asked to read aloud and then relax for ten minutes, by looking at a bare wall, before looking at a tropical fish tank. The researchers observed that their blood pressure then dropped. Moreover, afterwards, when they were asked to read aloud, their blood pressure did not go as high as it went when they read aloud, before the experiment. The findings were consistent with observations that children's blood pressure lowered when a dog was present compared to when a dog was not present. The conclusion was that, aside from talking and touching, seeing an animal and being in its presence was enough to deliver physiological benefits.

Charnetski and Riggers (2004) investigated changes in immune function (immunoglobulin A (IgA)) when participants petted a dog. Participants were randomised either to pet a dog, to pet a stuffed dog or to sit quietly. Salivary IgA was sampled pre- and post-intervention. Participants who petted the real dog had significantly higher levels of IgA post-intervention than the other two groups did. The enhanced psycho-neuroimmunological response gained from petting a dog may have positive health implications, such as improving ability to fight off infection.

Turning to AAIs involving children in school settings, most of the research confirms the physical benefits enjoyed by adults. However, Brelsford et al.'s (2017) literature review points to the need for more robust and larger scale studies while also emphasising the need for stronger risk assessment and safeguarding of all involved. Kropp and Shupp's (2017) literature review focused on the potential benefits of using therapy dogs in the classroom. In terms of physical well-being, their findings show that the presence of dogs increased children's gross motor skills (e.g. walking, jumping, running). The reason why the use of therapy dogs with children is successful is largely attributed to children's natural tendency to open up to animals, who provide a calm and non-judgemental presence (Jalongo et al., 2004). It is also the case that the power imbalance which traditionally exists between adult (such as a teacher) and child is removed. The non-hierarchical relationship between animal and child means that the latter is less likely to feel inferior, which opens up opportunities for learning.

There is wide-ranging evidence associated with the positive effects of pet ownership on a person's physical development. An obvious example is the physical benefits of dog walking. One recent study of 385 householders in the UK reports that dog owners are four times more likely than their peers to meet recommended guidelines for physical activity, namely 150 minutes of moderate-to-vigorous physical activity per week (Westgarth et al., 2019). While there is evidence that pet owners enjoy a range of physical health benefits - for example, stamina associated with dog walking - these cannot simply be transferred to AAIs in the classroom.

What is clear from both the generic educational research and that related to AAIs is that intrinsic motivation is key to improving children's physical (and all-round) development. When children are intrinsically motivated, they find activities enjoyable, interesting and challenging in their own right.

Tails from the classroom

In Burry Port Community Primary School, south Wales, Jade the 7-year-old Cavalier King Charles Spaniel frequently accompanies her owner Odette to school, where she works primarily with 4-, 5- and 6-year-old children. Jade's presence impacts on the children's physical development in a number of ways. For example, precision and coordination in fine motor skills are developed when the children pick up dog treats and fill Jade's treat ball with them. They use their fingers with increasing precision to fasten and unfasten her lead, to turn on the tap to refill her water bowl, and to build Jade houses and playgrounds in the small world area. They develop gross motor skills as they walk Jade around an obstacle course in the playground or throw toys to Jade during play with her.

Another volunteer, Grace, has noted the impact that physical contact with her dog, Hoola, can have on children (Box 5.1).

The thing that has really blown me away is the way that Hoola seems to know when physical interaction is required. Mostly, she lies and listens, allowing the child to stroke or cuddle her, but when she feels it necessary she physically interacts with the child, and the results have been astounding. A favourite is to touch the child with her nose or a very quick and gentle lick. She tends to do this when the child is struggling to read - it seems to break the cycle of frustration or distract the child from troubled thoughts, lifting their spirits and often making them laugh and magically giving them the ability to read.

Recently, though, I have noticed that she uses her whole body to calm children. One child that reads to her is very energetic, rarely staying still, continually flitting from one position to another, talking at great speed, but a highly intelligent child with a gift for reading. Hoola has worked out for herself that what this particular child needs is help in being calm and still. She started by placing her head in their lap or arm. They were so mesmerised by the physical contact that they stayed still, in the same position so as not to disturb Hoola. When needed she uses her whole body, pressing herself against them, and they visibly relax and calm down. Once in a reading position, she again rests her head on them and they are able to read calmly for ever-increasing periods of time. The sessions have also helped this child to learn about self-control, as the teachers have used the sessions as a reward for not interrupting, something they had difficulty doing before due to their effervescent nature. The child is so proud, regularly telling me how they have not interrupted in class so that they can read to Hoola.

Box 5.1. Grace Vobe and her therapy dog, Hoola

Drabble (2019) provides case studies of several children in her school who benefit from working with Doodles the school dog. For instance, Mason is a 10-year-old child who cannot walk. He needs to build upper body strength in order to use his wheelchair, and so staff try to encourage him to move around the school in his chair. Before Doodles was in school Mason sometimes lacked the motivation to make the long journeys down certain long corridors, but now that Doodles is based on one of these he is far more

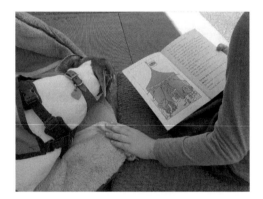

Figure 5.1. Subtle interaction between Hoola and a child

Source: Grace Vobe

willing. Eleanor is a 6-year-old girl who is just starting to walk around the school with a walking frame. Staff found that when Doodles was a few steps in front of Eleanor she was motivated to keep walking towards him.

Benefits can also be indirect. For example, when Carole and Sally visit Myrddin Special Needs Unit in south Wales, they interact with the children there in many ways. On several occasions Sally has accompanied the children to the school garden. There she gets involved in activities such as digging and planting, providing an incentive for the children to be physically active in the outdoor environment.

For the last eight years, Kim Jameson has been visiting a special school in west Wales with her golden retriever dogs: Toby, Willow and Robyn. All three dogs are qualified as both Pets As Therapy and BBYS dogs. Each dog has a different personality and qualities, and so each is better suited to some contexts than others. For the special school context, Willow and latterly Robyn proved to be the ideal dogs. They cope calmly with children who have learning difficulties and

Figure 5.2. Enjoying a calm interaction
Source: Burns By Your Side

also those with severe mobility restrictions. One example of the benefits the dogs bring was seen by Kim when visiting a young boy with very limited movement, and who is deaf and partially sighted. He reacts to touch and sees only shadows. He was laying on a bed when the dogs first visited, and it was difficult to get Robyn close to him. Kim asked her to do 'paws up' (which means she stands on her hind legs) and she put her front paws on the bed. The boy couldn't reach her, but without prompting, Robyn started inching herself up the bedside until the young boy was able to touch her. Kim said, 'The beam on his face as he rubbed her fur was priceless, and for Robyn her reaction was simple, wagging her tail and moving her head around the boy's hand, seemingly sensing that was all she needed to do.'

Another child who reacts positively to Robyn is confined to a wheelchair with severe cerebral palsy and little speech. When Robyn or Willow go into the classroom she follows them constantly with her eyes. She really makes an effort to stroke the dogs when they go up to her wheelchair and again just smiles with delight when she touches them. Kim remembers a visit that really meant something to all involved:

The real icing on the cake with this youngster was when she was laying on her mattress on the floor one day when we went in and she very clearly said 'Willow' and started laughing. Even the staff were surprised and asked her to say it again, which she did. This little girl has very little speech but her excitement at seeing Willow led to that magical and rare moment of speech. Priceless.

Summary

- There are global concerns over levels of childhood obesity and children's relative lack of physical activity.

- Interacting with animals can provide opportunities for children and young people to exercise outdoors and develop a range of physical skills.

- Case studies have shown that children with physical difficulties such as cerebral palsy benefit from equine-assisted therapy and other interventions.

- However, there is a need to build up evidence from such small-scale research.

Chapter 6

Tales of all creatures great and small: animals and the curriculum

I travelled with only those items that I thought necessary to relieve the tedium of a long journey: four books on natural history, a butterfly net, a dog and a jam jar full of caterpillars. (Durrell, 1956: 14)

Every year there is global excitement among young and old at the publication of the *Guinness World Records*. A significant section of the annual is devoted to animals, which reflects human interest in their world. And there are some very odd records. For example, in 2015, Caspa the llama achieved a world record by jumping over a bar measuring 113 cm, the highest jump ever recorded for a llama. Mochi, a female St Bernard, holds the record for the longest tongue measured in a dog – 18.58 cm in total. In 2017, JiffPom, a tiny Pomeranian, achieved world fame for being the most-followed dog on social media.[1] These examples illustrate how animal records can be used as a stimulus for children's curiosity and learning. For example, comparing Caspa's height and high-jump record with those of the children is a starting point for applying authentic mathematical skills. Could Caspa jump over them? Sometimes posing silly questions appeals to children and can motivate them to carry out simple investigations – for example, could Mochi's tongue reach the bottom of an ice-cream tub or could the dog lick her own nose? How do their own tongues compare? And what talking points arise from JiffPom's social media presence?

In this chapter we will discuss the potential learning gains associated with animals in the curriculum. We have chosen a sample of subjects – science, English, mathematics, history, art and design, and religious education – to illustrate the range of possibilities. It is by no means an exhaustive account. Neither have we tied the content to specific year groups, learning outcomes or success criteria.

1 @jiffpom. On Instagram alone, he has over 10 million followers. In 2014, he featured in a Katy Perry music video, 'Dark Horse', which has been viewed over 2 billion times on YouTube.

Rather, we have included a series of ideas so that teachers might research, plan and reflect further on the potential learning gains associated with the topic in their particular context.

Animals and science

Animals appear in the UK science curricula with reference to developing students' scientific knowledge and understanding of ecosystems, life cycles and living processes (Table 6.1). There is also an emphasis on gaining first-hand experience of scientific enquiry. Such learning should involve opportunities for students to closely observe animals and ask questions about what they see using a developing scientific vocabulary.

Pupils develop scientific concepts and skills through authentic, real-life learning experiences. For example, children (aged 4-5) in the reception class at Glyncollen Primary School in Swansea were excited to find out about life cycles when they undertook a topic called 'Grow: The Chicken and the Egg'. This offered opportunities for learning across the curriculum. As part of the work, an incubator with some fertilised chicken eggs was set up in the classroom. As well as careful observations of the eggs as they hatched, the children undertook activities based on the story of 'The Little Red Hen'. They watched a film of the story and talked about what they thought the main messages were – for example, the importance of working hard, being kind and helping others. They then compared and ordered the characters in terms of how hardworking they were and discussed their reasoning. They also used eggs to explore number bonds and one-to-one counting in a classroom area set aside for mathematical activities. They made chicks from a variety of materials in the creative classroom area and used books and the Internet to find out about other animals which lay eggs. Such activities required careful planning to enhance learning and safeguard child and animal welfare, and were reflected in the resourcing of the continuous provision in the classroom (see Appendix 1).

It is essential to research the suitability of hatching animals in your context and to prepare carefully. One of the main questions to ask is, what will happen to the animals after hatching? In some cases, returning them to the company who

Table 6.1. Animals in the UK national science curricula

England	Wales	Scotland	Northern Ireland
Science Key Stage 3 and 4	Science Progression Step 1	Forces, electricity and waves, e.g.	Science and Technology within the World Around Us
Sound waves	▦ I recognise that plants and animals are living.	▦ Through research on how animals communicate, I can explain how sound vibrations are carried by waves through air, water and other media.	Interdependence – key scientific ideas at primary level, e.g.
▦ Auditory range of humans and animals.	Science Progression Step 2		▦ Energy is needed by all living things to survive.
Cell biology	▦ Learners need to experience how things move, grow and sustain life (e.g. observing at first hand physical changes in humans and animals).		▦ The world has many different forms of animal and plant life.
▦ Stem cells in animals and meristems in plants.		Planet Earth – biodiversity and interdependence, e.g.	▦ We need to respect and care for all living things.
Health, disease and the development of medicines		▦ By exploring interactions and energy flow between plants and animals (including humans), I can develop my understanding of how species depend on one another and on the environment for survival.	▦ We can sort living things into categories based on their similarities and differences.
▦ Bacteria, viruses and fungi as pathogens in animals and plants.			▦ Living things have to change their behaviour over time in order to survive.
▦ Reducing and preventing the spread of infectious diseases in animals and plants.		Biological systems, e.g.	▦ Within an environment living things rely on each other to survive. These relationships take many different forms.
▦ The importance of selective breeding of plants and animals in agriculture.		▦ By investigating the lifecycles of plants and animals, I can recognise the different stages of their development.	

provided them will mean certain culling, particularly for male birds. At Glyncollen Primary School, Thereza Rees (a member of staff) keeps chickens, and so there was expertise available and the chicks would be homed by Thereza after the topic. Odette Nicholas, deputy head at Burry Port Community Primary School, hatched two geese (Daisy and Chip) with her class of 4- and 5-year-old children, but in the knowledge that she would be able to take the birds home with her at the end of the project. The eggs came from a friend's farm and the adult geese now live happily at home with her. In short, it is important to realise in advance that an activity that is planned for a half-term topic has implications for longer term commitment. Odette may share her garden with Daisy and Chip for up to seventeen years – the average lifespan of a goose!

Staff at Glyncollen and Burry Port also understood the requirements for safe and healthy hatching – for instance, eggs must be monitored and regularly turned to avoid chicks developing organs that stick to the inside of the shells. Mother chickens may turn an egg as often as thirty times a day, so schools must plan how this will be done during the busy school day and also over weekends and evenings. Odette took the eggs and incubator home with her every weekend – a short drive away – to ensure that these needs could be met. Hygiene was monitored carefully to avoid the risk of illnesses such as E. coli being passed on from chick to child, with children being reminded of good hand hygiene whenever they had contact with the chicks or equipment. The chicks came from reputable breeders and their health was continually checked.

There are a number of alternatives available for schools that are unable to provide the right conditions for hatching live chicks. These include life cycle models, high-quality photographic books and videos, such as the 4-H Virtual Farm.[2] Visits to farms may provide hands-on experiences without the added classroom responsibility that hatching entails. In the case of Glyncollen and Burry Port, teachers carefully documented the hatching process so that future classes can experience a virtual version of the activity. The recent coronavirus pandemic has meant rethinking how animals can be brought into classrooms. Brad and Mel Rundle, founders and directors of Therapy Animals Australia, now run live online sessions in which learners can meet and learn about a range of animals from

2   The 4-H Virtual Farm is based in Virginia, in the United States: https://www.sites.ext.vt.edu/virtualfarm/poultry/poultry_development.html.

shingleback lizards to parrots, fish and dogs.[3] These sessions can help engage and motivate learners, and the online format allows those in remote and rural communities, or overseas, opportunities to access the sessions.

Scientists estimate that there are some 10 quintillion individual insects crawling, hopping and flying around the Earth at any one time.[4] Put another way, there are around 200 million insects for *each* of us on the planet – the equivalent of more than three times the population of the UK. Although many people dislike bugs, insects are invaluable to human survival. They are key to the food web and eaten by everything from birds and small mammals to fish. Many insects also provide invaluable 'services' to humanity, such as plant pollination, while advances in genetics bring the hope that insects will prove to be the next major pharmaceutical breakthrough, supplying 'drugs from bugs' (Piper, 2017). However, increasing challenges to natural habitats, climate change and the use of pesticides have led to rapid decreases in insect populations, with some talking of a pending insect apocalypse (Jarvis, 2018; Main, 2019).

Education has a key role to play in overturning myths about insects and countering such labels as 'creepy crawlies'. For 8-year-old Ava Clements and her younger sister Ruby, learning about the life cycle of insects has inspired a great passion for these tiny creatures which extends far beyond the classroom (Box 6.1).

I really love butterflies and moths! For Easter, I was given a growing butterflies kit and we received some tiny caterpillars in a tub. I was so excited, but you couldn't touch them because they may have caught germs from us ... We had five caterpillars; Percy was the biggest and always reared up. We measured them nearly every day and marked each day on the calendar. They started at 6 mm and grew to 7 cm. They took over two weeks to turn into chrysalises and they climbed to the top of the tub, hung like a 'J' and then turned hard into chrysalises. You could really see them darken, harden and change shape and go from bumpy to smooth. As they all did it at

---

3   See https://therapyanimals.org.au.
4   See Langley (2016). It is worth writing out this figure for children to see:
    10,000,000,000,000,000,000.

different times, you could compare them and see what would happen next. A couple of them fell off but we gently placed them in the net.

An amazing thing happened when we were putting them in the net – they go crazy, they wriggle and shake. We thought they were hatching but it is a defence, the chrysalises wiggle and shake when they are disturbed to frighten predators. How amazing is that? It frightened me and my mum! There was lots of silk threads in there too which we had to remove from around the chrysalises as if they get tangled when they emerge, they can be deformed or strangled.

We missed them actually emerging, it is quick and only takes a minute or so, but we did see their wings getting bigger right in front of us as the blood pumped. We also saw meconium, which looks like blood but isn't, and shows that the butterfly is healthy. They were so beautiful when they opened their wings. They are called painted ladies and they did look so beautiful. You can get so close that we saw their tongue – it starts as two pieces then joins up into one – how fantastic is that and we saw it!

We gave them food and nectar to drink, they really like oranges, lavender from the garden, cucumbers and bananas. Three days after they had all hatched, we let them go. I was sad and happy, but it was my best day ever as they sat on my finger when I lifted them out. I think they knew I was their friend and that I loved them. I think I saw Percy in the garden at my school. Everyone should grow butterflies, they help flowers pollinate, eat weeds and scientists count them to see how healthy the environment is.

I have fifteen silkworms at the moment and I'm really excited to see what they do too (and they will be really fluffy).

Box 6.1. An 8-year-old's interest in insects

In fact, most insects are beneficial and completely harmless to humans. Children need to be taught about their real value so that they treat insects respectfully in their immediate environment and beyond. As noted in Chapter 5, young Japanese children learn about the unique role of insects (*mushi*), collecting and caring for the likes of fireflies and rhinoceros beetles. They listen to and play with insects, sing songs about them and complete homework assignments on them (Laurent, 2000).

Closer to home, at Millbrook Primary School in Newport, head teacher Lindsey Watkins houses a collection of stick insects in the school's family room. The school's motto of 'Learning about caring, caring about learning' is embodied in the approach towards looking after the animals to be found in the school. Children are timetabled to come to observe and care for the stick insects, learning about their needs. They take responsibility for aspects of their care. The insects also provide a good starting point for conversations between families, staff and pupils. Lindsey has noticed the positive impact that these intriguing creatures have had on parents and children. The school also has a giant African land snail (called Little Acorn), who lives in the nursery class with children aged 3-4 years. The children learn to care for Little Acorn, feeding him and cleaning his cage, and his presence sparks the children's curiosity and provides a sense of awe and wonder.

There are many resources to support the teaching of scientific ideas and skills relating to animals. For example, in the UK the Bumblebee Conservation Trust[5] produces a range of resources, and BugLife[6] have online guidance for schools and parents. The American Museum of Natural History[7] has a section devoted to following a real-life etymologist, while Friends of the Earth[8] provide information on how to build bug hotels. Organisations such as ZooLab[9] can bring animals into schools in the UK, allowing children the opportunity to see these creatures at first hand.

Research led by Professor Yamni Nigam at Swansea University aims to educate the general public about the benefits of an insect which has a poor image. The Love a Maggot! campaign highlights how maggot therapy helps humankind in the face of rising resistance to antibiotics. The maggots chosen for the medical treatment are the larvae of the green bottle fly (*Lucilia sericata*). The process works by forensically placing the clean and sterile maggots into wounds to quickly clear up the dead tissue. After three to four days, the maggots are removed, successfully

----

5   See https://www.bumblebeeconservation.org/bumble-kids/activities.
6   See https://www.buglife.org.uk/get-involved/children-and-schools.
7   See https://www.amnh.org/explore/ology/zoology/carly-s-adventures-in-wasp-land.
8   See https://friendsoftheearth.uk/bees/easy-bug-and-bee-hotel-kids.
9   See https://www.zoolabuk.com.

disinfecting the wound so that it can heal and close. Children and young people should be taught about the benefits of maggots for several reasons:

Figure 6.1. A maggot racing game

Source: Yamni Nigam, Swansea University

- As future decision-makers about the environment, children need to learn from a young age that insects are vital to our survival. While children may be aware of beneficial insects (e.g. pollinators like honeybees), most are unlikely to have been taught about another important and beneficial insect, the medicinal maggot.

- Maggots have been used to treat chronic wounds over many centuries. Aborigines, for example, have used them to successfully clean wounds for thousands of years, and so they have stood the test of time (Harding, 2017).

- Maggots represent an abundant and free resource at a time when health services have to cater for an ageing population and operate under considerable economic constraints.

- The use of maggots is an efficient and effective treatment, freely available via the National Health Service.

Of course, the challenge is to go beyond the 'yuck' factor and change perceptions. This is best done before negative associations with maggots are established, so that if children grow up and develop chronic wounds that require maggot therapy, they will not be repulsed and will more happily accept the treatment. To help overcome negative feelings, the research team at Swansea University have produced educational resource packs including lesson plans, videos, an interactive game and a maggot racing game (Figure 6.1).[10]

---

10 To find out more, see: https://www.swansea.ac.uk/humanandhealthsciences/research-at-the-college-of-human-and-health/research-impact-college-of-human-and-health/love-a-maggot. Maggots can be purchased through BioMonde: https://biomonde.com/en.

Animals and English

Chapter 4 discussed in detail the contribution animals can make to children's all-round language development. Animals have a strong presence in children's literature and can prove a key motivation to read. Authors around the world have been writing about whales, horses, rabbits, pigs and toads for centuries. These animals have become famous faces and familiar friends. Whether fact or fiction, fluffy, furry, fanged or feathered, there are many unforgettable literary animal characters that have formed an integral part of our childhoods and made lasting impressions on us. Famous animal characters such as Black Beauty, Joey the war horse, Hedwig the owl and Gelert the wolfhound appear in stories that convey strong moral messages about how to be better humans through their examples of loyalty, courage and friendship. Mythical animals such as the Gruffalo, the Jabberwock, phoenixes and dragons also ignite children's imaginations. Many of these stories have appeared as films, cartoons, TV shows and radio broadcasts, offering a range of media to introduce children to the main characters and compare representations. This can enhance their cultural knowledge of stories.

Animal heroes feature strongly in young children's picture books. *The Lion and the Bird* by Marianne Dubuc (2015) tells the story of a lion who finds a wounded bird in his garden one autumn day, which he then nurses back to health. He cares for her when the rest of her flock leave for the winter and the two quickly become friends. But what will happen to their friendship when the other birds return in springtime? The story celebrates how unexpected friendship helps very different characters to address their loneliness.

Foxes have a high profile in children's literature – for example, Roald Dahl's *Fantastic Mr Fox* (1974), Tod in Daniel Mannix's *The Fox and the Hound* (1967), the fox in Antoine de Saint-Exupéry's *The Little Prince* (1943) and, of course, Dr Seuss' *Fox in Socks* (1965). More recently, Zeb Soanes' *Gaspard the Fox* (2018) is a humorous story about a fox who sets out one summer evening in search of adventure and something to eat. On his travels he meets Peter the cat and Finty the dog, who help him to navigate the local canals, boats and people in his hunt for supper. The story is based on a real-life fox that regularly visited the author. Many children may be able to relate to animals they have seen, whether they are in a rural or urban context. Gaspard even has his own Twitter account and website! The book celebrates urban foxes and their relationship with the humans and animals with whom they share the city.

Many picture books open up cross-curricular opportunities for learning. For example, *Owl Babies* by Martin Waddell (1992) is an enchanting picture book about three baby owls who wake up to discover their mother has left the nest. Without her, they are scared and vulnerable. But then mum returns, and they feel comfortable and reassured. The story is a simple but powerful means of helping children to handle anxieties and fears about temporary separation.

Reading for information requires a context and a reason to read. Taking *Owl Babies* as an example, the story can inspire children to find out more about owls by following up on questions they may raise: why do owls hoot? How good is their eyesight? Is it possible to keep an owl as a pet? Will an owl attack my small dog or cat? Are all owls nocturnal? What is a group of owls called? How many different kinds of owls are there? What is the smallest and the biggest owl in the world? From the tiny elf owl (typically weighing 41 grams) to the Eurasian eagle-owl, which has a wing span of nearly 2 metres and can weigh almost 5 kilograms, owls are wonderful birds to stimulate children's research and engage their interest. Using reference books, magazines and online sources, animals can be used as a stimulus to teach children higher order reading skills, such as skimming to get the general idea about a species, and scanning for particular information.

Reading for information can follow on from practical hands-on experiences, such as a visit to an owl sanctuary. Examining owl pellets must be one of the most exciting and delightfully grisly activities (Figure 6.2)! Pellets are the undigested parts of a bird's food, such as hair or bones, which are regurgitated by being coughed up. By dissecting these, children can find out exactly what the owls have eaten. Organisations such as the Barn Owl Trust offer guidance and free downloadable worksheets to help teachers, as well as selling pellets ready for dissection.[11] We have discussed elsewhere a wide range of activities using birds, nests and eggs as starting points for learning (Grigg and Lewis, 2016, 2018).

---

11 See https://www.barnowltrust.org.uk/owl-facts-for-kids/owl-pellets. Genia Connell (2016) has also written a blog on how she organised this activity in her classroom.

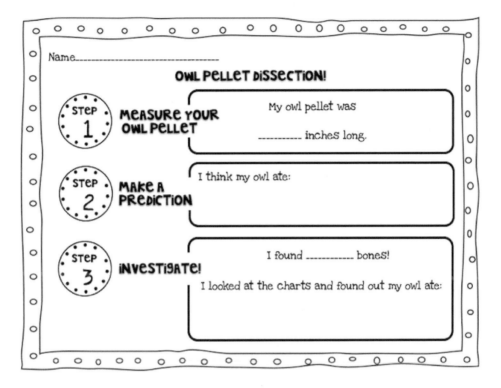

Figure 6.2. Example of an owl pellet dissection sheet

Source: Helen Lewis

Reading books for pleasure can also benefit teachers. We all have our favourite animal stories and it is important for children to hear teachers share their passion for reading. Picture books can provide a range of hooks into other curriculum areas, as explained by Jo Bowers, principal lecturer in primary education (literacy) at Cardiff Metropolitan University, using *Gorilla* by Anthony Browne (1983) as a starting point (see Box 6.2).

I love all Anthony Browne stories but *Gorilla* is one of my favourites. His picture books are particularly powerful for philosophical enquiry because of the themes within them. Spot-the-difference puzzles are often good starting points because a recurring theme in Browne's books is pictures that are spot-the-difference puzzles. This is where the illustrator paints two pictures the same but with some subtle and not-so-subtle differences. Sometimes the two pictures are side by side but sometimes they are set apart in different parts of the story. This allows the reader to compare different characters, explore their changing feelings, consider the different moods of the same character and how the story atmosphere has changed.

We see it in *Gorilla* in the meal scenes between Hannah and her father and Hannah and the gorilla. Compositionally they both show the back of Hannah's head but:

- The perspectives are different in that Hannah seems much further away from her father than the gorilla.

- The colours in the gorilla meal are much more vibrant and warmer than the one with her father, suggesting joy, whereas the blue with her father suggests sadness and coldness.

- We can see the food on the table with the gorilla, but although we know it is mealtime with her father, we can't see any food.

Spot the difference happens again when there is a back view of Hannah walking hand in hand with the gorilla and her father at the end. This time it links the gorilla with Hannah's father as they are both wearing the same clothes. They are more similar than different this time to emphasise the change in the relationship between Hannah and her father at the end of the book.

Box 6.2. Jo Bowers' reflection on the educational
value of *Gorilla*, one of her favourite animal stories

Bowers and Davies (2013) suggest that if teachers read for pleasure, it helps them to use texts creatively and gives them confidence when exploring these books with pupils. If they feel secure in their subject knowledge of children's literature, this in turn supports teachers' well-being.

Animals and mathematics

The ability to think mathematically has long been considered a trait of humans only. Studies in the early twentieth century explored whether mammals and birds possessed numerical skills. Koehler (1941), for example, concluded that pigeons, jackdaws and budgerigars were able to internally tag the items they had seen or responded to. He suggested that while they could not count in the way that we do, using a fixed series of symbolic labels (e.g. one, two, three), they could learn what he called 'unnamed numbers', so that four items might be represented by a series of inner marks or tags. The birds tended to lose accuracy between five and seven items.[12] Critics argued that these experiments had subjective bias. It became clear that the 'correct' responses of animals were the result of following human cues rather than animals' innate ability. More recent research has isolated the animal so that it cannot be directly influenced by its handler or experimenter, with computers recording the animal's responses.

Nonetheless, the basic conclusions remain that animals seem to have a kind of 'number sense' (Pepperberg, 1987a) and can undertake what scientists call 'almost' or 'rough' mathematics. What this means is that although animals cannot count in the conventional sense (i.e. 1, 2, 3), they are able to deal with simple mathematical operations. For example, researchers have trained chimpanzees to select the corresponding set of pieces of food for a given numeral in English and other languages (Frey et al., 2011). Birds can also perform a variety of number-related tasks when provided with visual stimuli – for example, continuous areas of colour or mixtures of numerous coloured items. Pepperberg (1987a) trained Alex, an African grey parrot, to identify up to six objects. He could also discriminate more than eighty different objects based on their colour, shape and material, demonstrating an understanding of the relational concepts of same and different. In other words, he could respond correctly to a question such as, 'What's same?' (e.g. for a red wooden triangle and a green rawhide triangle) or 'What's different?' (e.g. for a red wooden square and a blue wooden square). His success rate varied, depending on his familiarity with the objects, but overall was around 75% (Pepperberg, 1987b).

. . . .

12 For details of these early experiments, see Emmerton (2001); see also Milius (2016).

The wonders of the African grey parrot are delightfully conveyed to children through Dick King-Smith's story *Harry's Mad* (1986). King-Smith had been a farmer in Gloucestershire for twenty years and he authored many award-winning animal-related stories.[13] In *Harry's Mad*, he tells the story of Maddison, an African grey parrot, who is left as a gift to 10-year-old Harry Holdsworth by his eccentric American great-uncle. But 40-year-old Maddison is no ordinary parrot. He can not only mimic but hold conversations and solve real-life problems.

Animal stories are a highly effective way of introducing a range of mathematical concepts and skills to children. For example, Eileen Browne's story *No Problem* (1993) is about a mouse and the problems she has putting together a mysterious construction kit. The animals try to solve the problem in different ways. Shrew, for example, follows instructions systematically to make an aeroplane. The attraction of the story is that it introduces the problem-posing and problem-solving sequence in an accessible, engaging way. It illustrates the importance of giving children the opportunity to solve problems in different ways, thereby modelling flexible thinking. McGrath (2003) highlights how stories about animals can be used in the early years to convey mathematical concepts. She reminds us that 'the essence of a story can be richly mathematical if we choose to seek this out' (McGrath, 2003: 22). Emily Gravett's *The Rabbit Problem* (2009) explores the dilemmas facing two rabbits and their ever-expanding family. Each calendar-like page offers starting points to explore mathematical concepts such as sequencing, multiplication, weight, length and more.

Stories such as Eileen Browne's *Handa's Surprise* (2006) are not written by authors for the purpose of teaching mathematics, but they can illustrate concepts such as 'one less than' each time an animal takes a piece of fruit: one less than seven is six, one less than six is five, and so on.

The world of animals offers extensive possibilities to illustrate to children aspects of the mathematics curriculum in real life, including the application of number, problem-solving, understanding shapes, space and measure, and handling data. Many excellent classroom resources are available via organisations such as the World Wildlife Fund, the Royal Society for the Prevention of Cruelty to Animals, the Royal Society for the Protection of Birds, the National Trust, the

---

13 These include *The Sheep-Pig* (1983), filmed as *Babe* (1995), *The Hodgeheg* (1987) and *Harriet's Hare* (1996).

Woodland Trust, and the Wildfowl and Wetlands Trust. Possible topics to explore further with children include:

- The geometry of spider webs observed in the school grounds.
- Flight statistics of birds, some of whom migrate thousands of miles non-stop.
- Handling and contributing data to national surveys – for example, the Royal Society for the Protection of Birds' Big Schools' Birdwatch.[14]
- Studying hibernation patterns of animals such as hedgehogs and dormice.

While these examples relate generally to the topic of animals, there is no reason why specific AAIs should not focus on promoting children's confidence and skills in mathematics. One teacher relates how she worked with Copper, a therapy dog, and an occupational therapist to support students who were very anxious about mathematics. Their behaviours included crawling under tables, multiple requests to visit the toilet, and crying. The students were asked to complete a simple pre- and post-intervention survey on a 5-point scale of how much they liked mathematics class so the teacher could collect measurable data. Copper then spent ten to fifteen minutes each week helping to 'teach' mathematics – for example, Copper would demonstrate 180 degrees by rolling over for a belly rub, while a 360-degree roll brought him back to his tummy. The students were allowed to pet Copper while reading their mathematics question out loud and explaining to him how they would solve it. After six weeks, the teacher and therapist observed a significant reduction in negative behaviours and an increase in how much students enjoyed the classes.[15]

Animals and history

Chapter 1 highlights how animals have played an important part in our history – for example, as fellow hunters, companions, sacrifices and sources of entertainment. For teachers, animal stories offer an opportunity to bring to life topics within the history curriculum. For example, the heroic deeds of animals during

14 See https://www.rspb.org.uk/fun-and-learning/for-teachers/schools-birdwatch.
15 See https://www.schooltherapydogs.org/animal-assisted-therapy.

the First and Second World Wars are likely to simulate children's interest in finding out more about the past and provide the opportunity to raise historical questions. The Imperial War Museum is one of a number of museums and galleries that recognises the educational potential of animals to promote historical skills and understanding. It has produced a range of animal-themed resources which provide valuable starting points for classroom discussion – for example, regarding the ethical and moral questions of involving animals in warfare.[16] Generally speaking, animals undertook work such as transportation, protection and pest control during their war service, but they also had an important role in maintaining the morale of troops. There are also stories of individual heroes such as Cher Ami (French for 'Dear Friend'), one of 600 carrier pigeons in the United States Army Signal Corps. During the First World War, she delivered important letters in the American sector in north-eastern France, but her most notable exploit was her final and most daring delivery. Despite being wounded in the breast and legs by enemy fire, Cher Ami still managed to return to her loft and deliver a message that informed American forces of a battalion stranded behind enemy lines and separated from their allies. Cher Ami's valiant effort saved the lives of the 194 soldiers who were brought back to safety.

One of the most challenging but interesting aspects of teaching history involves understanding that the past is open to interpretation rather than fixed in stone, and animals can be a useful context to illustrate this. Steven Spielberg's film *War Horse* is based on Michael Morpurgo's novel about a boy called Albert and his horse, Joey, who is sent to fight on the bloody battlefields of France in the First World War. The book was published in 1982 without much acclaim, before becoming a West End play in 2007. The life-sized horse puppets intrigued audiences. In 2011, when Spielberg released his film, it was billed as an extraordinary true story. Richard van Emden, an expert on the war, pointed out that in the film there was 'a lot of artistic licence, shall we put it that way' (see Wilson, 2012). But he acknowledges that the central theme, the role of horses in the First World War, is worthy of recognition. The real horses were the star performers, more so than Emily Watson, Benedict Cumberbatch or Jeremy Irvine. As one critic put it, audiences were gripped by 'their gleaming flanks, flowing manes and hooves thundering through history' (Kellaway, 2012).

16 See https://www.iwm.org.uk/search/global?query=animals&pageSize=.

For some critics, the film conveys the pointlessness of war and represents a pacifist sermon released at a time when the western world wanted to bring service personnel home from the conflicts in Iraq, Libya and other foreign fields and deserts (Cox, 2012). Horses, depicted heroically galloping across no-man's land, had played their part in shaping people's attitudes towards war.[17]

Another example of the need for careful interpretation of historical events can be found through an exploration of the events of the 'Great Race of Mercy' which took place in Alaska in 1925. Gripped by an outbreak of deadly diphtheria, the tiny town of Nome was without medicine and the doctor radioed an urgent message for supplies of antitoxin to be delivered. The only way to get this medicine across the frozen land in time was via sled dog teams. The dog most recognised for playing a part in this life-saving adventure is Balto, whose statue stands in New York's Central Park. However, careful analysis of the evidence reveals that Balto just happened to be the lead dog for the final fifty-five miles of the journey and the dog who contributed most to the effort was 12-year-old Togo. He led his team for over 200 miles, crossing the perilous Norton Sound in temperatures as low as -30°C (Steinmetz, 2011).

Stories about animals in the past are a way in for teachers to discuss controversial issues in history. For example, horses were reportedly thrown overboard when water rations ran low on board the ships of the Spanish Armada. One legend has it that some of the horses managed to swim to shore and subsequently established the herds of wild ponies that roam the New Forest today. Another says that the Scottish Shetland pony is descended from the few Spanish horses that escaped from the wrecks. In reality, horses transported by sea during this period were often in a poor physical state and, in any event, were too far out at sea to have any hope of reaching land.

One of the aims of teaching history is to ensure that children 'know and understand significant aspects of the history of the wider world'.[18] This includes the nature of ancient civilisations, in which animals were an important feature of everyday life. Museums can offer pupils insights into how different cultures had

---

17 The charge scene was rehearsed on the Duke of Wellington's estate at Stratfield Saye, Hampshire. In reality, the horses crashed through foam chairs, collapsible tents and rubber barbed wire. Animatronics were also used.
18 See https://www.gov.uk/government/publications/national-curriculum-in-england-history-programmes-of-study/national-curriculum-in-england-history-programmes-of-study.

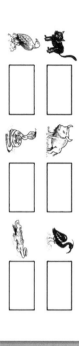

PAGE 1 ANIMALS IN ANCIENT EGYPT
(Key Stage 2)

There were lots of different animals that lived in Egypt, but not all of the types of animals we see today lived in Pharaoh's Egypt. As a class, we will try and guess what the animal is. We will put a ✓ in the box next to the animals that lived in ancient Egypt and an X for those that didn't.

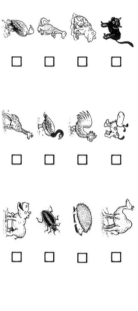

Look at the different animals in the display case. How many of these can you find? Write the number in the box. Include parts of animals as well.

PAGE 2 ANIMALS IN ANCIENT EGYPT
(Key Stage 2)

Now we have looked at the animals in the cases, what do you think some of them were called in ancient Egypt? We'll give you one clue: a frog was called KERER. The ancient Egyptians believed many of their animals were sacred because their gods could take animal form and behave like the animal.

The Egyptian gods were often shown as part animal, part human (zoomorphic). Can you work out the animal that each of the following Egyptian gods have transformed into? Write the name of the animal beside each picture.

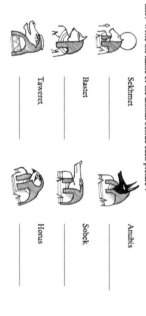

Sekhmet _____	Anubis _____
Bastet _____	Sobek _____
Tawaret _____	Horus _____

The animals that were considered sacred were mummified when they died. Animals, as small as beetles and as large as bulls have been found mummified. If you were rich even your favourite pet could be mummified!

In the case there are three animal mummies can you name one of them? _____

Figure 6.3. Animals in ancient Egypt activities for Key Stage 2

Source: Egypt Centre, Swansea University

different views of, and relationships with, animals. For example, the Egypt Centre at Swansea University reveals how the ancient Egyptians linked some animals with their gods, seeing them as part human and part animal (zoomorphic). Hannah Sweetapple, the museum's education and events officer, explains that the ancient Egyptians did not worship animals as such; rather, they believed that the god could take the form of the animal. Many Egyptians also kept different pets, and some were considered sacred and mummified after death. The museum provides practical, object-based sessions to engage children in this topic (Figure 6.3).

Table 6.2 shows how very young children's skills and understanding of ancient Egypt can be developed through hands-on activities involving animal-related concepts.

Table 6.2. Skills relating to the foundation phase in Wales (children aged 3–7 years)

Language and communication skills	Listening and responding to others by discussing the different types of gods the ancient Egyptians worshipped as well as discussing the different animals in ancient Egypt and how they compare to today's animals. Children are also encouraged to guess types of animals in ancient Egypt. Encourage children to ask and answer questions and to increase confidence when speaking using a growing vocabulary (e.g. goddess, Osiris, donkey).
Knowledge and understanding of the world	Encourage their historical curiosity as they begin to understand how people of a different culture lived very differently a long time ago in another country. Comparing ancient Egyptian animals with animals today, especially pets. Awareness of change and difference over time (e.g. most people only believe in one god but in ancient Egypt they believed in many gods).

Physical development	Gross motor skills – walking and moving around the museum. Putting the headdresses on and off as well as feeling the animals in the bags all help to develop children's motor skills. They will also develop their motor skills while holding the buckets, torches and magnifying glasses to explore the gallery.
Creative development	This activity encourages the children to use their imagination and get involved in the story of Osiris and Seth by wearing headdresses. It also encourages children to use their imagination and think about what it would be like to have so many gods and goddesses. The children then have to use their imagination to guess what animal is in the bag!
Personal and social development	Children are expected to listen attentively and take turns in answering questions. They are encouraged to help each other think about the animal in the bag as well as guessing the sorts of animals found in ancient Egypt. Certain behaviour is expected as there are other visitors in the museum: they have to listen to others, to wait their turn and to share. This helps children to recognise and gain a positive awareness of their own and ancient cultures by developing an empathy with a past civilisation. They are encouraged to make links with prior knowledge, which enables them to succeed and build self-esteem.

Source: Egypt Centre, Swansea University

Similar starting points can be found in museums across the country and beyond. At the British Museum, younger children can learn to identify the African animals represented in a range of objects in the museum's collection.[19] They can then learn to program animal robots and photograph their visit to the African galleries.

---

19 See https://www.britishmuseum.org/learn/schools/ages-3-6/digital-session-coding-animals.

It is important not to lose sight of the point that history is primarily about people, so whenever animals feature in history lessons, the focus should be on how people interacted with them and what this tells us about individuals and societies in the past. Learning about dinosaurs and other creatures may be of interest, but it should not be confused with historical learning because natural history is not the same as history. Nonetheless, our fascination with animals is reflected in many museum exhibits all over the world, and children should understand the essential role animals have played in human societies, past and present.

Animals in art and design

The teaching of art and design aims to inspire children so that they develop the knowledge and skills to experiment, invent and generate their own ideas. It also aims to raise their awareness of the significant historical contribution art and design make in our world. Many artists, craft makers and designers have drawn inspiration from animals. By exploring their works, children can learn about different artistic techniques, develop observational skills and understand how animals are depicted in different cultures.

In ancient caves, such as those in Lascaux, France, early humans painted images of hunting scenes on the walls - including animals such as bison, stags and equines. These were discovered in 1940 and provide an insight into life many thousands of years ago. They can inspire children to explore mark-making using natural materials such as crushed berries and sticks or to experiment with designs drawn onto natural backdrops such as stones, sand and mud (Grigg and Lewis, 2016). Images of animals carry significance in many cultures. For example, in North American First Nation communities the bear represents strength, family, vitality, courage and health; the eagle signifies focus, strength, peace, leadership and ultimate prestige; and the wolf represents loyalty, strong family ties, good communication and intelligence (Arthurson, 2013).

Animals of all shapes and sizes appear in many works of art, depicted in different artistic styles and mediums (see Table 6.3). Archaeologists continue to unearth animal-themed objects from distant times, such as the discovery in 2013 of a Roman eagle sculpture in the City of London. It is regarded as one of the best-preserved pieces of Romano-British art ever found (Kennedy, 2013). Animals have had a strong presence in paintings. Albrecht Dürer's *Rhinoceros* has been described as the most influential animal picture in history (Sherwin, 2016). In subsequent centuries, many artists used the picture as a basis for their own work. In reality, Dürer never saw a rhinoceros. Rather, he based his drawing on a written description and sketch by an unknown artist. The poor Indian rhinoceros had been selected as a gift for the king of Portugal, who then sent it on as a present to the Pope, but the ship transporting the rhinoceros sank en route and the animal drowned. To ensure that ordinary people could afford his work, Dürer created a woodcut because it was cheaper to reproduce than an engraving. Artists have also used animals to convey a sense of majesty, power and awe. Sir Edwin Landseer's *Monarch of the Glen* is widely regarded as the epitome of the majestic wildlife of the Scottish Highlands. The stag became a marketing emblem for many products, from Scotch whisky to soap, mineral water, shortbread and soup, increasing its global recognition.

Table 6.3. Examples of artwork focusing on animals

Artist	Work	Date	Details
Unknown	Lascaux Cave paintings	15,000 BC	Mineral pigments and charcoal
Ancient Egyptian	Gayer-Anderson Cat	After c.600 BC	Sculpture mainly of bronze, 42 cm high
Ancient Celts	Uffington White Horse	c.800 BC– AD 100	Crushed chalk, 112 m long
Probably Anglo-Saxon female embroiderers	Bayeux Tapestry	11th century	Embroidered cloth, 70 m x 50 cm
Albrecht Dürer	*The Rhinoceros*	1515	Woodcut, 24.9 x 30.3 cm

Artist	Work	Date	Details
Hans Holbein the Younger	*Portrait of a Lady with a Squirrel and a Starling*	c.1626	Oil on oak, 56 cm x 38.8 cm
Carel Fabritius	*The Goldfinch*	1654	Oil on panel, 33.5 x 22.8 cm
Sir Edwin Landseer	*The Monarch of the Glen*	1851	Oil on canvas, 163.8 x 168.9 cm
Rosa Bonheur	*The Horse Fair*	1852–1855	Oil on canvas, 244.5 × 506.7 cm
Henri Rousseau	*Tiger in a Tropical Storm*	1891	Oil on canvas, 130 cm × 162 cm
Pablo Picasso	*The Bull*	1945	Lithograph (plate 11), 29.2 x 39.5 cm
Richard Avedon	*Dovima with Elephants*	1955	Gelatin silver print, 48.4 × 38.2 cm
Jeff Koons	*Rabbit*	1986	Stainless steel, 104.1 x 48.3 x 30.5 cm
Katharina Fritsch	*Rat-King*	1993	Polyester and paint, 2.8 m x 13 m
Damien Hirst	*Away from the Flock*	1994	Glass, stainless steel, Perspex, acrylic paint, lamb and formaldehyde solution, 96 × 149 × 51 cm

Artist	Work	Date	Details
Banksy	*Love Rat*	2004	Screen-print, 50 x 35 cm
Sam Rowley	*Station Squabble*	2020	Digital photograph, unknown

Many artists have taken inspiration from their own pets. The eccentric French artist Suzanne Valadon fed caviar (rather than fish) to her 'good Catholic' cats on Fridays and kept a goat in her studio to eat up any of her drawings that she thought were poor. The style of *Two Cats* (1918) and her other paintings is characterised by rich colours and bold, open brushwork and she would outline her figures in firm black lines.

Through careful observation, children can imitate particular artistic techniques and styles to learn how artists conveyed meaning. For example, Francisco de Goya's *The Dog* (1820), Charles Burton Barber's *Suspense* (1894) and Mary Anne Aytoun-Ellis' *Dog* (2012) use a range of techniques such as blending to bring texture to their paintings, and deploy shade and tone to bring them to life. The paintings could be compared and contrasted, looking for similarities and differences in subject or technique. Pablo Picasso's suite of eleven lithographs, known collectively as *The Bull* (1945), formed a masterclass in the step-by-step creation of a masterpiece. Picasso seeks to reveal the animal's 'spirit' by portraying its development in successive stages. Among his innovations was the use of his fingers to make marks, instead of a brush or lithographic crayon. Picasso liked the way lithography allowed him to easily erase, rework and amend his work. Today, designers of Apple computers use Picasso's work in their training as an inspiration for simplicity.

Photography is an immediately accessible medium for children to explore. For many young people taking photographs of animals is a quick, everyday experience. But as an art form, photography can be a painstaking process. Richard Avedon's *Dovima with Elephants* is a remarkable photograph taken in Paris in the summer of 1955. The model, Dovima, wears a Dior dress, which contrasts beautifully with the rough texture of the elephants behind her. Sam Rowley's stunning *Station Squabble* (2020) captures the scene when two mice fight over a morsel of food on a London Underground platform. Rowley spent a week overnight in the underground lying on various platforms and waiting for the right moment, which was over in seconds.[20]

Works of art, by their creative nature, can be controversial. Damien Hirst's *Away from the Flock* (1994) is a case in point. The glass-walled tank is filled with formaldehyde solution in which a dead lamb is fixed so that it appears to be alive and caught in movement. Hirst had already attracted controversy for his formaldehyde-preserved sharks, dissected cows and calves. When *Away from the Flock* was exhibited it sold in the first week for £25,000, a purchase that *The Sun* newspaper described as 'Baa-rmy'. When interviewed about his work, Hirst said that he didn't mind what people thought about it, as long as they got involved in the debate. The following week, an unemployed artist from Oxford removed the top of Hirst's tank, poured black ink into it and changed the title to *Black Sheep* (Walsh, 1999).

Banksy, the anonymous street graffiti artist, is another controversial figure with an interest in animals, particularly the rat (an anagram of art). *Love Rat* (2004) is one of his most iconic works, depicting a rat holding a large paintbrush in his paws having just completed the painting of a heart. The first impression is that the message is about spreading love on the streets. However, the dripping red paint from the heart is a popular street art technique, representing pain and suffering.

Approaches such as Visible Thinking Routines (Ritchhart et al., 2011) could be used to explore works of art in more detail. For example, the routine 'main-side-hidden' could encourage learners of all ages to explore the complexity and depth of a painting, sculpture or photograph. The artworks need to be chosen carefully, ensuring there is sufficient detail and complexity to allow the children to engage with the routine fully. A painting such as *Returning from the Bois de Boulogne, Lady with Dog* by Giuseppe de Nittis (1878) is a good example. After closely looking at the painting, the children could be invited to consider:

▨ What is the *main* story being depicted, and who are the main characters?

▨ What is the *side* story (or stories) happening around the edges that may not necessarily involve the main characters?

20 You can see more of Sam Rowley's photographs at https://www.sam-rowley.com.

■ What is the *hidden* story – another story that may be obscured, neglected or happening below the surface that we aren't readily aware of initially?

Thinking in this way allows the children to generate new questions and also encourages them to identify additional points of view, beyond those of the central characters. The different stories present in the painting might be exciting starting points for some creative writing.

Another useful routine to support children to look more closely at works of art and design is 'colour-shapes-lines'. This encourages them to think carefully about the decisions the artist has made when creating their work and the reasons why they may have done so. For example, Chinese artist Hua Tunan's paintings, such as *Prairie Fire*, use techniques from traditional Chinese art and western graffiti to create abstract shapes of animals, employing ink splashes, colour, shape and line in an original and intriguing manner.[21] After looking closely at the artwork, children can be asked to describe the colours, shapes and lines that they notice in detail. They can then select one or two of these and consider how it contributes to the artwork's overall feel, mood, appearance, story and ideas. By taking time to think deeply about these details, children may develop new ideas about art and the choices they make when they create their own.

Animals also appear in many sculptures, from the marble 'Jennings Dog' in the British Museum to the less well-known sugarcraft replica of a dog named Rufus II, created for his owner Winston Churchill's seventy-ninth birthday cake. Animals have also influenced the design world – for instance, Japan's Shinkansen bullet trains are modelled on a kingfisher's beak and George de Mestral was inspired to invent Velcro after seeing how tiny burrs attached themselves to his dog's fur. In the village of Lacock, Wiltshire, the fourteenth-century George Inn has an example of a dog wheel – an object in which the running of short, specially trained 'turnspit' dogs turned the spit to roast the meat evenly.

Looking closely at animals' fur, feathers and skin can present opportunities to investigate pattern and texture. Julia Ocker's film *Zebra* is a good starting point to explore and describe pattern.[22] Chameleons are fascinating masters of disguise and a wonderful way to introduce and study the concept of camouflage,

21 See https://www.demilked.com/animal-paintings-ink-on-paper-hua-tunan.
22 See https://www.youtube.com/watch?v=VwQDjmzdQlg.

as well as colour, shade and tone. Unfortunately, this fascinating creature is also one of the world's most trafficked animals, a fact which can trigger a debate over moral issues.

Animals in religious and moral education

All the world's major religions acknowledge that humankind depends on nature for its survival and teach love of all living creatures. For example, Buddhism is based on a universal idea of compassion for all life and Judaism embraces the Hebrew concept of *tsa'ar ba'alei hayim* – noting the importance of preventing the 'sorrow of living creatures' (World Animal Net, n.d.). Hindus regard all living creatures as sacred and many Hindus adopt a vegetarian diet. They acknowledge this reverence for life in their special affection for the cow. To a Hindu, the cow is a symbol of the Earth, the ever-giving, undemanding provider. The cow represents life and the sustenance of life. Many Sikhs believe that humans and the world of nature have a great deal in common. God created everything, therefore animals are important and valuable. Sikhs do not believe that animals should be worshipped but they do believe that they should be respected as a part of God's creation. Sikhs believe in reincarnation and that all animals have souls. Although animal life is valuable, it is only in a human body that the soul has the chance to reach God, because only humans know the difference between right and wrong.

Many religions have stories which contain reference to animals – for example, in the Bible we can read about Noah's ark, Jonah and the whale, Daniel in the lion's den and, perhaps less well known, Elijah and the ravens and Aaron and the serpent. In Islam there are stories such as 'The Prophet and the Ants' and 'The Crying Camel', which teach us that animals need to be cared for no matter how big or small they may be. In Hinduism, many gods have animal characteristics. For example, Ganesha has the head of an elephant. His large head symbolises knowledge, intelligence and thinking, his trunk represents power and his large ears denote his attentiveness. Hanuman the monkey god is one of the most popular deities in Hinduism, exemplifying courage, strength and devotion.

Furthermore, issues around animal rights provide excellent opportunities for debate, discussion and reflection. The BBC Bitesize website has a unit of work which covers a variety of issues from animal rights in the law to animal rights in world religions.[23] Debating moral and philosophical questions relating to the rights of animals and the moral and ethical duties we have towards them can also be done using philosophical enquiry approaches such as Philosophy for Children (e.g. Lipman, 1988).

Summary

- This chapter outlines the wide-ranging potential gains associated with learning about animals across the curriculum.

- Students can develop scientific knowledge, skills and understanding through observing animals in authentic, first-hand contexts.

- Interacting with animals affords opportunities to promote children's all-round language development, while they can be motivated to read and write about animals which appear in a wide range of genres.

- Animal stories and observations are a highly effective way to introduce a range of mathematical concepts and skills, such as measures, shapes and problem-solving.

- Although the teaching of history is primarily about people, their interaction with animals in the past opens up opportunities to convey knowledge about events such as the First and Second World Wars.

- Animals are a key source of inspiration for artists and designers. Students can learn about artistic techniques and materials that focus on animals, from ancient cave paintings to modern-day sculptures.

- In religious and moral education, students can learn about the central role animals play in world religions and the ethical issues that provoke debate and reflection.

---

23 See https://www.bbc.co.uk/bitesize/guides/zys3d2p/revision/2.

Chapter 7

Tales of snails, wolves and teddies: animals as starting points for cross-curricular approaches

The current vision for schools is for every student to be an engaged learner, whose attention, energy and intellect are completely focused on the object of learning in the lessons. (Ng, 2017: 130)

Much of the learning and teaching that emerges from using animals as inspiration is cross-curricular by nature, and most early years settings and many primary schools plan using themes, topics or cross-curricular projects. This chapter briefly describes three examples of how educationalists have used AAIs to promote cross-curricular knowledge, skills and dispositions. The arguments for and against cross-curricular teaching have been well rehearsed (Kerry, 2015). What is clear is that excellent teachers make links explicit to their students – for example, between what they are learning in one subject and in another, between classroom learning and the outside world, and within subjects themselves (Siraj and Taggart, 2014).

Case study 1: Snail tales

Jude Penny is a senior lecturer in primary education at the University of Gloucestershire who has a passion for science. While snails may not be the most attractive of creatures, and despite their traditional association with slothfulness and extravagance, Jude suggests that they provide incredible learning opportunities and a powerful resource to engage children. For Jude, they have proven to be the basis for her most enjoyable and memorable lessons with children and student teachers alike. This case study draws on some of her experiences.[1]

Science: habitats and life processes

After carefully collecting snails from their natural habitats, or creating a habitat in the outdoor classroom, children can learn about the basic needs of these animals. A clear plastic container can be filled with soil and plant material. Ventilation holes are required and the environment needs to be kept moist through misting every couple of days or by keeping a damp paper towel in the container. Scraps of vegetables and peelings can be placed on the soil. The children can then observe the habits of the snails over a given period. To give children an opportunity to observe snails close up, Jude advises that the snails are gently placed on a piece of black paper so that their slime trails can be seen clearly. If a snail is reluctant to come out of its shell, place it in a shallow dish of water and it will slowly emerge. Snails love to nibble a small piece of banana, and if you dip the tip of a paintbrush in vinegar and hold it near (without touching) the snail's antennae, they will retract as they are not keen on acetic acid!

Snails are living things and do all the things that living things do (the life processes of movement, respiration, sensitivity, growth, reproduction, excretion and nutrition), so snail watching gives children the opportunity to make observations that link to the life processes. For example:

- 'It's eating the banana. I didn't know it had a mouth!' (*Nutrition*)

- 'Oh, Miss, he just did a poo!' (*Excretion*)

- 'He can smell the vinegar, Miss!' or 'He just pulled in his tentacle.' (*Sensitivity*)

- A snail once laid some eggs while the children were observing, leading to a conversation about life cycles. (*Reproduction*)

....

1   The snail is the common name for gastropod molluscs, which can be split into three groups: land snails, sea snails and freshwater snails. Common garden snails are most active in warm, damp weather and are usually seen at night.

Children can gain first-hand evidence that can help them to make sense of the criteria for living things. They can then compare these behaviours with other animals they are familiar with, including themselves.

Scientific skills

When given the opportunity to interact with snails, children use a range of scientific enquiry skills, including making observations, raising questions, performing simple tests and gathering evidence to help answer their questions. Children raise a variety of questions about the snails that are potential starting points for scientific enquiry, and these can be collected on a 'question wall' or poster. It is important that time is spent considering what would be the best way for the children to address their scientific questions – for example, a question such as, 'Do snails prefer damp or dry areas?' can be investigated through a simple test, whereas, 'What is the largest/smallest snail on Earth?' requires the use of research. The children can learn about the different types of scientific enquiry to which their questions can lead.

Art and design

Since ancient times, snails have featured as artistic body decoration, for ornamentation, as religious motifs (Figure 7.1) and as sources to inspire architecture.[2] Other more unusual connections to art include the fact that gravestones are sometimes etched with snail images because they are seen as creatures that undergo 'resurrection' when, after a long period of drought, it rains and snails that appeared to have dried up start crawling around (Jones, 2014). Dutch still-life artists often included snails as a reminder of human mortality, with around 500 paintings featuring them identified from the sixteenth and seventeenth centuries alone (Breure and Heer, 2015).

Snails provide rich stimuli for children to experiment, invent and create their own works of art, craft and design. They can produce observational drawings, collages, models and 'snail trail' patterns on black paper using a range of mark-making equipment. Empty shells can be collected and decorated, or filled

2 See, for example, https://www.trendhunter.com/slideshow/snailinspired-designs.

with soil and used to make tiny fairy gardens.

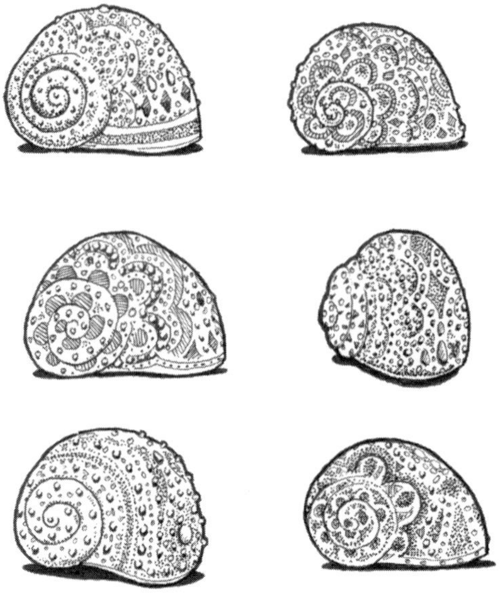

Jo Saxton's *Snail Trail: In Search of a Modern Masterpiece* (2009) is a stimulating starting point to introduce children to some of the great works of modern art that include snails, such as pieces by Pollock, Rothko, Mondrian, Dali, Picasso and Matisse. Children should enjoy running their finger along the silvery trail of an art-loving snail searching for a picture that best represents them. Perhaps inevitably, this leads to a discussion of *The Snail* by the French artist Henri Matisse.

Figure 7.1. Decorated prayer shells

When Matisse created *The Snail*, which he worked on between 1952 and 1953, he was in his eighties and experiencing failing health (he died in 1954). Confined to bed, Matisse relied on assistants to help him assemble coloured bits of paper to form a loose spiral on a white backdrop. The scale of the work is impressive – at nearly 3 square metres. At first, paper was painted in vibrant colours with an opaque gouache paint. Then, Matisse directed his assistants to cut and tear the paper into specific shapes. Finally, the shapes were arranged on a plain white sheet of paper and slowly moved into position until Matisse was satisfied with the overall composition. Reflecting on his technique (*gouaches découpées*), which he had experimented with since the 1940s, Matisse explained: 'I first of all drew the snail from nature, holding it. I became aware of an unrolling, I found an image in my mind purified of the shell, then I took the scissors' (Verdet, 1952: 64-65).

Mathematics

As we have seen, Matisse was among those who admired the geometry of snails. Children could create their own geometric designs using circles and 'near' circles, rather than quadrilaterals and 'near' quadrilaterals. A snail can be gently placed on a piece of graph paper and measured to see how wide it is and then a mark made to show how long its 'foot' is when fully extended. Children can be asked to think about such questions as, 'Do snails with bigger shells always have longer bodies?', 'How far does your snail travel in one minute?' or 'Do bigger snails travel faster than small snails?' Measurement skills and concepts relating to time and distance can be promoted through snail racing. The annual Snail Racing World Championships typically attracts around 200 snails who commence their race to the words, 'Ready, steady, slow'.[3]

There are various snail-themed mathematical resources available to teachers. NRICH is a professional collaboration between the faculties of mathematics and education at the University of Cambridge which seeks to enrich and enhance the mathematical experiences of children aged 3–18. It offers free online resources on its website, which include some snail-related mathematical challenges for the primary school.[4] The American Mathematics Society also has a section on its website dedicated to more advanced study of the mathematics underpinning shells.[5] Similarly, the New Zealand Ministry of Education website has a few mathematical activities related to snails.[6]

Literacy

Snail watching provides a stimulus for a range of genres of writing, including poetry, story and non-fiction fact files. Children can explore Julia Donaldson's story of *The Snail and the Whale* (2003) for similes and create some for their own snails. They could focus on one of the pictures, without the accompanying text, and write about that part of the animal's adventure. They could also create speech or thought bubbles from the animal's viewpoint. At the end of the story, the snail recounts his adventure to his friends. The children might then write the story of the snails that have visited their school, detailing where they have been and where they will be off to next. Other titles featuring snails include Chris

3   See http://www.snailracing.net.
4   See https://nrich.maths.org/216.
5   See http://www.ams.org/publicoutreach/feature-column/fcarc-shell1.
6   See https://nzmaths.co.nz/resource/snails.

Raschka's *Snaily Snail* (2000), Judy Allen's *Are You a Snail?* (2003), Joyce Sidman's *Swirl by Swirl: Spirals in Nature* (2011) and Mary Murphy's *Slow Snail* (2013).

Personal and social development

While observing snails, children demonstrate authentic responses because they are genuinely intrigued and curious about them. Children may also have the opportunity to develop interpersonal skills as they share the experience with their peers. They learn that snails must be treated with respect and not be subjected to unreasonable or extreme conditions. After a short time in school, snails can be returned to where they were collected. This might raise some important issues to be explored with the children, since snails are often considered to be pests. Having interacted with them, the children may demonstrate increased sensitivity towards the snails and should understand that they are well adapted to cope with a range of conditions in the outside world.

Children should also be taught about health and safety issues when working with snails. Both children and adults should always wash their hands soon after coming into contact with snails. Cuts and abrasions on the hands and arms should be covered to minimise the risk of infection, and containers and surfaces should be properly washed and disinfected after use.

Jude Penny sums up the educational value of snails as follows: 'Student teachers often grimace when I present them with snails. However, it is not long before they are totally engrossed in "snail watching". Whatever your opinion of these amazing invertebrates, if you make the effort to bring them into your classroom, the children's responses alone will make you wonder why you had never done it before!'

Case study 2: The wonder of wolves

Wolves were once a common sight in Britain before they were hunted to extinction towards the end of the seventeenth century. Folklore has it that Sir Ewen Cameron shot the last wild wolf in 1680 in the Scottish Highlands (Weymouth,

2014). Unfortunately for wolves, they have suffered a poor press through the ages because of their natural tendency to prey. In fact, sheep and cattle have often fallen victim to domesticated dogs that have gone feral rather than wild wolves. Nonetheless, the wolf has long been cast in negative tones. In the New Testament we are warned, 'Beware of the false prophets, who come to you in sheep's clothing but inwardly are ravenous wolves' (Matthew 7:15) and the Qur'an references a wolf eating Joseph. The oldest known piece of western prose, *The Epic of Gilgamesh*, is said to contain the first mention of a werewolf: Gilgamesh jilts a potential lover because she had turned her previous mate into a wolf.

Children's stories are hardly much kinder to wolves. The notion of the big bad wolf can be traced back more than 2,500 years to when the wolf featured in twenty-five of Aesop's fables.[7] Through such stories, generations of children have been brought up with a negative view of wolves. However, in recent years there have been attempts to address the imbalance and undo the 'Little Red Riding Hood' legacy, particularly through children's information books and films which stress, for example, the unlikelihood of being attacked by a wolf (Mitts-Smith, 2010). The general intent is to make 'the wild' less threatening and more intriguing.

The loyalty, intelligence and self-sacrificial love of wolves are among their qualities and attributes. These are illustrated in the remarkable story of Marcos Rodríguez Pantoja. In 1953, at the age of 7, he was abandoned in the Spanish mountains and left to fend for himself. With no one to talk to, he began to howl, bark and chirp. He survived only because he was protected and cared for by a pack of wolves. Twelve years later, police found him and he was taken by a priest to a convent. In 2010, a rather romanticised film, *Entrelobos* (Among Wolves), was made about his life as a 'wolf man' (Bremner, 2018). Pantoja found it easier to live with wolves than humans.

Laura Braun is one teacher who has set about trying to educate children about the realities of wolves. Her Year 5-6 class project at Bury Church of England Primary, a small school in West Sussex, focused on whether wolves should be reintroduced to the South Downs National Park. The children undertook

---

7   See https://aesopsfables.org/C2_aesops_fables_about_wolves.html.

preliminary research and engaged in a range of activities designed to increase their knowledge and understanding of wolves.

In science, the class learned about wolves' life cycles, habitats and habits. They looked closely at their endangered status across the world, and learned about the reintroduction of wolves into Yellowstone Park in the United States and other rewilding projects across the world. As none of the class had seen wolves in the wild, it was important to Laura that they read materials and watched films to increase their knowledge and understanding, and so they read newspaper reports about rewilding in Norway, Belgium and Ireland and watched some video clips about wolf behaviour, thereby developing their language and literacy skills.

In English lessons, the class read a range of literature, exploring how wolves are portrayed in classic stories and fables as well as modern books such as Neil Gaiman's *The Wolves in the Walls* (2003), Katherine Rundell's *The Wolf Wilder* (2015), William Grill's *The Wolves of Currumpaw* (2016) and Jim Field's *The Way Home for Wolf* (2018). Gaiman's story was inspired by his 4-year-old daughter's nightmare that wolves were in her bedroom walls. Naturally, the family do not believe her until one day the wolves come out!

The final part of the project was to make clay wolves. For logistical support, Laura engaged the help of parents and governor volunteers. Laura says:

This would have been difficult if the children hadn't spent so much time 'getting to know' wolves before making them. Initially we looked at wolf photos and at how their body parts were 'joined together', especially considering the fact that their heads don't sit on top of their bodies but extend forward. To start with I showed the children a model I had made previously and we discussed what was good about it and what I'd like to have improved. We also looked at what would happen if the clay wasn't used properly, and they were appalled to see a wolf I had made that had exploded. This is always a good reminder at the start of clay work – it is a natural substance and you can't always rely on it to behave!

The children gained artistic skills in handling the tools and material correctly, collaborating together and problem-solving – for example, deciding whether their wolf should be standing, sitting or lying down. Laura used a visualiser to model the process and then the children made each section of the body, using cross-hatching and slip to join the pieces of clay together, propped up using a ball of clay to keep the models stable. Once the wolves had been created, the children used surface decoration techniques to create life-like fur, using photographs of wolves as reference points. This prompted much discussion about why wolf fur grows in different directions as it does. The final pre-firing stage was for Laura to 'gut' the wolves, scooping out a large amount of the middle of each wolf so that they could dry out entirely before firing. After the first firing the children looked once again at images of wolves to plan their colouration. This prompted much discussion as to why wolves are not uniformly one colour, raising the concepts of camouflage, habitats and food chains.

Through these activities the children gained a firm and broad knowledge on which to base their arguments for the re-introduction of wolves. They produced thoughtful opinion pieces designed to convince their audience and the letters were sent to the National Park authorities, providing an authentic external audience. Although wolves will not be making an appearance in the South Downs National Park in the near future, the letters were detailed and convincing in nature. In 2019, two wolverines were reintroduced alongside bears and lynx to a 10,000 square-metre paddock near Bristol, the first-time bears and wolves have lived side by side in Britain for a thousand years (Snaith, 2019).

Figure 7.2. Clay wolves

Source: Laura Braun

Reflecting on the learning, Laura thinks that by using wolves as the focus for the project the children were motivated from the outset, which gave them a thirst to find out more. And because the class looked at all aspects of wolves, from their diet to their habitat and how they are portrayed in literature, this not only gave them a much clearer understanding of the animal itself but also deepened their learning across the curriculum. Other predators can also be the basis of powerful learning across the curriculum – for example, the World Wildlife Fund's Tiger Toolkit provides starting points for learning in science, language, art, physical education and citizenship.[8]

Case study 3: Teddy bear tales

Bears are another animal which fascinate us and feature in many much-loved tales, from familiar stories such as Michael Rosen's *We're Going on a Bear Hunt* (1993), Jill Murphy's *Peace at Last* (1980) and 'Goldilocks and the Three Bears' (various editions), to Emily Gravett's unusual *Orange Pear Apple Bear* (2006). And then there is the long line of bears who have starred in cartoons and films, including Winnie-the-Pooh, Paddington, Baloo, Rupert, Iorek Byrnison, Yogi and Fozzie.

In real life, there are eight species of bear found across the world: sun bears, sloth bears, spectacled bears, American black bears, Asian black bears, brown bears (which include the subspecies grizzly bear), polar bears and giant pandas. All are threatened either by a loss of habitat or by hunting and other cruel practices such as dancing for tourists and bile farming. A number of charities offer the opportunity to adopt a bear, which can be an inspirational starting point for learning about sustainability, conservation and citizenship.[9]

A project on bears provides various possibilities for learning across the curriculum. The iconic teddy bear is an obvious starting point for early years practitioners. Teddy bears and other soft toy bears feature in the lives of many children, meaning there will be a personal connection and some prior experience that practitioners can build upon.

There are lots of stories about toy bears that can be used to promote children's language and literacy skills. While many are fictional, there are examples from real-life events. For example, in 1903, 3,000 of the first teddies ever manufactured were sent from Germany to the United States by ship. They never arrived.

8   See https://www.worldwildlife.org/teaching-resources/toolkits/tiger-toolkit.
9   Examples include https://www.bornfree.org.uk/adopt-a-bear, https://support.wwf.org.uk/adopt-a-polar-bear, https://www.durrell.org/wildlife/adopt/andean-bear and https://www.animalsasia.org/uk/donate/sponsor-a-bear.

However, exactly what happened to these Steiff bears remains a mystery, with some wondering if they became shipwrecked. Considering what might have happened to the bears would be an ideal way to engage children's imaginative thinking. Possible scenarios as to the fate of the teddies could be explored: children could retell the story of the shipwreck in a drama lesson, they could create a desert island camp in the outdoor area or think about other people's point of view if they imagine how the teddy bears might have felt if they arrived in a new country. Older pupils could write letters to the manufacturer requesting further information about the order or create a video news bulletin based on discovering the missing teddies over 100 years later.

Other activities that could link to a topic on teddy bears include tasks required for a teddy bear picnic. This is particularly suitable for very young children, and holding a picnic can be a good way to promote family engagement. Older children could help younger ones to prepare for a picnic and develop a range of skills and understanding by, for example:

- Helping to identify a date and venue for the picnic, deciding on what would be a suitable location and the reasons for this.
- Writing for a purpose (e.g. creating invitations and shopping lists).
- Preparing a menu suitable for the different guests, considering dietary requirements and healthy eating options.
- Planning some activities for the picnic, taking into account the needs of the children and parents attending.
- Budgeting for the picnic (e.g. by accessing a supermarket website and calculating the quantities and costs involved in catering for a given number of guests).
- Undertaking a visit to a local shop to buy ingredients.
- Making food for the picnic.
- Planning for the unexpected (e.g. poor weather).
- Following instructions and teddy bear footprints around obstacles in the outdoor provision.
- Creating dens for teddies in the small world or construction area.
- Attending the picnic and reporting back on what happened.

Michael Rosen's much loved tale *We're Going on a Bear Hunt* offers inspiration and opportunity for a range of activities. For example, going into the outdoors to recreate the adventure is one option to develop listening, gross motor and creative skills. If your outdoor provision lacks trees, rivers and mud, then you can provide shallow trays or buckets and the children can step into these as the story progresses (this is also useful in inclement weather as the activity can take place in a hall). Equally, fine motor and imaginative skills could be developed by recreating the grass, stream and mud in the small world area. For example, one pupil (Gabriel Brown) created the different elements of the story using little figures to retell the tale in the outdoor environment, supporting playful learning and imagination.

Figure 7.3. Small world bear hunt

Source: Sharon Smith

Although there are many templates and worksheets available for developing skills such as cutting, sticking and pencil control, try to use the opportunity to develop individual creativity and imagination. For instance, the children could be encouraged to compose an accompanying soundtrack for their story by collecting grass, water, mud, sticks and ice (or cotton wool) in separate, recycled plastic bottles and exploring the sounds these materials make. They could then find out whether there are musical instruments that could represent these sounds. The children could retell the story with the accompanying music, perhaps recording the finished performance for parents and other children to enjoy.

Another option is to create hibernating bear caves from paper bags and natural resources, prompting the children to explore and decide what materials might provide a comfy bed for a bear. The role play area could be turned into a cosy den complete with sleeping teddy bears. This idea could be adapted for the outdoor area, with the children challenged to create dens using materials found in the grounds. Building dens promotes a wide variety of skills, including gross and fine motor skills, problem-solving, communication, collaboration and language skills. If they work closely as a team to create their den, the children will need to take turns in conversation, explain and justify their ideas, and negotiate with others. As well as sticks, rope and other natural materials, resources such as blankets, sheets, wooden pegs, boxes or ribbon can be used to create dens. Older children could design and evaluate their dens in greater depth, promoting an opportunity for some analysis and reflection on what worked well. Organisations such as the National Trust[10] and the Eden Project[11] produce practical guides and lesson plans for den building.

Creating a display of old and new teddy bears in the classroom might inspire some close observation and lead to a range of art activities such as sketching, collage and printing. This would also generate discussion about 'then' and 'now', looking at how materials and designs have changed over time. For example, in Figure 7.4 Mildred's panda is from the 1930s, while Janet's was bought recently. Although the pandas share many similarities, they are also different in various ways.

Children could be encouraged to use their observational and thinking skills to look closely at the bears. For example, they could complete a thinking frame (known as a 'describing frame' – see Figure 7.5) to

Figure 7.4. Mildred's and Janet's pandas

Source: Helen Lewis

describe one of the bears in detail.[12] This supports the development of description, close and detailed observation and a rich vocabulary.

10 See https://nt.global.ssl.fastly.net/hatfield-forest/documents/den-building---key-stages-1-2-and-3.pdf.

11 See https://www.edenproject.com/learn/schools/lesson-plans/den-designers.

12 This is one of numerous thinking frames developed by Thinking Matters – see https://www.thinkingmatters.com.

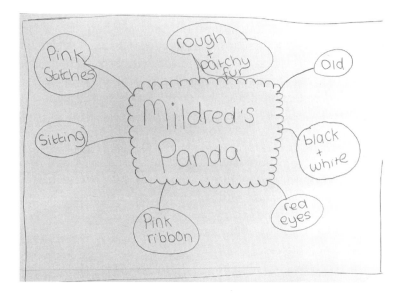

Figure 7.5. An example of a describing frame to describe a toy panda

Source: Helen Lewis

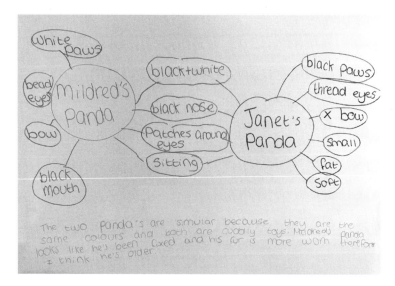

Figure 7.6. Example of a comparing contrasting frame

Source: Helen Lewis

Further discussion could promote critical thinking skills. For example, the children could look closely at both the old and the new bear to find similarities and differences, and record their observations on a thinking frame called a 'comparing contrasting frame' (Figure 7.6). This could be completed practically or as a written activity, depending on the age and stage of development of the children.

Traditional tales and modern versions of much-loved stories can provide excellent starting points for learning across the curriculum. Possibly one of the most famous of these is the cautionary tale of 'Goldilocks and the Three Bears'. Retelling the story, exploring the morals and messages contained in it and considering alternative endings, are familiar classroom activities. Again, exploring fairy tales is not suitable only for young children. Older learners can be equally engaged if the 'hook' is right. For instance, they could investigate the essential elements of a good fairy tale, create 'wanted' posters based on characters or write letters of apology from the repentant villains. In Grigg and Lewis (2018), we discuss a range of other activities that could be inspired by the story - for example, developing a range of breakfast oat recipes for different individuals inspired by Goldilocks' porridge.

Alternative versions of familiar stories offer children the chance to consider different viewpoints and other people's perspectives. For example, in a topic on fairy tales, Toby Forward's *The Wolf's Story* (2005) provides an unusual viewpoint on the story of Little Red Riding Hood - perhaps the wolf was simply misunderstood?[13] The visible thinking routine 'circle of viewpoints' (Ritchhart et al., 2011) allows students to explore multiple perspectives and encourages them to see that people may think and feel differently about things (Figure 7.7). After reading different versions of a familiar tale, children could be encouraged to identify the different characters and perspectives in the story. These are noted around the edge of the circle - which might be drawn on paper or created using a hoop. In small groups, each child can identify one character to discuss. They then stand by this character and take turns to discuss the story, using the following scaffold:

- I am thinking of (the topic) from the point of view of (character).

- I think (describe the topic from their viewpoint) because (reasons and justifications).

---

13 Other examples of alternative versions of traditional tales include Eugene Trivizas' *The Three Little Wolves and the Big Bad Pig* (1993) and Jon Scieszka's *The True Story of the Three Little Pigs* (1991).

■ One question that I have from this viewpoint is …

Thinking about the thoughts, feelings and experiences of different people can encourage pupils to look at different perspectives and is useful for exploring characters, events and controversial subjects.

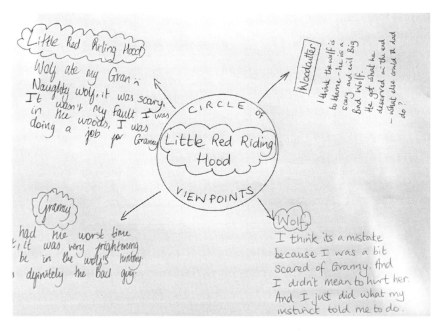

Figure 7.7. Circle of viewpoints example

Source: Helen Lewis

After carrying out a circle of viewpoints activity, the children could role play news reporters and interview different characters from the story. They could undertake philosophical debates (Grigg and Lewis, 2018) around questions such as, 'Who would you rather live with – Goldilocks, Little Red Riding Hood or the Three Little Pigs?' or consider some possibility thinking (Craft, 2000) based on questions such as, 'What if Cinderella hadn't dropped her shoe?'

Summary

- This chapter describes three examples of cross-curricular projects that focus on animals: snails, wolves and bears. Each of the projects has the potential to enrich children's learning.

- A project on snails allows students to develop a range of scientific and mathematical enquiry skills such as observation, questioning and measuring.

- A project on wolves enables students to learn about how animals can be unfairly portrayed in a negative light. They can learn about the realities behind the traditional casting of wolves as dark, menacing figures.

- The iconic teddy bear is an excellent starting point for practitioners to develop children's understanding of this endangered and inspirational animal, as well as broader educational experiences including developing creative and critical thinking.

Chapter 8

Cautionary tales: considering the practicalities and ethics of animal-assisted education

When I grow up and keep a dog

He'll try to understand me,

And then I'll think, how should I like

A tyrant to command me? (Carrington, 1907: 104)

I (HL) started my teaching career in a large inner-city primary school in London, and inherited Sandy, an albino rat, from the teacher before me. I had never met a rat before but Sandy quickly won me over. She was gentle, friendly, clean and curious, and a real asset to a newly qualified teacher like me. When I arrived in the morning she would be keen to come out of her cage, and while I prepared for the day she was great company, busily investigating the classroom. She was often fascinated by the resources I was setting out. She particularly liked the wooden Dienes blocks which I used in my maths lessons – she would move the tiny cubes around the table. At first, I would put her back in her cage when the children started to arrive, as I always worried that she might get lost in the hustle and bustle of registration. But as that difficult first term as a teacher progressed, I found that I needed to develop some techniques to motivate and manage a busy, challenging class. Sandy was to become a valuable ally in this.

I started greeting the children at the door with Sandy perched happily on my shoulder, encouraging them to enter the class calmly. This had an almost immediate quietening effect, transforming what had been a loud and chaotic part of the day. Rotas to feed Sandy and clean out her cage developed responsibility among the children, and gaining a place on the week's 'rat rota' became something valued by the class. During carpet times, if the children demonstrated appropriate behaviour, Sandy would roam around freely, encouraging them to be quiet, still and relaxed. Several of the children had significant additional needs, and spending time with Sandy was a positive intervention for them. For example, while Gary struggled with speech and language development, he embraced the opportunity to teach Sandy some simple tricks, like coming when he called her name. This encouraged him to make some independent decisions, such as what treat to reward her with, as well as to speak clearly and for a purpose. Caitlin, who was living in a women's refuge with her mum, found social situations very difficult. However, she took great pleasure in trying to teach Sandy to 'stand up' when asked – something inquisitive rats like to do. Once she had done this, she spent time with a small group of children, researching other tricks to teach Sandy, and this was a real step forward in her social development.

Sandy was part of my classroom for nearly three years and reached a good age for a rat. She was buried in the school grounds when she died. I would like to think that Sandy had a good life. There is no doubt that she was much loved by all the children, and by me and other staff. She had a large cage filled with clean and comfortable bedding, and wherever possible was given choices as to when she came out of and went back into it. We explored what a rat needed to eat to keep healthy, so her diet was good – her favourite treat was a piece of dried banana. She had regular enrichments: the classroom provided lots of places to explore and she was regularly able to have the run of it. During holiday times, Sandy and I would brave public transport and head back to my home for the break, and at weekends the caretaker would pop in to feed her. I think Sandy's quality of life was good compared to that of many small animals kept as pets.

However, on reflection, Sandy could have had a better life. Firstly, rats are highly social animals and naturally live in groups. Although Sandy had plenty of human interaction during the school day, ideally she should have had rat as well as human company. Secondly, although she was a very clever rat, I couldn't explain to her about weekends. She seemed to like routine, and during the school day there was plenty of routine and plenty going on. I wonder how she felt on Saturdays and Sundays; whether she felt lonely or anxious. Or perhaps she welcomed the peace. My classroom was a busy place, and although I like to think Sandy enjoyed the hustle and bustle, it was loud and bright. Ultimately, Sandy had not chosen to be there, so I wonder now if it was ever overwhelming for her.

Considering the needs, wants and emotions of animals brought into educational settings is crucial. In this chapter we will consider these as well as some of the ethical, cultural and practical issues relating to keeping animals in schools.

Ethical issues: should we have pets in school?

It is important to acknowledge that not everyone supports the idea of animals being used in educational contexts. For example, animal welfare organisations such as People for the Ethical Treatment of Animals (PETA) and the RSPCA are not generally supportive of the use of animals in schools. Feinberg (2019), writing on behalf of PETA, suggests ten reasons why it 'sucks' to be a class pet (Box 8.1).

1   Being kept in unnatural conditions – for example, small nocturnal rodents in brightly lit, noisy classrooms.

2   Health concerns – for example, what happens to animals in cold, deserted classrooms at weekends.

3   A lack of enrichment opportunities – for example, if kept in a small cage all the time.

4   It is not the role of an animal to teach responsibility to children, and young children cannot be relied on to be truly responsible for an animal's needs.

5   Classroom conditions can cause stress for animals, particularly small 'prey' species such as mice and rabbits.

6   If children are allowed to take the class pet home there is no way of knowing the conditions they will encounter away from school.

7   Most schools do not have emergency evacuation plans in place for their pets, so what will happen in the case of a flood, fire and so on?

8 Not only are there health and safety concerns relating to handling animals, but children may have also allergies that can be triggered by classroom pets.

9 Accidents and abuse can happen. Feinberg refers to the following examples from the United States: in Texas, some high school students strangled a 'pet' ferret during class; in Arkansas, a classroom snake was 'cooked to death in a school microwave'; in Kansas, a rabbit died after his tail was 'pulled off'; and in California, a goldfish in a middle school died from bleach poisoning.

10 Many classroom pets come from pet shops and other breeders who may not have exercised careful breeding policies. The animals may therefore be unhealthy, under-socialised and temperamentally unsuitable for classrooms.

Box 8.1. Ten reasons why it 'sucks' to be a class pet

Source: Adapted from Feinberg (2019)

These are significant concerns which should not be ignored or minimised. We would argue that some schools are not appropriate contexts for animals. Some of these concerns relating to animal welfare have been noted as challenges for many years. For example, the famous British theorist Susan Isaacs described a tragic incident that took place in her nursery school in the 1930s. The children were changing the water in the goldfish bowl when one boy, Frank, had a sudden 'burst of cruelty'. Before the teacher could intervene, the fish were thrown into the sand and stamped on. The children were immediately remorseful, with Frank suggesting, 'Now let's put it into water, and then it'll come alive again' (Isaacs, 1930: 204). While this group of young children learned a difficult lesson about the impact of their behaviour, it came at an unacceptable cost to the goldfish.

Many concerns can be addressed through careful research, planning, preparation, communication and a commitment to put the welfare of the animal first. In carefully managed contexts, both animals and children can benefit from relationships together, and being part of school life can bring enrichment to the animal. In situations in which having an animal on school premises is not the right choice, school excursions to settings such as farms can be arranged, while there is also educational value in the use of toy and virtual animals.

Animals as feeling, sentient beings

Animals are not simply resources or pedagogical tools. They are sentient beings and, as such, possess feelings and emotions that we need to recognise, understand and anticipate. Research in the area of cognitive ethology seeks to explore how animals think and what they feel, and this includes their emotions, reasoning and self-awareness. As long ago as the 1870s, Charles Darwin (1872, cited in Bekoff, 2007: 43) suggested that there are six universal emotions – anger, happiness, sadness, fear, disgust and surprise. These emotions evolve in both humans and animals to further social bonds: 'just because dog-joy and chimpanzee-joy and human-joy aren't exactly the same doesn't mean that that any of these animals don't experience joy' (Bekoff, 2007: 34). For example, Bekoff suggests that animals experience joy in a range of situations. Rats will chirp with joy, play hide-and-seek with their owners and, if they are tickled, will actively seek out more tickles. Understanding how these emotions manifest themselves should allow us to connect and empathise with animals when we interact. So, before bringing animals into your classroom context, some careful research needs to be done.

While we may be increasingly convinced that animals bring value to a child's life, we must also consider whether interactions with children add to or decrease an animal's quality of life. Mills et al. (2012) report that animals in many therapy contexts enter into environments that are complex in nature, and this may mean that their sensory systems are taxed by novel and potentially arousing stimuli. This could have long-term effects on the animal's well-being. For example, Hall et al. (2019) carried out a systematic review of research that explored the effects that interactions with children had on dogs' psychological, physical and social quality of life. They found that being given unprovoked attention, such as during children's tantrums, caused stress to dogs. Other stressors included children cuddling the dog, a lack of predictable routine, loud noises and unpredictable games. This kind of behaviour resulted in dogs showing signs of stress, such as avoidance behaviours, lip-licking, panting and yawning. While the children may have benefited from and enjoyed the interactions, for some dogs these were stressful experiences. Both adults and children need to learn to recognise the signs of species-specific stress and act to remove the triggers or remove the animal from the context.

Practical considerations

In this section, we explore some of the practical aspects that should be considered before bringing animals into classrooms, from both the human and animal perspective. All animals can pose risks to health and well-being, because all can be unpredictable and even the smallest will act to protect themselves. All animals require high standards of husbandry and hygiene. We need to be aware, for example, that reptiles such as turtles can carry salmonella, rodents can pass on leptospirosis and, of course, nearly all small animals can nip, scratch and kick. Children must be taught how to handle animals appropriately, and at a basic level how to wash their hands well after touching them or cleaning out their living areas.

Animals are a commitment, both in terms of time to care for them but also their life expectancy. Perhaps the most overlooked factor is the failure to prepare for the long-term obligations that animal ownership brings (Table 8.1). That cute baby rabbit could live for up to ten years, goldfish can live to be twenty-five and a tortoise could be part of the school community for over seventy years. In short, who will take responsibility for looking after these animals should you move school, change career or retire?

Table 8.1. Average life expectancy of common pets

Type of pet	Average life expectancy	Further details
Dog	8-13 years	Generally, the smaller the dog the longer the average life span. An Irish Wolfhound (average 115 lbs) has an average lifespan of seven years, while a Jack Russell Terrier (average 15 lbs) can live up to 13-16 years old. However, much depends on the breed and the quality of care. Spayed or neutered dogs usually live longer, and these procedures can reduce the chance of certain cancers.
Cat	10-15 years	Indoor cats generally live three times longer than those kept outdoors, although the latter enjoy more freedom to explore. Siamese, Persian and Burmese cats can live up to the age of 15-20.
Goldfish	3-10 years	Goldfish kept in a bowl are likely to die younger than those in a large tank because of stunted growth. A goldfish named Tish from Yorkshire lived to the age of 43!

Type of pet	Average life expectancy	Further details
Bird (e.g. budgerigars, macaws, parrots)	5-60 years	The average lifespan of pet birds varies considerably among different species. Some species of budgerigars live only for five years, while African grey parrots, macaws and cockatoos might typically live to 40-60 years old.
Guinea pig	4-8 years	Long-haired breeds such as Silkies or Peruvians tend to have shorter life spans than hairless or skinny guinea pigs, but it is not clear why. The oldest caged guinea pig, Snowball, lived to nearly 15 years old.
Rabbit	8-12 years	The Netherland Dwarf rabbit can live to the age of 10, while larger ones, such as Flemish Giants, don't usually live beyond 8 years old.
Mouse	1-3 years	Mice are sociable creatures who can live for up to five years, if well cared for.
Hamster	2-3 years	The most popular hamster, the Syrian, is most active at night and typically lives for one to two years, although some have been known to live for six to seven years.
Gerbil	2-4 years	Mongolian gerbils, the most common breed, live two to four years on average, with some reaching 5 years old.

Type of pet	Average life expectancy	Further details
Rat	2–4 years	The fancy rat, a form of domesticated brown rat and the most popular pet rat, typically lives for two to three years. However, some mole rats can live for ten to twenty years.
Hedgehog	4–6 years	The African pygmy hedgehog can live for eight to ten years in captivity. However, it is estimated that half of all hedgehogs die in their first year.
Ferret	5–10 years	Most ferrets live for around six years, although longer life spans are not so rare.
Snake	13–30 years	The life expectancy of snakes varies considerably according to the species. Constrictors and pythons might live to 30 or 40, whereas corn and milk snakes typically live for thirteen to twenty years.
Lizard	3–20 years	Small lizards live only for a few years, while the largest can live for twenty years or more. Lizards are very agile, shed their skin and are 'sunseekers'.
Turtle/tortoise	40–60 years	In 2019, the world's oldest living pet was reported to be a female tortoise called Tommy (aged 121 years), who was bought at a market in 1909 aged 11.

Type of pet	Average life expectancy	Further details
Chicken	5–10 years	Jersey Giants, Golden Comets and Cornish Cross have the shortest life spans, typically living only for a few years. Matilda, a variation of the Old English Game breed, lived until she was 16 to become the world's oldest chicken on record.
Horse or pony	25–30 years	Ponies tend to live longer than horses, possibly because they do not run as fast and are less prone to accidents. A few horses live into their forties.

Table 8.1. Average life expectancy of common pets

Even among the same species there can be great differences in terms of life expectancy. For example, if considering a school dog then it is worth bearing in mind that, on average, a Great Dane lives for between six to eight years, whereas a Yorkshire Terrier may exceed 15 years of age.

Researching carefully the type of animal you think would be most appropriate in your school is crucial. All animals have complex needs relating to diet, housing, health and enrichment, as well as varied temperaments and personalities. Not all animals will be suited to your individual context, so you need to read and research thoroughly, and be honest in what you know you can offer.

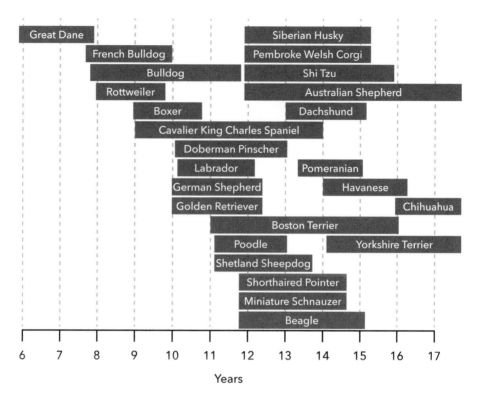

Figure 8.1. Dog breed life expectancy

Source: Adapted from Alt (2018)

Meeting basic needs

Some of those working in the field of animal ethics advocate a 'capabilities approach', developed by Martha Nussbaum and Nobel Prize-winning economist Amartya Sen. Nussbaum (2004) argues that if we are committed to justice then we should take a stance on the quality of an animal's life and ensure that they have opportunities to flourish. The protection of animals is seen in terms of their capacity for sentience – that is, valuing their feelings, perceptions and experience of sensations (Regan, 1983; Singer, 1990).

In the UK, the concept of animal freedoms has been around since the 1960s, culminating in the 'five freedoms' advocated by the former Farm Animal Welfare Council (1979-2011):

Freedom from
hunger and thirst.

Freedom from
discomfort.

Freedom from fear.

Freedom from pain,
injury, disease.

Freedom to perform natural behaviours.

Figure 8.2. The five freedoms

The RSPCA has since developed these freedoms into animal needs: for a suitable environment; for a suitable diet; to be able to exhibit normal behaviour patterns; to be housed with, or apart from, other animals; and to be protected from pain, suffering, injury and disease.[1] It is important to reflect on how each of these needs can be met *all* of the time. This means throughout the year, including weekends and school holidays, and to have a plan in place in case of unexpected school closures – for example, on snow days.

One of the challenges for practitioners in educational settings is making a judgement on whether the animal is enjoying such freedoms, both at any given moment and across the duration of the intervention. This is why a well-read and experienced handler or owner is so important.

More generally, animal rights is a complex and emotive field and one which is beyond the scope of this book. As Anthony (2009: 272) asks, in the context of farm animals, 'What is the baseline standard for morally acceptable animal welfare?' As educators, this question must be foremost in our minds when we evaluate whether our context is right for animals.

Financial considerations

On a practical level, one important factor relates to the cost of keeping animals. Although many animals can be bought for a relatively low cost, or even given 'free to a good home', there will still be financial considerations. For example, cheaper priced cages, hutches and tanks are usually too small to meet all of the animals' needs, and more appropriate housing costs more. Almost all animals will need routine veterinary care, including neutering and vaccination, which can be expensive, particularly for larger animals. For instance, Davis (2018) estimates that from the food to the hutch, vaccinations and insurance, the average cost of owning a rabbit is around £500–£1,000 a year. Since rabbits are social animals, and should be kept in groups of two as a minimum, the total cost is likely to be at least double this. Animals will often need insurance and meeting dietary requirements is an ongoing expense. During holidays there may be a need for

---

1   See https://www.rspca.org.uk/whatwedo/endcruelty/changingthelaw/whatwechanged/
    animalwelfareact.

the animals to be boarded, and equipment such as bowls, brushes and bedding all contribute to expenditure.

To take a more detailed example, the initial costs involved in housing, feeding and buying three guinea pigs could amount to around £470 (Table 8.2).

Table 8.2. Average set-up costs for housing three guinea pigs

Buying the guinea pigs	£20 (x 3)
Indoor cage (at least 1.2 m long by 70 cm wide)	£150
Outdoor hutch (at least 1.3 m long by 70 cm wide)	£120
Outdoor run (at least 1.2 m long by 70 cm wide)	£100
Food for the first week	£10
Bowls, drinking bottles and toys	£25
Bedding for the first week	£5
Total	£470

Further to these initial costs, the budget will need to take into account ongoing health issues which can involve costly trips to the vet. In 2018, insurance company Exotic Direct had a wide range of claims, including:

- £418 for the treatment of a guinea pig suffering from weight loss.
- £363 for the treatment of a guinea pig with respiratory problems.
- £222 for a guinea pig with eye problems.
- £285 for a guinea pig with bloody urine. (Wells, 2018)

Insurance is highly recommended for even the smallest animals. Typically, insurance with companies such as Exotic Direct costs around £60 a year for one guinea pig. Being clear about how and who is responsible for meeting these costs if an animal is being brought into an educational environment is essential from the outset.

Dealing with animal behaviours

One important aspect of preparation is to research the kinds of animal behaviours to be expected, some of which may be off-putting or seem unsavoury but which are perfectly natural. These can include sexual activity, territorial behaviour or unusual dietary habits. Rabbits and guinea pigs, for example, are coprophagic – essentially meaning that they eat their own poo. While this is normal for these animals, it is helpful to anticipate children's reactions and questions. Such behaviour should be discussed in a matter-of-fact way, with organisations such as the RSPCA providing appropriate guidance (Figure 8.3).

It is also important to prepare to meet the emotional needs of animals, and to recognise abnormal behaviours which can arise from boredom, stress or illness. It is therefore essential to know enough about the animal to identify what are normal and what are abnormal behaviours. We may be good at recognising significant and distressing stereotypical behaviours in some animals. For instance, in 1979, the arrival of Misha, a rescued polar bear, caused controversy for Bristol Zoo (*Shropshire Star*, 2019). Misha had been a circus bear, confined to a tiny crate, and even when released into a larger enclosure in the zoo he would pace backwards and forwards until his feet bled. The zoo received hundreds of complaints about his condition, which led to an overhaul of how polar bears are kept in captivity.

However, other abnormal behaviours in our companion animals may be harder to spot because they seem to be natural. For example, while pecking is a normal, inquisitive behaviour in chickens, when they are stressed or bored they may peck their own feathers or become aggressive with other chickens (Dixon, 2008). Guinea pigs can inject a slurry of food pellets into the tubes of their sipper bottles when bored or stressed by a change of routine (Pollock and Arbona,

Why do rabbits eat their own poo?

To obtain as much nutrition as possible from their food

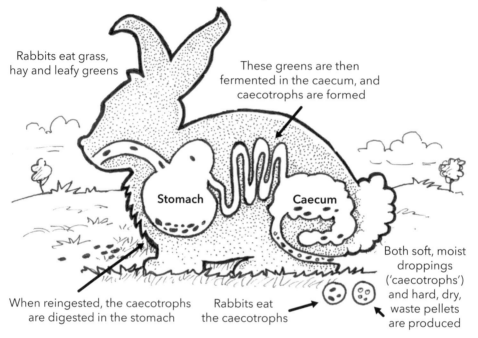

Rabbits eat grass, hay and leafy greens

These greens are then fermented in the caecum, and caecotrophs are formed

Stomach

Caecum

When reingested, the caecotrophs are digested in the stomach

Rabbits eat the caecotrophs

Both soft, moist droppings ('caecotrophs') and hard, dry, waste pellets are produced

Rabbits eat large quantities of low-quality food and digest it through a process called 'caecotrophy'. This produces the caecotrophs, which the rabbits then eat directly from their bottom. This cycle of reingestion means that rabbits can obtain maximum nutrition from their food. This digestive process is similar to a cow chewing its cud, and is perfectly normal rabbit behaviour.

Figure 8.3. Why do rabbits eat their own poo?

Source: Adapted from https://www.rspca.org.uk/webContent/staticImages/
RabbitPooInfographic.jpg

2017). The US researcher Temple Grandin notes that while gerbils love to dig and tunnel, many develop stereotypical digging behaviours when kept in small cages (Grandin and Johnson, 2009). Gerbils can spend up to a third of their lives digging in the corners, which is not how they would spend large amounts of time in their natural environment. Although owners may feel they are providing a suitable physical environment, and the gerbil is behaving naturally, any stereo-typical, overly repetitive behaviour shows that the animal is unhappy in some way. Grandin explains that in the wild a gerbil digs because it needs to create tunnels and nests. In a cage, the action of digging does not result in tunnels, and most captive gerbils do not build their own nests underground, which means that the emotional need of the gerbil to dig in order to hide is not fulfilled. This leads to repetitive behaviours. So, while digging is a behavioural need, continuous, repetitive digging is symptomatic of needs not being met. Understanding the natural behaviours of any animal that you bring into your classroom, and how you can enrich their lives to incorporate these, is therefore imperative.

Choosing the right animal for your context

Animals used in educational contexts should be selected on the basis of a number of factors, such as age, sex, temperament and typical behaviours, and the animals should be treated as equal partners in the process. Animals and children should be carefully prepared in advance of the interventions. This is particularly important since research suggests that behaviour is often governed by context (e.g. Boissy, 1995; Lanier et al., 2000). For example, in equine therapy situations in which sessions are provided for people with disabilities, it is crucial that the horse is well-schooled and has a smooth gait, but it must also have a calm temperament so it is not fazed by unusual equipment or unpredictable movements and noises (Fredrickson-MacNamara and Butler, 2010).

One possible challenge in selection, particularly when thinking about dogs, is that behaviour and temperament tests may not capture the full profile of a dog required to work in varied contexts (Binfet and Struik, 2018). For instance, Fredrickson-MacNamara and Butler (2010) suggest that a key factor in the selection of animals is that they need to be able to cope with the encroachment of strangers, while Binfet and Struik (2018) add that this may be nuanced - for instance, a dog may react differently to the approach of a male or female stranger or to people wearing hats, glasses or face masks. Therefore, considering the intended aims of the intervention is vital. For instance, if the goal is to develop nurturing skills, a small herbivore such as a guinea pig might be ideal because of their need to eat frequently, but we also need to take into account the participants and the environment:

Consider, for example, an educational program designed for adolescent boys. Boys of this age may be more motivated to learn about reptiles and arachnids than common household pets. Selecting dogs for this group because the organization only works with dogs may reduce participant motivation. In a medical facility where hallways are very narrow and crowded with equipment, the animal-handler team must be highly mobile and able to get out of the way quickly. Thus, given these dynamics, a rabbit in a basket may be more suitable than a golden retriever walking beside a handler. (Fredrickson-MacNamara and Butler, 2010: 125)

MacNamara and MacLean (2017: 185–186) suggest that those considering an animal in educational settings should draw up an 'animal job description'. They suggest this should include:

- The goal of including an animal.
- Session logistics (e.g. duration and type of contact).
- Optimal animal characteristics (physical and behavioural).

The authors provide an example of a job description which includes some of the following criteria (Box 8.2).

Wanted

• Calm disposition

• Happy to work with small groups of 7–8-year-olds

• Willing to work for fifteen to twenty minutes three times a day

• Willing to be petted and given treats by children

• No scratching or nipping allowed

• No other skills necessary

• Open to animals of any colour or coat texture!

Box 8.2. An animal's job description

Source: Adapted from MacNamara and MacLean (2017: 186)

By considering these sorts of requirements in detail, selecting the most appropriate animal for the role should be possible. Well-socialised guinea pigs or rats, for example, might fit the bill for the description in Box 8.2. So, while as an individual you may have a preference for a certain type of animal, your preparation needs to ensure that your environment can cater for its needs. Table 8.3 includes some key facts about the basic needs of animals commonly found in schools.

Table 8.3. Some key information about school pets

Animals and their average lifespan	Enrichment	Diet	Housing and health
Dog 8–13 years	Social. Different breeds are bred for different purposes so some may be more or less suited to school life. Regular exercise, socialisation, mental stimulation and consistent, reward-based training.	No raw diet because of the risk of passing on bacterial infections.	Secure and quiet place to sleep. Should not be crated for long periods. Vaccinated, microchipped and neutered. Regular grooming, teeth checks and nail trimming.
Rabbit 7–10 years	Social in a bonded group. Territorial with complicated social structures. Love objects that they can move and manipulate for stimulation and exercise.	Hay and grass are the most important part of a rabbit's diet. Chewing this helps to wear down their teeth, which grow continuously. Supplement with leafy greens and rabbit pellets. No light-coloured lettuce (e.g. iceberg).	A traditional small hutch will not meet the need for exercise and stimulation. Although indoor rabbits can thrive, an outdoor area provides an opportunity to exercise natural behaviours. Regular grooming and nail trimming is required. Should be vaccinated and neutered.

	Behaviour / enrichment	Diet	Care requirements
	Need space to run, stand, hide and burrow. Hide food under flowerpots and in cardboard boxes or tubes with the ends stuffed with hay or shredded newspaper. Hanging up their greens so they have to stand on their back legs to reach them provides enrichment.	Carrots are high in sugar so are best kept as a treat.	
Guinea pig 4–8 years	Social in a bonded group. Rabbits not good companions. Guinea pigs need space to run and hide. They love to forage. Toys that hide treats (and can stand up to a good gnaw) are perfect.	Hay and grass are crucial as a source of vitamin C.	Do not cope well with extremes of temperature or damp. Regular grooming and nail trimming is required. Long-haired varieties need daily grooming. Should be neutered. Minimum requirements for a pair of guinea pigs is an enclosure 2 m x 0.5 m x 25 cm, but ideally their enclosure should be larger than this.

Animals and their average lifespan	Enrichment	Diet	Housing and health
Chicken 8–10 years	Social in a bonded group. There are hundreds of different breeds of chicken to choose from, and of these many have slightly different requirements. Orpingtons, Brahmas and Silkie Bantams are known for their gentle dispositions, while rescuing factory farm chickens can be very rewarding.	Formulated complete poultry feeds are the easiest way to ensure chickens are getting the correct diet. Grit is needed to grind food in the chicken's gizzard – they don't have teeth. Household scraps are technically no longer allowed to be fed to chickens, but 'allotment scraps' can provide greens, etc. Treats such as fruit and corn should be fed sparingly.	Need space to forage, scratch and perch. Housing must be predator- and rat-proof. Coops need to be breezy enough to prevent respiratory diseases but not too draughty. Coops need to be easy to clean so bugs and bacteria don't fester. Chickens need access to a dust bath to keep their feathers in good condition. Provide 'roosting poles' and one nest box for every four or five chickens. Nest boxes should be raised off the ground by at least a few inches, but lower than the lowest roosting pole. They should also be dark and 'out of the way' to cater to hens' instinct to lay in a safe place. Chickens need at least 4 square feet if they are able to roam freely during the day, and at least 10 square feet per bird if they are permanently confined.
Goldfish 5–10 years	Social. Ideally kept in groups of three or four fish. Different species may not live well together. Need space and environment in which to hide.	Goldfish require more carbohydrates than other fish species, therefore specialised goldfish food should be used. They will constantly look for food.	Ideally goldfish should be kept in a tank that is a minimum of 200 cm x 60 cm x 60 cm. The more fish you have, the larger the tank needs to be. Water should be kept at 23-24°C. Filtration is vital for removing waste from the tank. A partial water change of 25-30% is strongly recommended at least once every two weeks.

		They should only be fed what they can eat within a few minutes, once or twice a day. Remove uneaten food to reduce waste build-up.	The tank should have gravel and ideally live plants as a food source and to add oxygen to the water. Plastic plants and ornaments can supply the fish with shelter.
Hamster 2-3 years	Solitary (unless dwarf variety). Nocturnal.	Pelleted mix supplemented with a variety of other items, including fresh vegetables. Hamsters should be fed once a day. Remove any fresh food that has not been eaten within a few hours. Provide water in a bottle, not a dish.	Need space to burrow and hide. Cage should be well-ventilated, with a place to hide and opportunities for exercise. Never underestimate a hamster's ability to escape.
African land snail 6-8 years	Solitary. Nocturnal.	Kale, cabbage, and leafy greens. Small chunks of cuttlefish bone for added calcium. Feed salad daily.	A glass tank is best – at 20-29°C. Provide soil for them to burrow in. Snails are hermaphrodites, which means that a single snail possesses both male and female reproductive organs. It is rare but not unheard of for them to self-fertilise.

Meeting the needs of all: animals and inclusive classroom practice

The age and needs of children should impact on the choice of animal. For example, although hamsters are often seen as ideal pets for young children, they need to sleep during the day, so busy classrooms may not be the ideal environment for them. Since some of the dwarf varieties are only 5 cm in size, they are also very small for young children or those with poor fine motor control to handle safely and carefully.

Not everyone in a class is likely to love animals. Moreover, for some individual pupils, the presence of an animal may be detrimental to their educational experiences. For example, Grandin (2008: 7) reminds us that for children with a diagnosis of ASD, sensory issues can outweigh any potential benefits of spending time with animals. Some may find that loud noises, such as a barking dog, cause stress, for some the smell of an animal can be overbearing, while others may be anxious due to the unpredictability of animal behaviour.

Other children may have allergies to different species, such as cats, dogs, guinea pigs, rabbits and even fish. Allergic reactions can differ in severity from itchy eyes and a runny nose to severe respiratory failure. There are a number of ways in which symptoms can be addressed, but if you have an animal in school the potential for a reaction will always be there. Considering what species to choose, where animals will be housed in school and who will have contact with them must all be considered as part of any risk assessment process. Taking proactive action such as regular grooming (which includes wiping the animal with cleaning wipes) will help to remove loose hair and dander. It is also imperative to clean the animal's environment weekly, including all toys and any other items inside the habitat. Good hand hygiene is also essential. Children and adults should wash their hands immediately after touching an animal or any part of their habitat. Soap and water are best, but antibacterial wipes or hand sanitiser can also be used. Vacuuming the classroom daily using a machine with a built-in high-efficiency particulate air (HEPA) filter can help to remove traces of hair and dander, and a portable HEPA filter can be used in the classroom to help remove tiny airborne particles (see Chapter 9 for more about allergies and school dogs).

There are also cultural and religious sensitivities to consider when engaging with animals. For example, while Islam teaches its followers to be merciful to all creatures and forbids animal cruelty, many Muslim scholars agree that the saliva of a dog is impure and that objects or people that come into contact with it should be washed seven times (Huda, 2018). However, other Muslims argue that dogs are loyal. One story in the Qur'an (Surah 18) is about a group of Muslims who seek shelter in a cave and are protected by a dog. Based on such teachings, many Muslims find that it is a matter of faith to be kind to dogs and believe that dogs can be beneficial in our lives. While Muslims are among the most avid of pet owners, there are conditions that they follow: such animals should not be potentially dangerous to other humans (e.g. venomous snakes), should be permissible according to the Islamic faith (e.g. not pigs) and should be treated with kindness. Muslims who own pet dogs usually keep them outside in the garden.[2] Service animals, such as guide dogs, may be important companions to Muslims with disabilities. Working animals - such as guard, hunting or herding dogs - are also often viewed as useful and hard-working. In the United Arab Emirates, visitors to Abu Dhabi can go to the Arabian Saluki Center, which honours the traditions of hunting, training and breeding Salukis - a distinctive breed of dog found in desert regions.

The implications of these varying attitudes for those schools with children from Muslim families on roll show how clear communication with parents is essential to avoid offence, however unintentional. Some parents might be willing for their children to have contact with a working dog, as long as the children can wash thoroughly afterwards, others may allow their child to watch but not touch the dog and others may wish for no contact at all.

Tuning into animal communication

Animals communicate in complex and sophisticated ways. For example, prairie dogs can 'describe' the size, hair colour and clothing of human intruders, marmosets take turns in conversation, and honeybees can tell other bees the distance to and quantity of nectar they have found. Kingfishers will bring gifts to

2   This is based on the Hadith which says: 'Angels do not enter a house which has a dog or picture in it' (Sahih Bukhari 3:515).

their mate and fiddler crabs attract females by using their large claws in a dance (Meijer, 2019). However, because very few animals communicate using human words it is easy for us to miss what is being said. If animals are to be brought into classrooms, then time needs to be spent learning about how they communicate to ensure a safe working environment and to provide appropriately for their needs.

Different species have different language systems, but many combine body language and scent with vocalisation. For rabbits, social grooming and body language are key communication tools. For instance, a rabbit lying with one or two rear legs stuck out sideways, with the body often stretched out, is indicating that it is very comfortable.[3] In a classroom context where there are rabbits, they should be observed regularly to ensure they are comfortable in the environment. Hamsters use body language, chemical signals and high-pitched sounds to communicate. A hamster with laid-back ears may be feeling frightened or aggressive, while one with a relaxed, stretched out body usually signals a sense of calm. Chickens are vocal communicators but also use objects. A mother hen will repeatedly pick up and drop food in front of her chicks to demonstrate what is good to eat. Mother hens also communicate with chicks before they hatch, 'purring' to the eggs so that the chicks inside can recognise her voice after they hatch. Chicks even begin peeping inside their eggs, so the mother can feel and hear them too.

Many companion animals develop a vocabulary specific to their human carers. For example, while kittens may meow, older cats do not communicate with one another with a meow - they use body language, scent, facial expressions and touch instead. Cats meow specifically at humans, and specifically to get something that they want - like food (Raidhan, 2018). But we need to understand the subtlety of these communications because they are also accompanied by body language signals. For example, if a cat meows and arches her back to meet your hand when being stroked, this is likely to mean she's enjoying the contact and is inviting more. Conversely, if she meows and shrinks under human touch, she is signalling that she has had enough (Antoniades, 2015). Chapter 9 includes more information about communication in dogs.

----

3   See http://language.rabbitspeak.com for more information on rabbit communication.

Touching is an integral part of almost every AAI, but we must remember that this is an intimate act and should not be forced on an animal. The animal should be allowed to seek out this friendly contact; it should not be demanded of them. Different species maintain rigid rules of communication and being unaware of those rules can be perceived as disrespect or intimidation. For instance, small animals such as rabbits and guinea pigs have instinctive vulnerabilities associated with being prey animals. Predators often hover, swoop in, grab and carry off their prey. Any intervention that places a person physically over an animal such as a guinea pig may therefore cause stress and discomfort to the animal. We must stay attuned to our animal's communication, habits and behaviours so that we can be aware of what they are telling us at all times.

Summary

- Animals can bring a rich range of benefits to educational contexts.

- However, any interventions involving them must be carefully planned, monitored and regulated.

- The needs of animals as sentient beings should always take priority over seeing them as teaching resources.

- We must read an animal's cues and act accordingly.

- Careful research at a species-specific level is needed, taking into account emotional, practical and financial constraints and the role the animal will undertake.

- The long-term commitments that animals bring and planning for their lifelong care are essential factors to consider when deciding on animal-assisted education.

Chapter 9

Tales of 'the dog in the playground': making the most of dogs in schools

Dogs are just wolves in sheep's clothing. (Coren, 2007: 13)

In June 2013, tragedy struck a small school in Ballymena, Ireland. After teaching a topic about pets, one of the teachers brought her dog in to meet her class. This was a well-intentioned event, designed as a treat. The dog was a calm and well-mannered family pet, and the children were allowed to come up and stroke it. Unfortunately, for some reason the dog felt insecure, but no one recognised this until it was too late. The dog turned on a 5-year-old boy, biting him on the face. The dog was put to sleep and all involved were naturally very upset and shaken by the incident (Porter, 2013). What started as an enrichment experience changed the lives of all involved.

This is not an isolated incident. A recent study has indicated that in the UK alone there are approximately nineteen dog bites per 1,000 people per year, and although only a very small proportion require hospital admission the impact can nonetheless be shocking (Westgarth et al., 2018). Due to their relative sizes and the manner of interaction, dog bites to children are often on the face or neck. These are rarely 'unprovoked', and it is likely that the dog has been trying to communicate that it is stressed. Unfortunately, we are just not very good at reading their non-verbal cues (Pavlides, 2008).

There has been a growing interest in school dogs in recent years. In 2019, Sir Anthony Seldon recommended that every school should have a dog, but we would urge caution. This final chapter explores how a number of schools and other educational providers have carefully prepared for bringing dogs into classrooms. The examples show how decisions varied according to the context, but all share a commitment to detailed planning and preparation. The step-by-step process is shown in Figure 9.1.

| Undertaking research | Selecting a suitable dog | Risk assessment |

| Informing parents | Implementation | Evaluation |

Figure 9.1. The process of preparing for a dog in school

1. Undertaking research

The first stage is to undertake thorough research about what it means to bring a dog into your setting. Julie Carson, head of the Woodland Academy Trust in Bexley, was a firm believer in the benefits that dogs can have on children but carried out extensive research before going ahead. For example, she initially contacted charities that bring dogs into schools to see if they could work with her. However, this led her to realise that this was not an appropriate option for her schools, as not only were there lengthy waiting lists but she had children who would benefit from daily rather than weekly contact with the dog. This resulted in her investigating the possibility of having a team of dogs for the Trust. She read about and visited schools which had taken this path but found that many of these had a member of staff who was going to get a dog anyway, and this dog would then become the school dog. She didn't feel this would work for the Trust as most of the staff who wanted a dog already had one. Julie recalls:

We decided to take a different approach to this, as my concern was that most of our staff who wanted and could afford dogs had them already, and there was a large group of staff who might want a dog but could not afford one. We therefore decided that the Trust would own the dogs and that they would live with handlers. Before we could go ahead with the scheme, I had to ensure that we actually had members of staff who would be willing to take on the responsibility of looking after a dog. The dog would live with them all the time, and come into school with them, and they would be responsible for some financial aspects of looking after the dog and the Trust would be responsible for other aspects. I sent out expressions of interest, which set out the expectations of the role of a handler (including the fact that they would remain at the Trust for at least three years), and the responses were then used to identify the person who would be best suited to being responsible for the dog.

Julie also created a report for the executive board at the Trust, which focused on benefits, risks, costs, role within the school and management of the dogs. In this she considered aspects relating to health and safety but also practical considerations such as where and how the dogs would be housed during the day and their timetables, so they were not overworked and therefore stressed. She also had to look at wider aspects such as illness and old age, and what would happen if, after the three years, the handler wanted to leave the school. With such detailed preparations in place the executive board agreed to the plan.

2. Selecting a suitable dog

A successful school dog needs to possess a range of qualities. Fredrickson-MacNamara and Butler (2010: 126) suggest that these are: 'the capacity to recover from the encroachment of strangers, cope comfortably in the environment and respond appropriately to interactions'. Sarah Ellis is an experienced and highly skilled dog trainer who had one of the first reading dogs in Wales. She is one of only two people in the UK trained and affiliated with US-based READ. She was involved in establishing the BBYS scheme in west Wales. This currently has over 80 volunteers and 150 dogs working in schools, libraries, colleges and universities. This gave Sarah great satisfaction as she believes that dogs thrive when given 'work' to do, and many of the Burns dogs anticipate what is going to happen as soon as their uniform (a jacket or bandana) comes out. Sarah has also seen how special the relationship between dog and owner becomes as they take part in the scheme. To qualify as a Burns dog there is an initial temperament assessment and then dogs and handlers must complete the Bronze and Silver Kennel Club Good Citizen awards. Training is provided based on the positive reinforcement of desired behaviour. Sarah assesses a number of qualities when looking for a suitable dog:

- A calm, happy dog with polite body language.
- A dog which is happy to be touched all over its body, with no sensitive areas.
- A dog which enjoys being stroked and asks Sarah to carry on when she stops (e.g. with a nudge).
- A dog which does not jump up.
- A dog which walks calmly on the lead.
- An outgoing dog but not one which demands attention boisterously (or, equally, not one which hides behind its owner).

Sarah's training approach is based on positive rewards, although she points out:

This takes time and dedication from the owner. If the dog is positively rewarded for a behaviour, he will offer it again. With slow, gentle training and lots of fabulous treats the dog will begin to learn what is required.

Watching the volunteers working so hard to train the dogs in preparation was very impressive; many of these people had never trained or even thought about training their dogs before. We had several dogs between 8 and 10 years old who had never even been to puppy school who have gone on to succeed.

One important question to consider is whether to select a puppy or an older dog. The age at which an animal is introduced into an educational context also needs consideration, particularly if this is to be a school dog. There are many who advocate bringing a puppy to school from a very early age, so that she can grow up in a school environment and become familiar with the physical and social routines. However, bringing a puppy into school presents particular challenges. Although early behaviour in a puppy can provide indications as to whether she will be bold and confident or shy and retiring, many factors influence how a puppy develops, and it may be that life in school does not suit the puppy you choose.

Many trainers suggest that the influences a puppy has between three and seventeen weeks of age can shape their behaviour well into adulthood. During this socialisation period it is crucial to provide puppies with positive, varied experiences that will give them the best possible start in life. In the UK, the Dogs Trust and the Kennel Club provide guidance as to the sorts of things puppies need in the form of a Puppy Socialisation Plan.[1] A puppy in a school environment may have a range of valuable new experiences, but these need to be carefully managed. Negative incidents during this period can also shape behaviour, and so a puppy who gets scared and overwhelmed in a loud and noisy playground or who starts to chase the cleaner's vacuum may subsequently develop hard-to-break, negative habits or become fearful or withdrawn.

In terms of behaviour, this period of socialisation may be more important than selecting a particular breed of dog. Pedigree dogs generally have a specific breed type, so a Labrador will look similar to other Labradors and show certain behavioural traits – for example, retrievers frequently like to carry objects in their mouths. However, dogs of the same breed are individuals and have their own personalities, even if they come from the same litter and have the same

1   See http://www.thepuppyplan.com.

experiences as puppies. The personality of any individual dog is shaped by a combination of many factors, including breed, genetics, owner characteristics and early experiences. Bennett and Rohlf (2007) studied the relationship between demographic variables (e.g. the amount of experience the owner reported having with dogs, the owner's age and their family size) and dog behaviour by looking at 413 adults and their pets. They found that problematic behaviours were associated with a range of both owner and dog characteristics, although most differences were small. For example, the number of people in the household positively correlated with aggression and disobedience in the dog, with larger households generally having more-disobedient dogs. Dogs acquired from pet shops or puppy farms had more problematic behaviours, although involvement in professional training courses and other shared activities decreased the occurrence.

In another study of over 14,000 dog owners, Kubinyi et al. (2009) found that owners who had previously owned two or more dogs reported having calmer dogs than owners who had not owned a dog before or had only had one. Experienced owners also had more-trainable dogs. Dogs living in larger families were reported as being less social than dogs living in smaller families. Additionally, a higher number of people in the household was associated with significantly bolder dogs. The research also found that people who played with their dog every day perceived their pet to be calmer, more trainable and more social than those who played with them less.[2]

Svartberg and Forkman (2002) tested the personalities of thousands of dogs and concluded that there is evidence of five narrow personality traits in all dogs tested: playfulness, curiosity/fearlessness, chase-proneness, sociability and aggressiveness. These are relevant to understanding dog behaviour. However, when selecting a puppy it is important to bear in mind that there are no guarantees as to the personality it may develop. Thus, selecting a puppy specifically to become a school dog may be problematic, and appropriate socialisation and training are essential. Personality in a dog should always be seen as an interaction between the dog and the environment and should be assessed in a particular context: 'If this happens, or in this type of situation, the dog usually behaves in this way.' Unfortunately, not all dogs are suited for working with

---

2   This could be interpreted in two ways. People may prefer to play with calmer, more sociable dogs or dogs could become calmer and more sociable as a result of frequent play.

people with whom they are not familiar, even if they are good-natured and confident when with their own family. A dog that is unsure of strangers will often exhibit sad or depressed behaviour, since they often feel anxious in these situations, and this may lead to withdrawal or aggression (Johanna, 2018). Thus, there is a need for knowledge of dog personalities on several levels as well as an understanding that must go beyond breed to consider a wide range of factors.

There are also practical issues to consider if you want to have a baby animal such as a puppy in school for longer than an hour. Puppies, no matter how cute, need huge amounts of sleep, need to feed every four hours, chew and nip, and need toileting at least once an hour. This might be manageable during a one-off visit, but it is important to consider whether you can meet these needs all day, every day and still give sufficient attention to your pupils within the constraints of the timetable.

The experiences and skills of the animal's handler also have a key bearing on the success of any intervention. For example, there is an increasing trend for bringing therapy dogs onto university campuses to support students, but to maximise the experience for students it is essential that adults are suitably trained (e.g. Gallard and Taylor, 2017; Binfet and Struik, 2018). The dog's owner needs to have a blend of dog training and management skills but also to have the social skills needed to interact with the people with whom they will work. Depending on the nature of the interactions, they will need to be able to build rapport, have appropriate conversations with students and staff, respond to signs of distress and so on. When selecting a dog, it is important to remember that you are actually selecting a partnership. Bekoff (2019, original emphasis) notes that we must be aware that there is no 'universal' dog, and *the unique personality of each dog, each human and their relationship must always come first* … Each and every dog–human relationship needs to be considered on a case-by-case basis.'

We would therefore urge caution when choosing a puppy with the express intention of it becoming a permanent school dog. There are many tales of this working very successfully. However, even if you select a breed typically known for being gentle and calm, and ensure that you socialise it well, other factors such as the owner's own experience with dogs and the dog's individual personality will also contribute to shaping the behaviour of the adult dog. There are no guarantees. This is why many organisations that train therapy dogs only work with dogs over 1 year old, when much of their personality can be observed.

3. Risk assessment

A detailed risk assessment must be completed before any animal can come into school. This should cover, for example, practical and health-related matters such as whether some children are allergic to animals (see Box 9.1). Julie Carson ensured that thorough risk assessments were in place before each dog was allowed into school. These included non-negotiable aspects such as:

- The dog must always be on a lead.
- The dog must always be with its handler when it works with children.
- The room the dog is based in must have a sign on the door to state that a dog is inside.
- The room where the dog is kept must have an external bolt, out of children's reach.

Julie set clear rules for the children around approaching the dog – they adopted an 'ask, approach, pet, leave' model, with no more than three children with the dog at any one time. This model was introduced in assemblies, as were the rules of behaviour to follow when around the dog. Children were taught to recognise signs of dog stress, using puppets to help them understand. Initially the dogs were just seen around school and had interactions with the children in order to socialise, but they did not have a 'working' timetable until they were older and settled. All of Julie's dogs have undergone dog training by accredited trainers and will continue to do so throughout their lives. We must also bear in mind scientific evidence when making decisions about whether a dog is a suitable companion for allergy sufferers (Box 9.1).

There is a growing trend, popularised in some books about school dogs, to view certain breeds such as poodles, Bedlington terriers and Spanish water dogs as 'hypoallergenic' and therefore suitable for children with allergies.

However, this is somewhat misleading. Whilst some breeds of dog such as poodles do shed less fur than others, most allergies are actually to skin and saliva, which all dogs produce. Furthermore, the very fact that some breeds do not moult their coat means that they require regular grooming to prevent the numerous health problems associated with matted fur. Studies such as those by Nicholas et al. (2011) found no difference in allergens in the home when comparing 'hypoallergenic' breeds to other breeds of dog, and thus are clear in their advice, which is that patients cannot rely on particular breeds to disperse fewer allergens into the environment. It must be recognised that for some individuals, no matter how many precautions are taken, the risks are too great and keeping animals may not be possible.

Box 9.1. Dogs and allergies

Carol Lincoln, who was responsible for the implementation of the BBYS programme, has provided us with an anonymised version of a detailed risk assessment form (see Appendix 2). It illustrates the different risks that need to be considered when preparing for volunteers to visit schools and libraries with their dogs, including trip hazards, waste disposal and diet. The challenge is the lack of regulation, which puts schools, dogs and owners at risk. Carol notes:

What became quickly apparent in the early days was the lack of any regulation in the UK for therapy dog volunteer teams in terms of minimum standards of training and assessment of dogs, or even any animal welfare guidelines. There was scant guidance for schools or libraries on what to look out for when seeking a therapy dog service and little information for volunteers willing to give their time. The Kennel Club's Bark and Read Foundation confirmed this rather shocking revelation when we visited them with our initial ideas. We were delighted to be main contributors to the setting of minimum standards and guidelines,[3] which were agreed and published by a number of therapy and assistance dog organisations coordinated by the Kennel Club in 2018.

3 See https://www.thekennelclub.org.uk/media/1159872/barkread_standardsofpractice_a4_8pp-booklet_web.pdf.

In the case of this particular programme, Burns also has a no-raw-food diet policy in place for the dogs they work with because of the risk of passing on infections. Indeed, across the sector there is debate about whether dogs being fed raw meat-based diets (RMBDs) should work in educational settings. While there are many who consider RMBDs to have benefits for their dogs, a recent study concluded that 'the presence of antibiotic-resistant bacteria in RMBDs could therefore pose a serious risk to both animal health and public health – not only because infections with these bacteria are difficult to treat, but also because of the potential of it contributing to a more widespread occurrence of such bacteria' (van Bree et al., 2019: 50). This is an important issue that schools must therefore consider in their preparations for having a school dog.

Figure 9.2. Burns identification card

Source: Helen Lewis

Figure 9.3. Burns volunteers and dogs in uniform

Source: Vanessa Thomas

One of the benefits of working within the Burns scheme is that they provide insurance for all volunteers and dogs that are part of the scheme. Carol Lincoln explains: 'The insurance underwriters described the idea in the beginning as a place where "angels may fear to tread", but became convinced of the integrity of the scheme when they saw for themselves the impact for a child with communication difficulties.' Insurance is now available. Burns volunteers carry identification with them and also wear a 'uniform' – a blue fleece or polo shirt, and the dog has a blue bandana or jacket. This ensures that they are visible and clearly identifiable when they are in the setting (Figures 9.2 and 9.3).

We would recommend that all schools who are investing in AAI examine what insurance is available to them. It is also important to consider the inherent risks to the animals involved in the intervention. Schools should invest in an animal first aid kit, for example, including essential items such as saline pods, dressing bandages, sterile gauze swabs, a foil blanket, disposable gloves, tick remover, tweezers and scissors. Emergency veterinary contact information should be easily accessible. Preparations for meeting the needs of the animal should be included in the assessment. Animal Assisted Intervention International provides detailed guidance on standards of practice, which were revised in 2019.[4]

4. Informing parents

When Joanna Thomas decided to introduce Georgie the Labrador into the Bishop of Llandaff secondary school in Cardiff she was aware of the need to consult with parents. A letter was sent out informing parents of the benefits that interactions with Georgie may bring (Figure 9.4). The letter informed parents of what the situation would be for children with allergies or phobias and also provided information about how Georgie would be cared for. Parents were given contact information so they could discuss any concerns face to face with staff. Georgie was welcomed by all and quickly became a valued member of the team.

Julie Carson followed a similar model when preparing for her dogs across Woodland Academy Trust. Parents and carers were sent information via letter, including a photo of the animal, before the dogs were brought into school. The letter had an opt-out clause so they could stop their child from interacting with the dog. It also gave them the option to discuss the presence of the dog with a senior member of staff if they had any worries or concerns. Across the four schools, Julie says that not one parent refused, and nor did anyone raise concerns over the presence of the dog. This is an ongoing process, so the school will also write to any parents of children who are working individually with the dogs to seek permission.

---

4   See https://aai-int.org/aai/standards-of-practice/.

The Bishop of Llandaff CiW High School
Ysgol Uwchradd Esgob Llandâf

Rookwood Close • Llandaff • Cardiff • CF5 2NR
Tel Ffôn • 029 20562485 **Fax** Ffacs • 029 20578862
Email Ebost • schooloffice@bishopofllandaff.org
Web Gwefan • www.bishopofllandaff.org **Twitter** @Bishop_Llandaff
Executive Headteacher Prifathro Gweithredol • Marc Belli
Head of School Pennaeth yr Ysgol • Sarah Parry

3rd July 2019

Dear Parent(s)/carer(s),

Re: Wellbeing Dog

We are very excited to introduce you to a new member of staff who we will be welcoming to our school over the next few weeks. Georgie was born on 9th May and she is an 8 week old Labrador Retriever who is in training to become a school dog and is set to become an integral part of our community. She will shortly be beginning her first set of puppy classes and, in time, we plan to train her to become a qualified 'wellbeing' dog.

Throughout the media, we hear significant stories about the increase in adverse childhood experiences and heightened anxiety. Georgie is joining the school to help support these students and will be based within The Marion Centre. However, she will be available to all members of our community who may benefit from her help. Georgie will settle into school life over the summer holidays in readiness for the new academic year.

There are many benefits of having a school dog. Wellbeing dogs have been working in schools for the past five years across the UK. However, they have been commonplace in other parts of the world for many years. Evidence indicates that benefits include

- Cognitive – companionship with a dog stimulates memory, problem-solving and game-playing;
- Social – a dog provides a positive mutual topic for discussion, encourages responsibility, wellbeing and focused interaction with others;
- Emotional – a school dog improves self-esteem, acceptance from others and lifts mood, often provoking laughter and fun. Dogs can also teach compassion and respect for other living things as well as relieving anxiety;
- Physical – interaction with a 'furry friend' reduces blood-pressure, provides tactile stimulation, assists with pain management, gives motivation to move, walk and stimulates the senses;
- Environmental – a dog in a school increases the sense of a family environment, with all of the above benefits continuing long after the school day is over; and
- Reading – reading to dogs has been proven to help children develop literacy skills and build confidence, through both the calming effect the dog's presence has on children as well as the fact that a dog will listen to children read without being judgemental or critical. This comforting environment helps to nurture children's enthusiasm for reading and provides them with the confidence to read aloud.

While there are numerous benefits to Georgie joining our community, we recognise there are some concerns you may have. Please be assured that the school has been working with external agencies to ensure these have been considered. A few of these are listed below

My child is allergic to dogs
It is understandable that some of you may be concerned about possible allergic reactions to a school dog. However, Georgie will be subjected to the most thorough cleanliness and grooming regime. She will also only be allowed in situations with students who voluntarily wish to work with her. Your permission will of course be sought in advance of Georgie having access to, and working with, your child in school.

Will Georgie be properly cared for?
Georgie will be extremely well looked after. She will live with Mrs Thomas (Assistant Head/Head of Marion Centre) and her family and will come to school most days but will stay safely in the offices until satisfactory training has been completed. She will then, in time, listen to students read in a controlled setting and will always be accompanied by a trained adult. Georgie will undergo thorough and rigorous training (beginning with puppy classes) so will be extremely well-behaved. Whilst Georgie is in school she will have access to a dog pen and crate in the offices where she can relax during her non-contact time. Georgie will visit the vet regularly for all her

injections as well as regular check-ups. If Georgie is unwell for any reason she will stay at home with a baby-sitter!

My child is scared of dogs

Some children may have had upsetting experiences and/or have a fear of dogs (or other animals). Georgie will only be in contact with children whose parents are happy for their child to work with her. However, Georgie's training will help her to be calm and gentle around children; she is already showing signs of a very loving and gentle nature. Experience and research have shown that, with proper guidance and handling, children can learn to overcome their fear of animals and grow in respect and appreciation for them.

The school has a 'no dogs' policy

Our school does have a 'no dogs' policy. However, as Georgie is training to be a 'wellbeing' dog, specific rules will apply to her, as a member of staff. She will be on a lead at all times when moving around the school site and will always be accompanied by a trained adult. Georgie will also be fully insured to carry out her role thus allowing her to be on the school site. Georgie will not be allowed to roam the site freely so there will be no issues with toileting etc.

We hope you will join us in welcoming Georgie to our family and embrace all that she has to offer. While Georgie will be introduced to the school in the coming week(s) via assemblies and walks of the site, should you not wish your child to come in to contact with our school dog then please do let us know. You can do this by getting in touch with Mrs Thomas, Assistant Head by email thomasj@bishopofllandaff.org.

I do hope you will see the benefits of this new addition of the team and we are certain Georgie will provide excellent support to our students.

Yours sincerely,

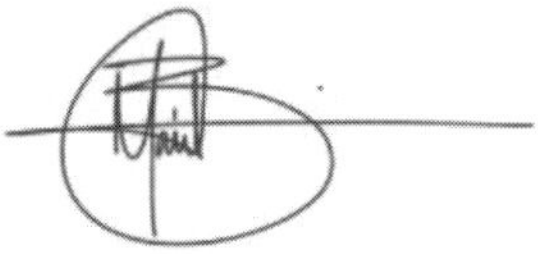

Marc Belli
Executive Headteacher

Figure 9.4. Letter to parents

In Chapter 8 we explored some of the cultural and religious considerations that need to be made when bringing a dog into school. Discussions with parents will help to ensure that the needs of all pupils and their families are considered.

5. Implementation

Schools employ animals in a variety of ways. For example, in Julie Carson's case, the four dogs are used in the following ways:

- Meeting and greeting on the gates to support children who are anxious about coming into school.
- Specific work with children (and adults) who are nervous around dogs.
- As an integral part of the school's behaviour policy.
- Working with speech and language and phonics groups.
- Listening to readers.
- Within the classroom as an emotional support and as part of the lesson – Betsy, one of the dogs, loved being part of the nursery's 'What big teeth you have' topic!
- Individual emotional support work.
- As a refocusing tool to help children who are finding it difficult to remain in the classroom and work.
- As a de-escalation support (obviously, not putting the dogs at any risk).

However, successful implementation needs careful preparation and planning. One factor to consider when implementing AAIs is the familiarity that a dog has with the setting. Clark et al. (2019) measured salivary cortisol levels in dogs making visits to hospital departments as part of a therapy scheme. When under stress, the body releases cortisol and this has potential detrimental effects for health and welfare. In the study, the levels of salivary cortisol were measured in the home environment and also after making a therapy visit. Four therapy dog teams were randomly assigned to one of four treatment frequency groups: two visits a week for four weeks, one visit a week for four weeks, two visits over four weeks and one visit over four weeks. Each visit lasted approximately fifteen minutes and took place at the same time of day. They were held in a quiet room and the dogs did not undertake any other therapy work during the study. Each dog undertook each treatment frequency over the course of the study. More frequent visits led to a decrease in cortisol, suggesting that the dogs who visited a familiar place regularly were better able to adapt to the visits. However, there were other interesting findings – for instance, male dogs with a female handler had lower cortisol levels.

Other practical matters should be considered. A recent study investigated the welfare of dogs during AAIs in Portugal (de Carvalho et al., 2019). Three welfare indicators related to stress were assessed in nineteen dogs of nineteen human-dog dyads: salivary cortisol concentration, heart rate and respiratory rate. Although analysis of the three indicators did not raise severe concerns about the welfare of the monitored dogs, it did identify some practices to avoid wherever possible. These included:

- Travelling for more than fifty minutes to the site.
- Working in excessively warm rooms.
- Entering schools during children's playtime, when the dog may be stressed by loud noises, unpredictable behaviour and a large number of children at one time.

These are all worthy considerations when planning visits from dogs.

When Nik Gardner (2019) decided to bring a school dog into Winford Church of England Primary School careful preparations took place. Through assemblies and modelling, the whole school learned how to approach a dog, how to recognise basic dog body language signals and how to be respectful towards animals. This is crucial for successful implementation because many children and adults do not use appropriate body language when greeting a dog. Previous guidance has suggested putting a hand out for the dog to sniff. In fact, this can be perceived as threatening by a nervous dog so it is better to give the dog time to come to you. A dog that wants to interact will move towards you. Even then, ensure that children learn to touch the dog gently on the chin or to the side of the neck or shoulder, not on the top of the head, which can be perceived as threatening. The key message to instil in all those who will interact with the dog is the need to consider the dog's comfort and personal space requirements. Not all dogs want to be touched by people they don't know, and those dogs should be respected for this and not forced into situations in which they are not comfortable.

The Kennel Club has produced a series of resources to educate us in how to meet and greet dogs more safely.[5] Sashi's Paw Plan, for example, includes guidance on the dos and don'ts of meeting dogs, and also provides advice on good body language to adopt if a dog jumps at you or knocks you over.

Dogs have developed a sophisticated communication system. They use body language as well as vocalisations to express how they feel and what they would like. However, we are not always effective in our interpretation of this language. This may be because certain dogs – for example, those with ears that are long or fluffy or tails that are permanently arched – are limited in their range of facial and bodily signals. Or it may be because we misinterpret or generally miss some of the highly sophisticated language that our dogs are using all of the time. We tend to generalise dogs' body language – for example, we think that a wagging tail is the symbol of a happy dog. In fact, this is not necessarily the case – the tail is used in a very complex way. Dog behaviourists suggest that we need to consider not just the movement of the tail, but also its position, speed and direction of movement (Coren, 2011). A dog that holds its tail horizontally is signalling that it feels relaxed, a vertical tail indicates dominance, a low position signals anxiety or submission and when tucked under the body fear. The faster the tail wags, the more excited the dog is, and a broad sweep of the tail suggests the dog is more friendly and secure than a tentative, narrow wag does. It has also been suggested that wags go more to the right when a dog is happy and relaxed, and more to the left when a dog is anxious or insecure. Tiny, high-speed tail vibrations can be interpreted as 'wagging' but are actually signs that the dog is alert and about to do something, usually run or fight. If the tail is held high while vibrating, the dog is communicating an active threat. Similarly, raised hackles on a dog's neck are not necessarily a sign of aggression – they are a sign of arousal and so could indicate fear, excitement, anxiety or anger. We need to look at the context and other body language cues to interpret what they mean.

Misunderstanding an animal's communications can have serious consequences. Meints et al. (2010a, 2010b) suggest that the majority of dog bite incidents

---

5   Interactive resources and posters are available to download at: https://www.thekennelclub.org.uk/training/safe-and-sound/safe-and-sound-for-parents-and-the-general-public.

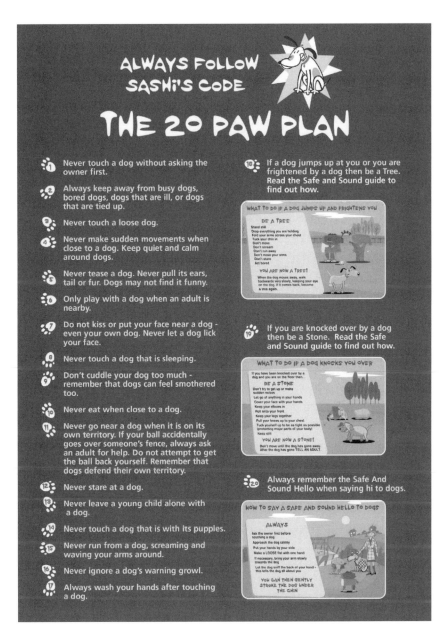

Figure 9.5. Sashi's Paw Plan

Source: https://www.thekennelclub.org.uk/media/20232/sashi20pawplan.pdf

happen to children when they are at home and involve a familiar dog. Children are also more likely to be bitten on the face. One possible reason suggested by the researchers is that young children are more likely to lean towards a dog and demonstrate intrusive facial proximity than older children. The researchers found that children at 2 and 3 years of age showed significantly more proximity behaviours than 4-, 5- and 6-year-olds.

In addition, the researchers found that children show clear 'leaning in' behaviour with small animals, even when the animal is desperately communicating that it is uncomfortable. For example, while some dogs do smile – my (HL) Irish setter Stanley used to show his teeth when he was excited to see us – this is unusual. Typically, most dogs show their teeth because they are communicating that they want to be given space. A wrinkled nose, growling and fixed eye contact usually accompanies such displays (whereas Stanley would greet us with relaxed body language, loose lips and a soft expression). Misunderstandings are understandable among children – after all, when a person shows their teeth it is usually in a smile, thereby inviting further communication. Indeed, one study found that 69% of 4-year-olds interpreted aggressive dogs' faces as smiling and happy (Meints et al., 2010b). Hence, they are at risk of moving closer to the dog and possibly getting bitten. They need to be trained to know what the dog is trying to tell them so they can respond appropriately.

Shepherd (2010) suggests that there is a 'ladder of aggression' in dog communication (Figure 9.6). The gestures are designed to avert any perceived threat and so to avoid escalation towards aggression. While all dogs entering schools must be assessed carefully and should not show any signs of aggression, we need to recognise that aggression is not always an offensive gesture. It can arise for a variety of other reasons such as fear, defence or protection and any dog can react should certain situations arise. The lower rungs show the behaviours a dog will try first when it feels uncomfortable, but these can escalate if ignored – and, of course, we must be aware that not all dogs display all of these reactions, and the order of some may shift and change depending on context. All dogs are individuals, with previous experiences and life histories. They are motivated by what works and doesn't work – so if a dog uses a raised paw to indicate it feels uncomfortable, but this is continually ignored, it may try a different signal. They are easy to miss – a yawn, a raised paw or an averted glance – so we must educate children and staff carefully.

Figure 9.6. Signs of progressive stress and anxiety in dogs

Source: Adapted from Shepherd (2010) and https://www.thebluedog.org/en/dog-behaviour/behaviour-problems/why-does-my-dog/ladder-of-aggression

Social media is awash with 'cute' pictures of dogs and people interacting, but many of these are concerning. When examined closely there are many examples of people behaving 'rudely' to dogs – for example, not maintaining appropriate social space, climbing on the dog, touching the dog when it is resting or eating, and following the dog as it tries to retreat. Research suggests that many adults have difficulty in reading behavioural signs of anxiety and fear in dogs that are interacting with children (Demirbas et al., 2016). These signs are often fleeting and subtle, and even owners may have difficulty recognising low-level arousal in their pets (e.g. Campbell, 2016).

Furthermore, there is a possibility of 'trigger stacking' occurring, which can lead to even the calmest of dogs responding negatively to a stressful situation (Hedges, 2015). A trigger is an experience that causes a dog to increase their awareness, fear or reactivity. A number of things can be classed as triggers, and these are not necessarily negative, such as sensory overload or simple, happy overexcitement. Dogs really like routines and so unexpected additions and changes to these can be a trigger. A visitor, even if well known to the dog, can add stress via excitement, so this becomes a trigger. Interacting at length with new people, regardless of the dog's comfort level with friendly strangers, can be seen as a trigger. A lengthy car trip can induce anxiety and so become a trigger. The stressor doesn't have to be an adverse activity to create a reaction. However, these stressors can stack up over the course of an hour or a visit. Once these reach a critical point the dog may react negatively (Figure 9.7). Therefore, it may be appropriate to consider the amount of time a dog spends with a child, particularly if the following behaviours are typically part of an interaction:

- The child being prone to tantrums.
- The child grooming the dog.
- The child being rough (e.g. tail-pulling).
- The child playing fancy dress with the dog.
- The child jumping around near the dog.
- The child playing with loud/wheeled toys near the dog.
- The child cuddling/kissing the dog. (Hall et al., 2017)

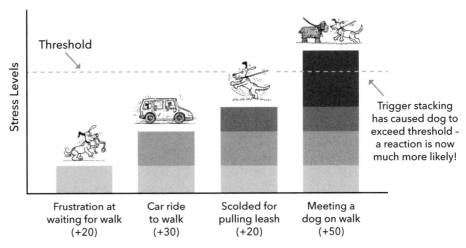

Stress Triggers Before and During a Walk

Figure 9.7. Trigger stacking in dogs

Source: https://www.thedogclinic.com/signs-of-stress

We should be aware that even a good dog can find itself in a bad situation – and if the triggers stack up, even the most patient dog can react adversely. For example, in Figure 9.8, while the dog is being very patient, it is displaying uncomfortable body language. The child should be gently removed from the situation immediately. If we imagine a dog visiting a school for the first time, there are a number of triggers that might be in action – from a car journey, inter-actions with unfamiliar people, overexcitement and a change in routine. We must monitor our animals carefully in every situation. The interaction in Figure 9.9 is much safer: there is a respectful distance between dog and student, the dog is being touched appropriately and there is no leaning into or over the dog.

Figure 9.8. Reading the body language of a dog

Source: Africa Studio – stock.adobe.com

We also need to learn to use an appropriate tone of voice with dogs. Increasing evidence suggests that effective 'dog-directed speech' is similar to the way we talk to babies. Puppies in particular respond well to high-pitched, dog-directed tones of voice. Recent research suggests that when we talk to dogs with appropriate tone and add dog-relevant content words we improve their attention, which may help to strengthen the bond between humans and their pets (Benjamin and Slocombe, 2018).

Figure 9.9. Subtle and respectful interaction

Source: Helen Lewis

6. Evaluation

Ongoing evaluation of a school dog, or any other animal-assisted initiative, is important to ensure that participants benefit and that the 'investment' has been worthwhile. The key questions to consider include:

- What impact are you hoping for? For example, is the focus on improving students' confidence and motivation to read? Or do you want to help students with particular physical disabilities or learning difficulties?

- How will you measure whether your objectives have been achieved? In other words, how will you gather data for evaluation purposes? For instance, do you intend to use pre- and post-tests, surveys or interviews with students, dog handlers, parents and teachers?

- Do you need to evaluate the processes involved as well as the outcomes? For example, if you have a volunteer coming into school, has communication been effective? Are the timings of sessions appropriate?

- How secure is your evidence base? Could it be improved by gathering a range of data from a variety of sources, or is it reliant on one type of data?

■ What will you do with your data? To whom will you disseminate the findings? How will it affect your future planning and provision?

Evaluation will often consider the progress in learning of targeted children, but impact can be broader in nature and scope. Julie Carson, for example, describes the impact in terms of fewer children arriving late at school and the attendance of specific children working with the dogs has increased. Parents have reported that children who were nervous around dogs are no longer showing this fear. The behaviour of many children has also improved. Julie notes that there are fewer instances of extreme emotional dysregulation from children working with the dogs. Furthermore, the well-being of staff has increased, with many being excited to interact with the dog. There is also a need to evaluate the scheme from the point of view of the dog and handler. Binfet and Struik (2018) suggest that dog therapy teams are regularly monitored for their interest, behaviour and temperament. Collecting regular observations and feedback from participants is vital.

How schools evaluate interventions will be context dependent. While standardised tests can provide useful information, there are a number of ways in which data can be gathered. Direct observation is a useful strategy. This might involve observing an interaction for a set time period and looking for specific behaviours, observing at regular intervals or observing an entire session. Notes can be kept in various ways – for instance, on checklists, as a narrative or by using photographs. Each method has advantages and disadvantages associated with it – for example, narrative records can be lengthy and photos can only capture an image at a specific moment in time. Observations also rely on the observer making accurate interpretations of what they see. Therefore, gaining some pupil voice data is also useful – perhaps by conducting small group conversations with a group of learners who have all been involved in an intervention.

Another approach is task analysis. For example, if the aim of an intervention is to encourage a child with a specific physical need to groom a therapy dog, the task may be broken down into smaller steps (e.g. reach for brush, pick up brush, put brush on dog's body, move brush over dog's body). Evaluation over time could examine how many of these steps the child completed independently. Data could also compare what happens when an animal is present compared to when it isn't. For instance, a simple checklist could be used to compare a child's social behaviour in the role play area in the presence of a dog to their behaviour in that situation when the dog is not there.

Anecdotal evidence can be very valuable. Arriving at school in the morning can be a difficult time for some children, and it can also be upsetting for parents if a child is unwilling to go into school and leave their mum or dad. Odette Nicholas at Burry Port Community Primary School has noticed that on the days when Jade the school dog is present in the foyer, the opportunity to greet, stroke and say hello to Jade has a positive impact. Odette can ask children who are finding the morning routine difficult to help Jade to walk to class, which encourages the child to be calm and also boosts their confidence as they feel helpful.

School dogs can be a wonderful addition to a school team, if steps are taken to thoroughly research, select, monitor and educate. Consider the following reflection from Carol Lincoln:

The personal best was the brief moment when I witnessed a very young boy, who very rarely spoke, march up to the most loving of golden retrievers, and in front of all his classmates, his simple words were cheerful, loud and clear for all to hear: 'Hello, dog'.

Summary

- School dogs can bring benefits to many children and adults, as previous chapters have outlined.

- However, to ensure that such gains are achieved, it is important to follow a careful evaluation process.

- We suggest that this begins with thorough research and preparation to ensure the right dog (and owner) are selected for your context.

- Risk assessment is essential and should be ongoing.

- All people within the school must develop an understanding of dog behaviour, body language and communication.

- Constant monitoring of human-animal interactions is vital to ensure well-being is maintained.

Conclusion

I'm not an animal lover if that means you think things are nice if you can pat them, but I am intoxicated by animals. (David Attenborough, in Gage, 2013)

This book is unapologetically supportive of AAIs in education. This is not simply because of our passionate interest in animals. The collective and emerging evidence presents a compelling case for schools, colleges and other educational contexts to explore ways of working with animals. We have outlined the potential benefits in terms of children's social, physical, language and emotional development. There are wider gains to be had for other participants too, such as animal owners and older generations. We have also acknowledged that there are practical challenges to overcome, which require careful planning and cooperation. Nothing should be taken for granted.

While we have focused on children and young people, it would be remiss to ignore completely what is known about the impact on animals. Pop et al. (2014) reviewed the literature on the physiological changes in dogs that correlate with welfare during and after positive interactions with humans. They report that most studies show that when the interactions are positive there is a significant decrease in the dog's blood pressure and cortisol levels, alongside a significant increase in the levels of β-endorphin, oxytocin, prolactin, phenylacetic acid and dopamine. This suggests that the benefits of the human–dog relationship are reciprocal.

The range of animals that have been the subject of educational research and therapeutic programmes includes cats, guinea pigs, cockatoos, African grey parrots, horses, goats, chickens, donkeys, pot-bellied pigs, rabbits, llamas and dolphins. We have tried to include references to a wide range of such animals. However, dogs have attracted the most attention and this is why we feature them so prominently.

The evidence emerging from systematic reviews is that AAIs bring a range of benefits in educational settings (Davies et al., 2015; Hall et al., 2016). Among teachers, there are various reported gains associated with the presence of animals, including: a reduction in student anxiety (Julius et al., 2012); enhanced social skills (McNicholas and Collis, 2000); empathy development and attachment (Zilcha-Mano et al., 2011a); enhanced language, imagination and self-reflection, especially among young children (Myers, 1998); and more motivated and engaged students (Wohlfarth et al., 2013; Fine, 2019). Much of the literature concentrates on how AAIs support students with special educational needs, particularly autism (e.g. Pavlides, 2008; O'Haire et al., 2013a).

Despite the challenges of researching human–animal interactions, one of this book's main conclusions is that AAIs are a valuable means of creating a calm, relaxed and welcoming learning environment. This has become particularly important in recent years with reports of high-stakes tests adding to pressures in children and young people's lives (Hutchins, 2015; Simpson, 2016). One of the unfortunate consequences of attainment pressures on schools is the reluctance of some teachers and leaders to be creative in their pedagogy and to move beyond the established canon of approaches. Yet, those who have had the experience of observing students reading to dogs, in contrast to reading during test conditions, comment on the notable difference in atmosphere. The mere presence of a dog in a classroom has been shown to improve children's attitudes towards learning (Gee et al., 2012), a theme which runs throughout our chapters.

While the general findings are clear in relation to the overall benefits, which this book has elaborated upon, we remain less certain as to exact cause and effect. This is not surprising given that educational research brings with it the challenges of working in non-clinical settings. Nonetheless, researchers are using innovative approaches to tease out different perspectives. These include the use of GoPro micro cameras strapped to a child's wrist or to a dog's harness to record photographs and videos, alongside children's drawings, paintings, artefacts and comic books (Carlyle, 2019). Such approaches go beyond words, which are frequently a barrier to those children who are experiencing emotional difficulties and who often are the participants in AAIs. Carlyle (2019: 208) refers to the 'canine-cam' generation of data which provides insight through a non-human lens.

Throughout this book we have also taken care to emphasise that any human–animal interaction must be a partnership which takes account of the animal's needs, emotions and natural behaviours. A useful premise is that if it's not beneficial to the animals involved, it's unlikely to be therapeutic to humans (Trujillo et al., 2011). While there is little evidence that AAIs are harmful to participants, there is a need to be precise in terms of any gains that accrue, why these happened and the implications for others, including the animals themselves. Careful research, preparation and education are crucial if animals are to be brought into settings. Not every educational environment is right for an animal, not every child will benefit and not every animal will enjoy the experience. All interventions must be closely monitored and reviewed.

All AAIs involve a partnership between animals and humans, and to be successful both parties must have confidence in each other. Fredrickson-MacNamara and Butler (2010: 137) suggest that each handler and animal comes with individual levels of comfort, talent, skill, experience and confidence in one another. A balancing act is therefore required between the animal and the handler at one end and the environment at the other (Figure C.1). Successful interventions maintain a balance, and this means that we need to know our animals, our environments and also ourselves well.

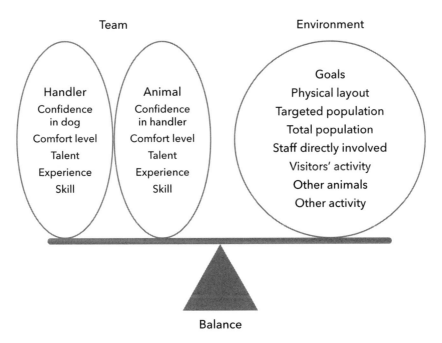

Figure C.1. The balance scale

For instance, a dog might possess a talent for interacting with young children and feel completely relaxed and comfortable when working with one child at a time reading out loud. However, the same dog might feel anxious and uncomfortable when walking through a crowded, noisy, unpredictable playground. An example of acting to maintain a sense of balance would therefore be for the handler to bring the dog into school through the playground after playtime has finished. An animal's level of confidence in the handler is based both on their relationship and on how the animal perceives the handler's behaviour in the specific moment. Talented handlers are able to deal with the reality of their current situation and act as their animals' advocates. Handlers who communicate frequently and appropriately with their animals demonstrate the bond that exists between them. Handler skill should reflect a loving partnership with the animal, while subtly suggesting that the handler is indeed in control and can easily redirect the animal's behaviour when necessary (Butler, 2004).

Talented animals are able to demonstrate behaviours appropriate to the intervention, such as the ability to relax and cope well when approached by strangers. Fredrickson-MacNamara and Butler (2010) remind us that just because an animal can be trained to deal with a situation, this does not mean it has the right 'talent' to be there. Just because some animals are willing to tolerate overwhelming environments does not mean people have a licence to exploit them; sometimes an environment imposes too much stress on an animal. We need to ensure that any animal we work with is comfortable, relaxed and not overwhelmed. We can only do this through understanding the species we are working with and the individual animal's personality and characteristics.

Evaluation and monitoring will best determine whether an animal and handler team can remain in balance within the specific educational environment we take them into. If an equilibrium can be achieved, then, as illustrated throughout this book, we should see genuine benefits for learners of all ages across social, emotional, behavioural, physical and cognitive aspects of development.

In conclusion, any decision to introduce an animal into an educational setting calls for serious discussion with all interested parties. The following questions might prove helpful to inform such an important decision:

1   Is your context a suitable environment for bringing an animal into?

2 How will you meet the needs and natural behaviours of the animal during its visit? How will you plan for weekends and holidays?

3 How will you inform parents, carers and stakeholders of your intentions? How will you deal with staff and students who don't love animals?

4 How will you reassure them that hygiene/risks will be managed appropriately?

5 What will you do if there are children, parents or staff with allergies?

6 What will you do if the intervention causes distress to an animal or a child?

7 What is your insurance policy? Any animal, no matter how gentle, can react instinctively in an adverse situation.

Example of a weekly planning sheet to enhance provision for young children's learning about the life cycle of birds

Writing area

- Write in response to a variety of stimuli on subjects that are of interest or importance to them.
- Explore the life cycle of a chicken – match key words to images, order and sequence.
- Use some ordering words (e.g. first, then) and write, independently, short sentences about the life cycle (challenge task).
- Develop handwriting skills and pencil control.

Maths area

- Count, compare and order numbers to at least 20.
- One-to-one recognition and number matching of plastic eggs in egg boxes.

Mark-making

- Fine manipulative skills:
  - Cutting.
  - Pencil control.
  - 'Snippy chicks' activity – yellow collage paper for the children to snip into small pieces themselves and add beaks, eyes, etc.

Creative area

- Experiment with different designs, colours and textures to decorate cardboard eggs using a variety of materials.
- Learn to manipulate small tools such as scissors.

See 'play dough' section on this planner for nest task.

Play dough

- Mix, arrange and combine materials, colours and shapes to create finished products.
- Use natural-coloured play dough as well as moss, twigs, chicks, lollipop sticks, etc. to create nests.
- Describe and explain choices of materials and evaluate the finished nest.

Round table (classroom)

- Use a variety of questions (e.g. 'Who?', 'What ?', 'Why?', 'When?' and 'How?') for a variety of purposes and to clarify understanding.
- Egg incubator – observe and discuss the hatching eggs.

ICT

- Use ICT such as digital cameras and book creator apps safely to create and store information about the hatching eggs.

Challenge area

- Vocabulary websites (e.g. https:// sightwords.com) can be used in

Role play

- Use an increasing range of appropriate and spontaneous vocabulary in play.
- Link to 'Little Red Hen' story – baker's shop set-up with baskets, bread, till/money, baker's outfits, etc.
- Use different combinations of money to pay for items up to 20p.
- Use written language for different purposes or functions within play and active learning, e.g. opportunities to write lists, orders.

Small world area

- Free play activities using small world farm figures, animals, etc.

Reading area

- Talk about features of books such as the contents page and title.
- Recall information in texts using their personal experiences to support understanding.
- Recognise familiar words and use strategies to decode others, tracking print with their eyes and starting to read punctuation expressively.
- Ensure a range of appropriate spring/ animal texts are available.

Personal and social development and well-being

- Take risks and become confident

- explorers of their indoor and outdoor environment.
- Demonstrate care, respect and affection for other children, adults and their environment.

order to create a variety of language games to suit pupil needs.

Outdoor

- 'We're Going on an Egg Hunt' – listen to and follow increasingly complex clues to find the location of laminated eggs.
- Link to 'construction' activity on this planner as these can happen outdoors in relevant habitats if the weather allows.

Water

- Use non-standard units to measure capacity and use the language of capacity accurately.
- Use spoons, jugs, containers and bowls of various sizes.

Construction

- Use a variety of materials and tools for experimentation and problem-solving. Big nest building: select a variety of stuffed animals that lay eggs (e.g. hen, crocodile, crab, fish, snake) and a range of construction equipment (e.g. boxes, bricks, crates, sticks, fabric). Can the children build a nest for each animal to lay its eggs in?

Cwtsh Cymraeg

- Welsh language development: speak clearly, using simple words, greetings and expressions relating to animals from the farm and numbers up to 10.

Source: Grace Thomas

Appendix 2:

Example risk assessment form

Location/Dept: Burns By Your Side	Date assessed: 16 July 2019
Task/Activity: Visiting schools and libraries	Review date: 31 July 2020

What are the hazards?	Who might be harmed and how?	What controls are already in place?
Slips, trips and falls Access and egress. Session potential to cause hazard in school environment. Ease of escape in event of emergency.	Children/handler/ school staff/Burns representative Injury may be caused by new hazards presented in school facility. *Original risk rating 5 x 4 = 20[1]*	▪ Provision of floor matting to be available for session duration. ▪ Quiet 'spot' to be predetermined by school staff for session duration. ▪ Session to take place in quiet environment away from busy areas – without causing obstruction to walkways or emergency exits. ▪ Any school policies/emergency procedures to be communicated to handler and staff on arrival. ▪ Handler and Burns staff to ensure they aren't causing trip hazard to any persons while session is taking place (bags, leads in walkways).
Child safety Ensuring children are kept safe and well during session.	Children/handler/ school staff/Burns representative Potential to cause stomach upsets, infections and/or toxocariasis. *Original risk rating 5 x 4 = 20*	▪ Teacher/teaching assistant to be present at all times during visit. ▪ Dog has completed assessment and testing process to ensure they are suitable for the task. ▪ Dedicated safeguarding officer from Burns in the vicinity at all times (handlers aware). ▪ Dog's temperament is suitable. ▪ Dog handler present at all times – session to be stopped at any time if there are concerns that dog well-being or child safety is compromised.

1   This provider uses a sliding scale to identify risk: the higher the number, the greater the risk.

	Severity (1-5)	Likelihood (1-5)	Risk/ Priority	Additional controls required	Action by whom?	Action by when?
Assessed by:						
Task coordinator:						
	5	2	10			
	5	4	20	▪ Children to receive assembly session on dog behaviours to help ensure they don't stress the dog during visits. ▪ Permission form to be completed by parent/ guardian prior to session (required to highlight any allergies which may affect child during session).		Prior to meeting

What are the hazards?	Who might be harmed and how?	What controls are already in place?
Child safety *cont*		▪ Child to wash hands with clean soapy water after each session. ▪ Teacher and handler to maintain good communication throughout session, ensuring it is run effectively and safely. ▪ DBS checks carried out by Burns for all volunteer handlers.
Dog safety Out-of-control dog causing undesired event while working with children or while in school environment.	Children/handler/school staff/Burns representative Dog bite potential (abrasions, bruising). *Original risk rating 4 x 4 = 16*	▪ Dog has completed assessment and testing process to ensure they are suitable for the task. ▪ Dog's temperament is suitable. ▪ Dog handler present at all times during the session. ▪ Dog to be kept on lead if not in session with child (handler to be present at all times). ▪ Physical contact with children during sessions must be under full guidance of the handler – outlined in the memorandum of understanding. ▪ Dog in full health at time of session. ▪ Session to take place in quiet and calm area.
Staff/volunteer welfare Burns staff and handler welfare.	Children/handler/school staff/Burns representative Potential for negative effect on person's health if welfare isn't protected. *Original risk rating 5 x 4 = 20*	▪ Any school policies/emergency procedures to be communicated to handler and staff on arrival. ▪ Regular breaks to be taken throughout sessions (toilet, water breaks). ▪ Handler to guide session duration (ensuring dog and handler welfare needs are met).
Fire/emergency procedure Burns volunteers working in schools.	Children/handler/school staff/Burns representative Serious or fatal injury may occur. *Original risk rating 5 x 4 = 20*	▪ Any school policies/emergency procedures to be communicated to handler and staff on arrival. ▪ Teacher/teaching assistant to be present at all times during visit. ▪ Teacher and handler to maintain good communication throughout session, ensuring it is run effectively and safely. ▪ Session to take place in quiet environment away from busy areas – without causing obstruction to walkways or emergency exits.

	Severity (1-5)	Likelihood (1-5)	Risk/ Priority	Additional controls required	Action by whom?	Action by when?
	4	3	12	▪ Dog expectation policy to be written up for handlers to follow at all times. ▪ Any signs of distress or undesirable body language from dog must end the session immediately.		3 weeks
	5	2	10			
	5	2	10	▪ Handler to be given full induction on emergency procedure for school.		On first session

What are the hazards?	Who might be harmed and how?	What controls are already in place?
Control of Substances Hazardous to Health (COSHH) regulations Dog waste/faeces being excreted on site while welfare breaks are taking place. Pathogenic organisms being transmitted from dog to environment or person – increased hazard following dog's consumption of raw food diet.	Children/handler/school staff/Burns representative Potential to cause stomach upsets, infections and/or toxocariasis. *Original risk rating 4 x 4 = 16*	▪ All dog waste to be bagged appropriately and disposed of adequately. ▪ Dogs to be kept up to date with vaccinations. ▪ Regular worm/flea treatment to be given to dog. ▪ Dog to be taken to an area away from children to excrete waste. ▪ All children/staff involved to wash hands post-session (with warm, soapy water) and ensure good hygiene methods are practised. ▪ BBYS dogs are not fed raw food diets – as per recruitment and volunteer policy.
Manager authorised:		

	Severity (1-5)	Likelihood (1-5)	Risk/ Priority	Additional controls required	Action by whom?	Action by when?
	4	2	8			

Source: Burns By Your Side

References and further reading

Abbott, F. (1912) *Society and Politics in Ancient Rome*. New York: Charles Scribner's Sons, pp. 187–188.

Abel, E. L. (2017) 'Therapy dogs help children's reading skills', *The BARk* (July). Available at: https://thebark.com/content/therapy-dogs-help-childrens-reading-skills.

Achenbach, T. M. (1991) *Manual for the Child Behavior Checklist and Revised Behavior Profile*. Burlington, VT: University of Vermont Department of Psychiatry.

Ainsworth, M. D. S. (1991) 'Attachment and other affectional bonds across the life cycle'. In C. M. Parkes, J. Stevenson-Hinde, and P. Marris (eds), *Attachment Across the Life Cycle*. Hove and New York: Routledge, pp. 33-51.

Albuquerque, N., Guo, K., Wilkinson, A., Savalli, C., Otta, E. and Mills, D. (2016) 'Dogs recognize dog and human emotions', *Biology Letters*, 12: 1-5. Available at: https://royalsocietypublishing.org/doi/pdf/10.1098/rsbl.2015.0883.

Allen, K., Shykoff, B. E. and Izzo, J. L. (2001) 'Pet ownership, but not ACE inhibitor therapy, blunts home blood pressure responses to mental stress', *Hypertension*, 38: 815-820.

Alt, K. (2018) 'Life expectancy of dogs: how long will my dog live?', *Canine Journal* (20 July). Available at: https://www.caninejournal.com/life-expectancy-of-dogs.

Anderson, K. L. and Olson, M. R. (2006) 'The value of a dog in a classroom of children with severe emotional disorders', *Anthrozoös*, 19(1): 35-49.

Anthony, R. (2009) 'Farming animals and the capabilities approach: understanding roles and responsibilities through narrative ethics', *Society and Animals*, 17: 257-278.

Antoniades, K. (2015) 'The cat's meow: understanding your feline friend', *Humane Society of the United States* (1 May).

Available at: https://www.humanesociety.org/news/understanding-feline-friend.

Arnold, J. M. (1996) *Animals in Roman Life and Art*. New York: Johns Hopkins University Press.

Arthurson, W. (2013) *Animal Spirits: The Wisdom of Nature*. Stony Plain, AB: Eschia Books.

Aston, R. (2018) *Physical Health and Wellbeing in Children and Youth: Review of the Literature*. OECD Education Working Papers No. 170. Paris: OECD.

Baker, L. and Wigfield, A. (1999) 'Dimensions of children's motivation for reading and their relations to reading activity and reading achievement', *Reading Research Quarterly*, 34(4): 452-477.

Barker, S. B. and Dawson, K. S. (1998) 'The effects of animal-assisted therapy on anxiety ratings of hospitalized psychiatric patients', *Psychiatric Services*, 49: 797-801.

Barkham, P. (2014) 'Do animals have emotions?', *The Guardian* (13 November). Available at: https://www.theguardian.com/lifeandstyle/2014/nov/13/if-only-they-could-talk-.

Barton, B. (2015) *I'm Trying to Love Spiders*. New York: Viking Books.

Beauchaine, T. P. and McNulty, T. (2013) 'Comorbidities and continuities as ontogenic processes: toward a developmental spectrum model of externalizing psychopathology', *Development and Psychopathology*, 25(4): 1505-1528.

Becker, M. B. and Morton, D. (2002) *The Healing Power of Pets*. New York: Hyperion.

Beetz, A. (2013) 'Socio-emotional correlates of a schooldog–teacher-team in the classroom', *Frontiers in Psychology*, 4: 1-7.

Beetz, A., Kotrschal, K., Turner, D. C., Hediger, K., Uvnäs-Moberg, K. and Julius, H. (2011) 'The effect of a real dog, toy dog and friendly person on insecurely attached children during a stressful task: an exploratory study', *Anthrozoös*, 24(4): 349–368.

Beetz, A. and McCardle, P. (2017) 'Does reading to a dog affect reading skills?' In N. R. Gee, A. H. Fine and P. McCardle (eds), *How Animals Help Students Learn: Research and Practice for Educators and Mental Health Professionals*. New York: Routledge, pp. 111–123.

Beetz, A., Uvnäs-Moberg, K., Julius, H. and Kotrschal, K. (2012) 'Psychosocial and psychophysiological effects of human–animal interactions: the possible role of oxytocin', *Frontiers in Psychology*, 3(234): 1–15.

Benjamin, A. and Slocombe, K. (2018) '"Who's a good boy?!" Dogs prefer naturalistic dog-directed speech', *Animal Cognition*, 21(3): 353–364.

Benjamin, N., Pattullo, S., Weller, R., Smith, L. and Ormerod, A. (1997) 'Wound licking and nitric oxide', *The Lancet*, 349(9067): 1776.

Bennett, P. C. and Rohlf, V. I. (2007) 'Owner–companion dog interactions: relationships between demographic variables, potentially problematic behaviours, training engagement and shared activities', *Applied Animal Behaviour Science*, 102(1–2): 65–84.

Bennett, P. C., Trigg, J. L., Godber, T. and Brown, C. (2015) 'An experience sampling approach to investigating associations between pet presence and indicators of psychological wellbeing and mood in older Australians', *Anthrozoös*, 28(3): 403–420.

Berger, P. L. and Luckman, T. (1966) *The Social Construction of Reality*. Penguin: New York.

Bekoff, M. (2007) *The Emotional Lives of Animals*. Novata, CA: New World Library.

Bekoff, M. (2019) 'Are therapy dogs always stressed?', *Psychology Today* (22 June). Available at: https://www.psychologytoday.com/gb/blog/animal-emotions/201906/are-therapy-dogs-always-stressed.

Binfet, J. T. and Struik, K. (2018) 'Dogs on campus: holistic assessment of therapy dogs and handlers for research and community initiatives', *Society & Animals*, 1: 1–21.

Bizub, A. L., Joy, A. and Davidson, L. (2003) 'It's like being in another world: demonstrating the benefits of therapeutic horseback riding for individuals with psychiatric disability', *Psychiatric Rehabilitation Journal*, 26(4): 377–384.

Bodio, S. J. (2009) 'Darwin's other bird – the domestic pigeon', *All About Birds* (15 July). Available at: https://www.allaboutbirds.org/news/darwins-other-bird-the-domestic-pigeon.

Bodson, L. (1983) 'Attitudes toward animals in Greco-Roman antiquity', *International Journal for the Study of Animal Problems*, 4(4): 312–320.

Boissy, A. (1995) 'Fear and fearfulness in animals', *Quarterly Review of Biology*, 70(2): 165–191.

Bowers, J. and Davies, S. (2013) 'Why teachers should read more children's books', *The Guardian* (25 July). Available at: https://www.theguardian.com/teacher-network/teacher-blog/2013/jul/25/teachers-read-more-childrens-books.

Bowlby, J. (1949) 'The study and reduction of group tensions in the family', *Human Relations*, 2: 123–128.

Bowlby, J. (1953) *Child Care and the Growth of Love*. Harmondsworth: Penguin.

Bowlby, J. (1969) *Attachment and Loss*. New York: Basic Books.

Brelsford, V. L., Gee, N. R. and Pfeffer, K. (2017) 'Animal-assisted interventions in the classroom: a systematic review', *International Journal of Environmental Research and Public Health*, 14: 669. Available at: https://pubmed.ncbi.nlm.nih.gov/28640200/.

Bremner, M. (2018) 'How to be human: the man who was raised by wolves', *The Guardian* (28 August). Available at: https://www.theguardian.com/news/2018/aug/28/how-to-be-human-the-man-who-was-raised-by-wolves.

Breure, B. and Heer, S. (2015) 'From a "domestic commodity" to a "secret of trade": snails and shells of land molluscs in early (mainly 16th and 17th century) visual arts', *Basteria*, 79: 81–97.

Buber, M. (2008) *I and Thou*. London: Simon & Schuster.

Burden, R. (2000) *Myself As a Learner*. Birmingham: Imaginative Minds.

Butler, K. (2004) *Therapy Dogs Today: Their Gifts, Our Obligation*. Norman, OK: Funpuddle Publishing Associates.

Buttelmann, D. and Tomasello, M. (2013) 'Can domestic dogs (*Canis familiaris*) use referential emotional expressions to locate hidden food?', *Animal Cognition*, 16(1): 137–145.

Cambridgeshire Community Services (2018) *Social Communication Difficulties and Autistic Spectrum Conditions*. Available at: https://www.cambscommunityservices.nhs.uk/docs/default-source/leaflets---community-paediatrics/0044---social-communication-difficulties-and-autistic-spectrum-disorders.pdf?sfvrsn=4.

Campbell, C. (2013) *Bonzo's War: Animals Under Fire 1939-1945*. London: Constable.

Campbell, E. J. (2016) 'Owners' abilities to recognise and comprehend signs or displays of aggression in their canine companions outwith the home environment', *Veterinary Nursing Journal*, 31: 329–333.

Carlyle, D. (2019) 'Walking in rhythm with Deleuze and a dog inside the classroom: being and becoming well and happy together', *Medical Humanities*, 45: 199–210.

Carr, N. and Cohen, S. (2011) 'The public face of zoos: images of entertainment, education and conservation', *Anthrozoös*, 24(2): 175–189.

Carr, S. and Rockett, B. (2017) 'Fostering secure attachment: experiences of animal companions in the foster home', *Attachment and Human Development*, 19(3): 259–277.

Carrington, E. (1907) *Our Animal Brothers*. London: Wells Gardner, Darton & Co.

Cassels, M. T., White, N., Gee, N. and Hughes, C. (2017) 'One of the family? Measuring young adolescents' relationships with pets and siblings', *Journal of Applied Developmental Psychology*, 49: 12–20.

Castano, E. (2012) 'Antisocial behavior in individuals and groups: an empathy-focused approach'. In K. Deaux and M. Snyder (eds), *The Oxford Handbook of Personality and Social Psychology*. New York: Oxford University Press, pp. 419–445.

Chaline, E. (2011) *Fifty Animals That Changed the Course of History*. London: David Charles.

Chandler, C. K. (2017) *Animal-Assisted Therapy in Counselling*, 3rd edn. Abingdon and New York: Routledge.

Chandler, C. K. and Otting, T. L. (eds) (2018) *Animal-Assisted Interventions for Emotional and Mental Health: Conversations with Pioneers of the Field*. Abingdon and New York: Routledge.

Charman, I. (2016) *The Zoo: The Wild and Wonderful Tale of the Founding of London Zoo*. London: Viking.

Charnetski, J. C. and Riggers, S. (2004) 'Effects of petting a dog on immune system function', *Psychological Reports*, 95: 1087–1091.

Children's Hospital of Eastern Ontario Research Institute (2018) 'Childhood physical inactivity reaches crisis levels around the globe', *ScienceDaily* (26 November). Available at: https://www.sciencedaily.com/releases/2018/11/181126123331.htm.

Clark, S. D., Smidt, J. M. and Bauer, B. A. (2019) 'Welfare considerations: salivary cortisol concentrations on frequency of therapy dog visits in an outpatient hospital setting: a pilot study', *Journal of Veterinary Behavior*, 30: 88–91.

Clements, H., Valentin, S., Jenkins, N., Rankin, J., Baker, J. S., Gee, N. et al. (2019) 'The effects of interacting with fish in aquariums on human health and well-being: a systematic review', *PLoS ONE*, 14(7): 1-36.

Available at: https://doi.org/10.1371/journal.pone.0220524.

Clutton-Brock, J. (1981) *Domesticated Animals from Early Times*. London: Heinemann.

Cole, K. M. and Gawlinski, A. (2000) 'Animal-assisted therapy: the human-animal bond', *AACN Advanced Critical Care,* 11(1): 139–149.

Cole, P. (2006) *All Children Ready for School: Health and Physical Well-Being* (Early Childhood Briefing Paper Series). Bloomington, IN: Indiana Institute on Disability and Community.

Connell, G. (2016) 'Owls across the curriculum: from books to pellet dissection', *Scholastic* (26 February). Available at: https://www.scholastic.com/teachers/blog-posts/genia-connell/owls-across-curriculum-books-pellet-dissection.

Coren, S. (2007) *Why Does My Dog Act That Way? A Complete Guide to Your Dog's Personality*. New York: Free Press.

Coren, S. (2011) 'What a wagging dog tail really means', *Psychology Today* (5 December). Available at: https://www.psychologytoday.com/gb/blog/canine-corner/201112/what-wagging-dog-tail-really-means-new-scientific-data.

Coren, S. (2013) 'Which emotions do dogs actually experience?', *Psychology Today* (14 March). Available at: https://www.psychologytoday.com/us/blog/canine-corner/201303/which-emotions-do-dogs-actually-experience.

Coren, S. (2018) 'No more corgis for Queen Elizabeth?', *Psychology Today* (2 May). Available at: https://www.psychologytoday.com/us/blog/canine-corner/201805/no-more-corgis-queen-elizabeth.

Covey, S. (2013) *7 Habits of Highly Effective People*. London: Simon & Schuster.

Cox, D. (2012) '*War Horse* tramples on western militarism', *The Guardian* (23 January). Available at: https://www.theguardian.com/film/filmblog/2012/jan/23/war-horse-western-militarism.

Craft, A. (2000) *Creativity Across the Primary Curriculum: Framing and Developing Practice*. London and New York: Routledge.

Crawford, J. J. and Pomerinke, K. A. (2003) *Therapy Pets: The Animal-Human Healing Partnership*. New York: Prometheus Books.

Crew, F. (1953) *Devoted to Dogs*. London: Frederick Muller.

Darwin, C. (1872) *The Expression of the Emotions in Man and Animals*. London: John Murray.

David, T., Goouch, K., Powell, S. and Abbott, L. (2003) *Birth to Three Matters: A Review of the Literature*. London: Department for Education and Skills.

Davies, N. (2016) 'Oppositional defiant disorder in the classroom', *Headteacher Update* (7 January). Available at: http://www.headteacher-update.com/best-practice-article/oppositional-defiant-disorder-in-the-classroom/112142.

Davies, T. N., Scalzo, R., Butler, E., Stauffer, M., Farah, Y. N., Perez, S. et al. (2015) 'Animal-assisted interventions for children with autism spectrum disorder: a systematic review', *Education and Training in Autism and Developmental Disabilities*, 50: 316–329.

Davis, A. (2018) 'How much do rabbits cost to keep?', *Money Advice Service* (27 September). Available at: https://www.moneyadviceservice.org.uk/blog/how-much-do-rabbits-cost-to-keep.

Davis, S. J. (1978) 'Evidence for domestication of the dog 12,000 years ago in the Natufian of Israel', *Nature*, 276: 608–610.

Davison, H. (2015) *An Exploratory Study of Primary Pupils' Experiences of Reading to Dogs*. Unpublished doctoral thesis, University of East London.

de Carvalho, I. R., Nunes, T., de Sousa, L. and Almeida, V. (2019) 'The combined use of salivary cortisol concentrations, heart rate and respiratory rate for the welfare assessment of dogs involved in AAI programs', *Journal of Veterinary Behavior*, 36: 26–33. DOI: 10.1016/j.jveb.2019.10.011.

de Milander, M., Bradley, S. and Fourie, R. (2016) 'Equine-assisted therapy as intervention for motor proficiency in children with autism spectrum disorder: case studies', *South African Journal for Research in Sport, Physical Education and Recreation*, 38(3): 37–49.

Dehaene, S. (2009) *Reading in the Brain: The Science and Evolution of a Human Invention*. New York: Viking.

DeLoache, J. S, Bloom, P. M. and LoBue, V. (2011) 'How very young children think about animals'. In P. McCardle, S. McCune, S. Griffin and V. Maholmes (eds), *How Animals Affect Us: Examining the Influences of Human–Animal Interaction on Child Development and Human Health*. Washington, DC: American Psychological Association, pp. 85–99.

Demirbas, Y. S., Ozturk, H., Emre, B., Kockaya, M., Ozvardar, T. and Scott, A. (2016) 'Adults' ability to interpret canine body language during a dog–child interaction', *Anthrozoös*, 29(4): 581–596.

Department for Education (DfE) (2012) *Research Evidence on Reading for Pleasure*. London: DfE. Available at: https://www.gov.uk/government/publications/research-evidence-on-reading-for-pleasure.

Department for Education and Skills (DfES) (2007) *The Early Years Foundation Stage Effective Practice: Respecting Each Other*. London: DfES.

Dew, B. L. (2000) 'Co-therapy with Moses', *Family Journal: Counseling and Therapy for Couples and Families*, 8(2): 199–201.

Dewey, J. (1938) *Experience and Education*. New York: Macmillan.

Dixon, L. M. (2008) 'Feather pecking behaviour and associated welfare issues in laying hens', *Avian Biology Research*, 1(2), 73–87.

Dixon, M. (2018) 'If our children can't recognise British wildlife, how can we expect them to look after it?', *The Telegraph* (4 February). Available at: https://www.telegraph.co.uk/news/2018/02/04/children-cant-recognise-british-animals-can-expect-look.

Dobson, R. (2009) 'Goldfish can feel pain, say scientists', *The Telegraph* (25 April). Available at: https://www.telegraph.co.uk/news/science/science-news/5219686/Goldfish-can-feel-pain-say-scientists.html.

Dogs Trust (2019) 'Our response to dogs in schools'. Available at: https://www.dogstrust.org.uk/news-events/news/2019/school-dogs.

Dowling, M. (2010) *Young Children's Personal, Social and Emotional Development*, 3rd edn. London: Sage.

Drabble, C. (2019) *Introducing a School Dog: Our Adventures with Doodles the Schnoodle*. London: Jessica Kingsley.

Durrell, G. (1956) *My Family and Other Animals*. London: Rupert-Hart Davies.

Dweck, C. (1986) 'Motivational processes affecting learning', *American Psychologist*, 41(10): 1040–1048.

Eckart, K. (2017) 'What the bond between homeless people and their pets demonstrates about compassion', *University of Washington* (16 June). Available at: https://www.washington.edu/news/2017/06/16/what-the-bond-between-homeless-people-and-their-pets-demonstrates-about-compassion.

Ecklund, B. K. and Lamon, K. M. (2008) 'Improving reading achievement through increased motivation, specific skill enhancement, and practice time for elementary students', *Education Resources Information Center*. Available at: http://files.eric.ed.gov/fulltext/ED503058.pdf.

Edwards, N. E. and Beck, A. M. (2002) 'Animal-assisted therapy and nutrition in Alzheimer's disease', *Western Journal of Nursing Research*, 24(6): 697–712.

Edwards, N. E. and Beck, A. M. (2013) 'The influence of aquariums on weight in individuals with dementia', *Alzheimer Disease and Associated Disorders*, 27(4): 379–383.

Eisenberg, N. and Strayer, J. (1987) 'Critical issues in the study of empathy'. In N. Eisenberg and J. Strayer (eds), *Cambridge Studies in Social and Emotional Development: Empathy and its Development*. New York: Cambridge University Press, pp. 3-13.

Eliot, G. (1857) *Mr. Gilfil's Love Story*. In *Scenes of Clerical Life*. Edinburgh: William Blackwood & Sons. Available at: http://www.searchengine.org.uk/ebooks/39/68.pdf.

Elliott, C. D., Smith, P. and McCulloch, K. (1997) *Technical Manual British Ability Scales II*. London: NFER-Nelson.

Emmert, J. (2013) 'Quantifying the impact of incorporating therapy dogs in an afternoon school program: a comparison of net change in reading fluency'. Oral presentation at the ISAZ Conference, Chicago, 17-19 July.

Emmerton, J. (2001) 'Birds' judgments of number and quantity'. In R. G. Cook (ed.), *Avian Visual Cognition*. Medford, MA: Tufts University E-book. Available at: https://pigeon.psy.tufts.edu/avc/emmerton/default.htm.

Endenburg, N. and van Lith, H. A. (2010) 'The influence of animals on the development of children', *Veterinary Journal*, 190(2): 208-214.

Evans, E. P. (1906) *The Criminal Prosecution and Capital Punishment of Animals*. London: Heinemann. Available at: http://www.gutenberg.org/ebooks/43286.

Fagan, B. (ed.) (2009) *The Complete Ice Age*. London: Thames & Hudson.

Farooq, M. A., Parkinson, K. N., Adamson, A. J., Pearce, M. S., Reilly, J. K., Hughes, A. R. et al. (2018) 'Timing of the decline in physical activity in childhood and adolescence: Gateshead Millennium Cohort Study', *British Journal of Sports Medicine*, 52: 1002-1006.

Feinberg, M. (2019) '10 reasons why it sucks to be a class pet', *PETA* (15 February). Available at: https://www.peta.org/students/student-life/why-class-pet-bad-idea.

Fine, A. H. (ed.) (2019) *Handbook on Animal-Assisted Therapy: Foundations and Guidelines for Animal-Assisted Interventions*, 5th edn. San Diego, CA: Academic Press.

Fisher, B. and Cozens, M. (2014) 'The BaRK (Building Reading Confidence for Kids) canine assisted reading program: one child's experience', *Literacy Learning: The Middle Years*, 22(1): 70.

Flynn, C. P. (2008) *Social Creatures: A Human and Animal Studies Reader*. Brooklyn, NY: Lantern Books.

Foltz, R. (2014) *Animals in Islamic Tradition and Muslim Cultures*. Oxford: OneWorld.

Foreman, M. (2015) *The Tortoise and the Soldier: A Story of Courage and Friendship in World War I*. London: Henry Holt & Company.

Fox, A. (2018) 'Pupils' bad behaviour causing teachers to quit, survey finds', *The Independent* (17 December). Available at: https://www.independent.co.uk/news/education/education-news/bad-behaviour-classroom-teachers-quit-childrens-education-disruption-a8685851.html.

Fraley, R. C. and Shaver, P. R. (2000) 'Adult romantic attachment: theoretical developments, emerging controversies, and unanswered questions', *Review of General Psychology*, 4: 132-154.

Fredrickson-MacNamara, M. and Butler, K. (2010) 'The art of animal selection for animal-assisted activity and therapy programs'. In A. Fine (ed.), *Handbook on Animal-Assisted Therapy: Theoretical Foundations and Guidelines For Practice*, 3rd edn. San Diego, CA: Academic Press, pp. 111-134.

Frey, U. J., Störmer, C. and Willführ, K. P. (2011) *Essential Building Blocks of Human Nature*. Dordrecht: Springer.

Friedmann, E., Katcher, A. H., Lynch, J. J. and Thomas, A. S. (1980) 'Animal companions and one-year survival of patients after discharge from a coronary care unit', *Public Health Report*, 95: 307-312.

Friedmann, E., Katcher, A. H., Thomas, S. A., Lynch, J. J. and Messent, P. R. (1983) 'Social interaction and blood pressure: influence of companion animals', *Journal of Nervous and Mental Disease*, 171(8): 461–463.

Friedrich, J. A. (2019) *The Role of Animal-Assisted Interventions in Communication Skills of Children with Autism*. Unpublished PhD thesis, Walden University.

Friesen, L. and Delisle, E. (2012) 'Animal-assisted literacy: a supportive environment for constrained and unconstrained learning', *Childhood Education*, 88(2): 102–107.

Gage, S. (2013) 'David Attenborough: I'm not an animal lover', *Metro* (29 January). Available at: https://metro.co.uk/2013/01/29/david-attenborough-im-not-an-animal-lover-3370670.

Gallard, D. and Taylor, E. (2017) 'Supporting students' mental health and wellbeing through the integration of companion animals into tutorial programmes at a teaching-led university', *Innovations in Practice*, 11(1): 39–49.

Gallup, G. G., Jr, Anderson, J. R. and Platek, S. M. (2011). 'Self-recognition'. In S. Gallagher (ed.), *The Oxford Handbook of the Self*. Oxford: Oxford University Press, pp. 80–110.

Gannon, W. (2012) 'Crows hold grudges in humanlike fashion', *Live Science* (11 September). Available at: https://www.livescience.com/23090-crows-grudges-brains.html.

Gardiner, J. (2006) *The Animals' War*. London: Imperial War Museum.

Gardner, N. (2019) 'Dogs in schools: getting it right', *Headteacher Update* (16 May). Available at: http://www.headteacher-update.com/best-practice-article/dogs-in-schools-getting-it-right/215066/.

Gee, N. R., Belcher, J. M., Grabski, J. L., DeJesus, M. and Riley, W. (2012) 'The presence of a therapy dog results in improved object recognition performance in preschool children', *Anthrozoös*, 25(3): 289–300.

Gee, N. R. and Fine, A. (2019) 'Animals in educational settings: research and practice.' In A. H. Fine (ed.), *Handbook on Animal-Assisted Therapy: Foundations and Guidelines for Animal-Assisted Interventions*. San Diego, CA: Academic Press, pp. 271–284.

Geist, T. S. (2011) 'Conceptual framework for animal assisted therapy', *Child and Adolescent Social Work Journal*, 28: 243–256.

Godfrey-Smith, P. (2017) 'Octopuses: playful, choosy and smarter than you think', *Science Focus* (12 September). Available at: https://www.sciencefocus.com/nature/octopuses-playful-choosy-and-smarter-than-you-think.

Grandgeorge, M., Dubois, E., Alavi, Z., Bourreau, Y. and Hausberger, M. (2019) 'Do animals perceive human developmental disabilities? Guinea pigs' behaviour with children with autism spectrum disorders and children with typical development. A pilot study', *Animals*, 9(8): 522.

Grandin, T. (2008) 'Foreword'. In M. Pavlides, *Animal-Assisted Interventions for Individuals with Autism*. London: Jessica Kingsley, pp. 7–9.

Grandin, T. and Johnson, C. (2009) *Animals Make Us Human: Creating the Best Life for Animals*. New York: Houghton Mifflin Harcourt.

Grigg, R. and Lewis, H. (2016) *A–Z of Learning Outside the Classroom*. London: Bloomsbury.

Grigg, R. and Lewis, H. (2018) *Teaching on a Shoestring: An A–Z of Everyday Objects to Enthuse and Engage Children and Extend Learning in the Early Years*. Carmarthen: Crown House Publishing.

Groves, C. (2012) 'Canine and able: how dogs made us human', *The Conversation* (7 June). Available at: http://theconversation.com/canine-and-able-how-dogs-made-us-human-7394.

Guthrie, J. T., Hoa, A. L., Wigfield, A., Tonks, S. M., Humenick, N. M. and Littles, E. (2007) 'Reading motivation and reading comprehension growth in the later elementary years', *Contemporary Educational Psychology*, 32: 282-313.

Hall, S. S., Finka, L. and Mills, D. S. (2019) 'A systematic scoping review: what is the risk from child-dog interactions to dog's quality of life?', *Journal of Veterinary Behavior*, 33: 16-26. DOI: 10.1016/j.jveb.2019.05.001.

Hall, S. S., Gee, N. R. and Mills, D. S. (2016) 'Children reading to dogs: a systematic review of the literature', *PLoS ONE*, 1(2): e0149759.

Hall, S. S., Wright, H. F. and Mills, D. S. (2017) 'Parent perceptions of the quality of life of pet dogs living with neuro-typically developing and neuro-atypically developing children: an exploratory study', *PLoS ONE*, 12(9): e0185300.

Hamilton, A. (2011) *Zen Mind, Zen Horse: The Science and Spirituality of Working with Horses*. North Adams, MA: Storey Publishing.

Harari, Y. N. (2011) *Sapiens. A Brief History of Humankind*. London: Vintage Books.

Harding, N. G. (2017) 'Maggot debridement therapy: the current perspectives', *Chronic Wound Care Management and Research*, 4: 121-128.

Harvey, J. (2019) *The Animal's Companion: People and their Pets, a 26,000-Year Love Story*. London: Allen & Unwin.

Hattie, J. (2012) *Visible Learning for Teachers: Maximizing Impact on Learning*. Abingdon and New York: Routledge.

Hawkins, R. D. and Williams, J. M. (2017) 'Childhood attachment to pets: associations between pet attachment, attitudes to animals, compassion, and humane behaviour', *International Journal of Environmental Research and Public Health*, 14(5): 490.

Hazan, C. and Zeifman, D. (1994) 'Sex and the psychological tether'. In K. Bartholomew and D. Perlman (eds), *Advances in Personal Relationships: Attachment Processes in Adulthood*. London: Jessica Kingsley, pp. 151-177.

Headley, C. W. (2019) 'The physical and emotional benefits of owning a pet', *Thrive Global* (10 April). Available at: https://thriveglobal.com/stories/physical-emotional-benefits-pet-ownership.

Hebb, D. O. (1949) 'Temperament in chimpanzees: I. Method of analysis', *Journal of Comparative and Physiological Psychology*, 42(3): 192-206.

Hedges, S. (2015) 'Advanced approaches to handling dogs in practice', *Veterinary Nurse*, 6(6): 308-315.

Heimbrod, C. (2019) 'Queen Elizabeth experienced "childlike escapism" after getting her first corgi at 7', *International Business Times* (18 August). Available at: https://www.ibtimes.com/queen-elizabeth-experienced-childlike-escapism-after-getting-her-first-corgi-7-2814763.

Hergovich, A., Monshi, B., Semmler, G. and Zieglmayer, V. (2002) 'The effects of the presence of a dog in a classroom', *Anthrozoös*, 15(1): 37-50.

Herzog, H. A. (2007) 'Gender differences in human–animal interactions: a review', *Anthrozoös*, 20(1): 7-21.

Hildyard, K. and Wolfe, D. A. (2002) 'Child neglect: developmental issues and outcomes', *Child Abuse and Neglect*, 26, 679-695.

Hills, A. M. (1995) 'Empathy and belief in the mental experience of animals', *Anthrozoös*, 8(3): 132-142.

Hines, B. (1968) *A Kestrel for a Knave*. London: Penguin.

Hoehl, S., Hellmer, K., Johansson, M. and Gredeback, G. (2017) 'Itsy bitsy spider …: infants react with increased arousal to spiders and snakes', *Frontiers in Psychology*, 8: 1710.

Horowitz, A. (2017) 'Smelling themselves: dogs investigate their own odours longer when modified in an "olfactory mirror" test', *Behavioural Processes*, 143: 17-24.

Horowitz, A. (2019) *Our Dogs, Ourselves*. London: Simon & Schuster.

Hosey, G. and Melfi, V. (2012) 'Human–animal bonds between zoo professionals and the animals in their care', *Zoo Biology*, 31(1): 13–26.

Hosey, G. and Melfi, V. (2018) *Anthrozoology: Human–Animal Interactions in Domesticated and Wild Animals*. Oxford: Oxford University Press.

Huda (2018) 'Islamic views regarding dogs', *Learn Religions* (1 October). Available at: https://www.learnreligions.com/dogs-in-islam-2004392.

Hunt, S. J., Hart, L. A. and Gomulkiewicz, R. (1992) 'Role of small animals in social interactions between strangers', *Journal of Social Psychology*, 132(2): 245–256.

Hutchins, M. (2015) *The Impact of Accountability Measures on Children and Young People*. London: National Union of Teachers.

Hyde, W. W. (1916) 'The prosecution and punishment of animals and lifeless things in the middle ages and modern times', *University of Pennsylvania Law Review and American Law Register*, 64(7): 696–730.

Ichitani, T. and Cunha, M. C. (2016) 'Effects of animal-assisted activity on self-reported feelings of pain in hospitalised children and adolescents', *Psicologia: Reflexão e Crítica*, 29: 43.

Isaacs, S. (1930) *Intellectual Growth in Young Children*. London: Routledge.

Ismay, J. (2019) 'Why whales and dolphins join the navy, in Russia and the U.S.', *New York Times Magazine* (30 April). Available at: https://www.nytimes.com/2019/04/30/magazine/beluga-whale-russia-military-dolphins.html.

Itoi, A., Yamada, Y., Nakae, S. and Kimura, M. (2015) 'Decline in objective physical activity over a 10-year period in a Japanese elementary school', *Journal of Physiological Anthropology*, 34(1): 38.

Jalongo, M. R., Astorino, T. and Bomboy, N. (2004) 'Canine visitors: the influence of therapy dogs on young children's learning and well-being in classrooms and hospitals', *Early Childhood Education Journal*, 32(1): 9–16.

Jarvis, B. (2018) 'The insect apocalypse is here', *New York Times Magazine* (27 November). Available at: https://www.nytimes.com/2018/11/27/magazine/insect-apocalypse.html.

Johanna, R. (2018) *Benefits and Challenges of Animal-Assisted Pedagogy: Aspects to Consider Before Bringing a Dog to School*. Unpublished bachelor's thesis, University of Oulu. Available at: http://jultika.oulu.fi/files/nbnfioulu-201811233107.pdf.

Johnson, R., Odendaal, J. and Meadows, R. (2002) 'Animal-assisted interventions research issues and answers', *Western Journal of Nursing Research*, 24: 422–440.

Jones, B. (2017) *Animal Assisted Therapies and Reading Interventions: Attitudes and Perceptions of Educators*. Unpublished thesis, University of Dayton, Ohio. Available at: https://etd.ohiolink.edu/!etd.send_file?accession=dayton1501664108849759&disposition=inline.

Jones, M. G., Rice, S. M. and Cotton, S. M. (2019) 'Incorporating animal-assisted therapy in mental health treatments for adolescents: a systematic review of canine assisted psychotherapy', *PLoS ONE*, 14(1): 1–27. Available at: https://doi.org/10.1371/journal.pone.0210761.

Jones, S. (2014) 'Snails in art and the art of snails', *Gresham College* (19 February). Available at: https://www.gresham.ac.uk/lectures-and-events/snails-in-art-and-the-art-of-snails.

Joseph, J., Thomas, N. and Thomas, A. (2016) 'Changing dimensions in human–animal relationships: animal assisted therapy for children with cerebral palsy', *International Journal of Child Development and Mental Health*, 4(2): 52–62.

Julius, H., Beetz, A., Kotrschal, K., Turner, D. and Uvnäs-Moberg, K. (2012) *Attachment to Pets*. New York: Hogrefe.

Kalof, L. (ed.) (2011) *A Cultural History of Animals in Antiquity*. Oxford: Berg.

Kean, H. (1998) *Animal Rights: Political and Social Change in Britain since 1800*. London: Reaktion Books.

Kean, H. and Howell, P. (eds) (2018) *The Routledge Companion to Animal-Human History*. Abingdon and New York: Routledge.

Kellaway, K. (2012) '*War Horse* author Michael Morpurgo on the hidden history behind Steven Spielberg's Oscar contender', *The Guardian* (8 January). Available at: https://www.theguardian.com/film/2012/jan/08/war-horse-michael-morpurgo-spielberg.

Kennel Club (2013) 'Reading to dogs transformed life of boy with dyslexia' (21 May) [press release]. Available at: https://www.littletongreen.staffs.sch.uk/admin/ckfinder/userfiles/files/Files%205/the-kennel-club.pdf.

Kennedy, M. (2013) 'Roman eagle found by archaeologists in City of London', *The Guardian* (29 October). Available at: https://www.theguardian.com/science/2013/oct/29/roman-eagle-found-archaeologists-london-sculpture-art.

Kerry, T. (ed.) (2015) *Cross-Curricular Teaching in the Primary School*. Abingdon and New York: Routledge.

Kessler, R., Amminger, G. P., Aguilar-Gaxiola, S., Alonso, J., Lee, S. and Ustün, T. B. (2007) 'Age of onset of mental disorders: a review of recent literature', *Current Opinion in Psychiatry*, 20(4): 359-364.

Keys, D. 'Roman eagle rises again in London after 2,000 years', *The Independent* (29 October). Available at: https://www.independent.co.uk/arts-entertainment/architecture/roman-eagle-rises-again-in-london-after-2000-years-8911721.html.

Kirnan, J., Siminerio, S. and Wong, Z. (2016) 'The impact of a therapy dog program on skills and attitudes towards reading', *Early Childhood Education Journal*, 44: 637-651.

Kistler, J. (2011) *Animals in the Military*. Oxford: ABC-CLIO.

Knapton, S. (2015) 'Fish tanks lower blood pressure and heart rate', *The Telegraph* (20 July). Available at: https://www.telegraph.co.uk/news/science/science-news/11770965/Fish-tanks-lower-blood-pressure-and-heart-rate.html.

Knight, S. and Edwards, V. (2008) 'In the company of wolves: the physical, social, and psychological benefits of dog ownership', *Journal of Aging and Health*, 20(4): 437-455.

Koehler, O. (1941) 'Vom Erlernen unbenannter Anzahlen bei Vögeln' [On the learning of unnamed numerosities by birds], *Die Naturwissenschaften*, 29: 201-218.

Kogan, L. R., Granger, B. P., Fitchett, J. A., Helmer, K. A. and Young, K. J. (1999) 'The human–animal team approach for children with emotional disorders: two case studies', *Child and Youth Care Forum*, 28(2): 105-121.

Kolb, D. (1984) *Experiential Learning: Turning Experience into Learning*. Englewood Cliffs, NJ: Prentice Hall.

Krachmalnicoff, P. (1977) *The Magic of the Animals*. London: Arlington Books.

Kranzler, E. (1990) 'Parent death in childhood'. In L. E. Arnold (ed.), *Childhood Stress*. New York: John Wiley & Sons, pp. 405-422.

Kretschmann, R. (2014) 'Student motivation in physical education – the evidence in a nutshell', *Acta Kinesiologica*, 8(1): 27-32.

Kropp, J. J. and Shupp, M. M. (2017) 'Review of the research: are therapy dogs in classrooms beneficial?', *Forum on Public Policy Online*, No. 2. Available at: https://forumonpublicpolicy.com/wp-content/uploads/2018/02/Final-Draft-Kropp-and-Shupp.pdf.

Kruger, K. A. and Serpell, J. A. (2006) 'Animal-assisted interventions in mental health: definitions and theoretical foundations'. In A. H. Fine (ed.), *Handbook on Animal-Assisted Therapy: Theoretical Foundations and Guidelines for Practice*. San Diego, CA: Academic Press, pp. 21-38.

Kubinyi, E., Turcsán, B. and Miklósi, Á. (2009) 'Dog and owner demographic characteristics and dog personality trait associations', *Behavioural Processes*, 81(3): 392–401.

Kwong, M. J. (2008) *Not Just a Dog: An Attachment Theory Perspective on Relationships with Assistance Dogs*. Unpublished PhD thesis, Simon Fraser University.

Lakey, B. and Orehek, E. (2011) 'Relational regulation theory: a new approach to explain the link between perceived support and mental health', *Psychological Review*, 118(3): 482–495.

Lane, H. and Zavada, S. (2013) 'When reading gets ruff: canine-assisted reading programs', *Reading Teacher*, 67(2): 87–95.

Langley, L. (2016) 'This is why insects rule the world', *National Geographic* (26 November). Available at: https://www.nationalgeographic.com/news/2016/11/bugs-insects-ants-evolution-beetles.

Lanier, J. L., Grandin, T., Green, R. D., Avery, D. and McGee, K. (2000) 'The relationship between reaction to sudden, intermittent movements and sounds and temperament', *Journal of Animal Science*, 78(6): 1467–1474.

Laurent, E. L. (2000) 'Children, "insects" and play in Japan'. In A. L. Podberscek, E. Paul and J. Serpell (eds), *Companion Animals and Us: Exploring the Relationships Between People and Pets*. Cambridge: Cambridge University Press, pp. 61–89.

Le Roux, M. C., Swartz, L. and Swart, E. (2014) 'The effect of an animal-assisted reading program on the reading rate, accuracy and comprehension of grade 3 students: a randomized control study', *Child Youth Care*, 43: 655–673.

Lenihan, D., McCobb, E., Diurba, A., Linder, D. and Freeman, L. (2016) 'Measuring the effects of reading assistance dogs on reading ability and attitudes in elementary schoolchildren', *Journal of Research in Childhood Education*, 30(2): 252–259.

Levinson, B. M. (1962) 'The dog as co-therapist', *Mental Hygiene*, 46: 59–65.

Levinson, B. M. (1969) *Pet-Oriented Child Psychotherapy*, 1st edn. Springfield, IL: Charles C. Thomas.

Levinson, B. M. and Mallon, G. P. (1997) *Pet-Oriented Child Psychotherapy*, 2nd edn. Springfield, IL: Charles C. Thomas.

Levinson, E. M., Vogt, M., Barker, W. F., Jalongo, M. R. and Van Zandt, P. (2017) 'Effects of reading with adult tutor/therapy dog teams on elementary students' reading achievement and attitudes', *Society & Animals*, 25: 38–56.

Lewis, H. (2017) 'Canines in the classroom: how dogs can support children with additional learning needs in the classroom', *SENCo*, 3(2): 46–47.

Lewis, H. (2018) 'Dogs and dispositions: how animal assisted intervention can improve children's views of themselves as learners'. Paper presented at the International Conference on Thinking, Miami, Florida, 16–20 May.

Lewis, H. (2019) 'The school dog, and why we need to "paws" for thought', *UKEd Magazine*, 55(6): 9–11.

Lewis, H. and Nicholas, O. (2018) 'Animal-assisted interventions in educational settings: exploring the impact of the "Burns By Your Side" reading with dogs scheme'. Available at: https://www.bera.ac.uk/wp-content/uploads/2018/08/BERAreadingdogsHLON.pdf?noredirect=1.

Linder, D., Mueller, M., Gibbs, D., Alper, J. and Freeman, L. (2017) 'Effects of an animal-assisted intervention on reading skills and attitudes in second grade students', *Journal of Early Childhood Education*, 46(3): 323–329.

Lindgren, E., Riordan, C. and Newton, E. (2019) *Exploring Shelter Access Among Animal Guardians: Experiencing Homelessness in New York City*. New York: NYC Street Clinic Research. Available at: https://www.mydogismyhome.org/streetclinic.

Lindon, J. (2003) *Childcare and Early Education*. London: Thompson.

Lipman, M. (1988) *Philosophy Goes to School*. Philadelphia, PA: Temple University Press.

LoBue, V., Pickard, M., Sherman, K., Axford, C. and DeLoache, J. (2013) 'Young children's interest in live animals', *British Journal of Developmental Psychology*, 31(1): 57–69.

Locke, J. (1693) *Some Thoughts Concerning Education*. London: A. & J. Churchill. Available at: https://archive.org/details/somethoughtscon02lockgoog/page/n7.

Loveridge, S. (2017) 'Reading confidence with "Tail Waggin' Tutors"'. Available at https://files.eric.ed.gov/fulltext/ED578670.pdf.

Lowndes, G. A. N. (1937) *The Silent Social Revolution*, 1st edn. Oxford: Oxford University Press.

Lubin, R. (2019) 'David Attenborough's most inspirational quotes and how he's fighting for the planet', *The Mirror* (7 April). Available at: https://www.mirror.co.uk/news/uk-news/david-attenboroughs-most-inspirational-quotes-14199273.

Ludy-Dobson, C. R. and Perry, B. D. (2010) 'The role of healthy relational interactions in buffering the impact of childhood trauma'. In E. Gil (ed.), *Working with Children to Heal Interpersonal Trauma: The Power of Play*. New York: Guilford Press, pp. 26–43.

Lynch, J. J. (1985) *The Language of the Heart*. New York: Basic Books.

MacDonough, K. (1999) *Reigning Cats and Dogs: A History of Pets at Court since the Renaissance*. New York: St Martin's Press.

MacNamara, M. and MacLean, E. L. (2017) 'Selecting animals for education environments'. In N. Gee, A. Fine and P. McCardle (eds), *How Animals Help Students Learn: Research and Practice for Educators and Mental Health Professionals*. Abingdon and New York: Routledge, pp. 182–196.

McClelland, D. (1988) *Human Motivation*. Cambridge: Cambridge University Press.

McGrath, C. (2003) *Teaching Mathematics Through Story: A Creative Approach for the Early Years*. Abingdon and New York: Routledge.

McLaughlin, K. (2016) 'The unintended consequences of dog shaming', *The Clever Canine, RI* (8 January). Available at: http://theclevercanineri.com/blog/2016/1/5/6jba881ue734dtagv1b1koo6h5g2n6.

McNicholas, J. and Collis, G. M. (2000) 'Dogs as catalysts for social interactions: robustness of the effect', *British Journal of Psychology*, 91(1): 61–70.

McSweeney, F. K. and Bierley, C. (1984) 'Recent developments in classical conditioning', *Journal of Consumer Research*, 11(2): 619–631.

Mader, B., Hart, L. A. and Bergin, B. (1989) 'Social acknowledgments for children with disabilities: effects of service dogs', *Child Development*, 60(6): 1529–1534.

Magrane, P. (2016) 'A brief history of dogs', *Daily Telegraph* (26 October). Available at: https://www.telegraph.co.uk/pets/life-and-style/history-of-dogs.

Main, D. (2019) 'Why insect populations are plummeting – and why it matters', *National Geographic* (18 February). Available at: https://www.nationalgeographic.co.uk/environment/2019/02/why-insect-populations-are-plummeting-and-why-it-matters.

Mallon, G. (1992) 'Utilization of animals as therapeutic adjuncts with children and youth: a review of the literature', *Child and Youth Care Forum*, 21(1): 53–65.

Marsa-Sambola, F., Williams, J., Muldoon, J., Lawrence, A., Connor, M. and Currie, C. (2017) 'Quality of life and adolescents' communication with their significant others (mother, father, and best friend): the mediating effect of attachment to pets', *Attachment and Human Development*, 19(3): 278–297.

Martin, F. and Farnum, J. (2002) 'Animal-assisted therapy for children with pervasive developmental disorders', *Western Journal of Nursing Research*, 24(6): 657–670.

Martínez, R. and Fernández, A. (2010) *The Social and Economic Impact of Illiteracy: Analytical Model and Pilot Study*. Santiago: UNESCO. Available at: http://unesdoc.unesco.org/images/0019/001905/190571E.pdf.

Maslow, A. (1954) *Motivation and Personality*. New York: Harper & Row.

May, D. K., Seivert, N. P., Cano, A., Casey, R. J. and Johnson, A. (2007) 'Animal-assisted therapy for youth: a systematic methodological critique', *Human–Animal Interaction Bulletin*, 4(1): 1–18.

Meadows, S. (2018) *Understanding Child Development: Psychological Perspectives and Applications*. Abingdon and New York: Routledge.

Medical Research Council (2004) *MRC Ethics Guide: Medical Research Involving Children*. London: MRC.

Meehan, M., Massavelli, B. and Pachana, N. (2017) 'Using attachment theory and social support theory to examine and measure pets as sources of social support and attachment figures', *Anthrozoös*, 30(2): 273–289.

Meijer, E. (2019) *Animal Languages: The Secret Conversations of the Living World*. London: John Murray.

Meints, K., Racca, A. and Hickey, N. (2010a) 'How to prevent dog bite injuries? Children misinterpret dogs facial expressions', *Injury Prevention*, 16 (Suppl. 1): A68.

Meints, K., Syrnyk, C. and De Keuster, T. (2010b) 'Why do children get bitten in the face?', *Injury Prevention*, 16 (Suppl. 1): A172.

Melson, G. F. (2001) *Why the Wild Things Are: Animals in the Lives of Children*. Cambridge, MA: Harvard University Press.

Mikulincer, M. and Shaver, P. R. (2003) 'The attachment behavioral system in adulthood: activation, psychodynamics, and interpersonal processes'. In M. P. Zanna (ed.), *Advances in Experimental Social Psychology*. New York: Academic Press, pp. 53–152.

Mikulincer, M. and Shaver, P. R. (2007) *Attachment in Adulthood: Structure, Dynamics and Change*. New York: Guilford Press.

Milius, S. (2016) 'Animals can do "almost math"', *Science News for Students* (12 December). Available at: https://www.sciencenewsforstudents.org/article/animals-can-do-almost-math.

Miller, C. (2001) 'Childhood animal cruelty and interpersonal violence', *Clinical Psychology Review*, 21(5): 735–749.

Miller, P. M. and Commons, M. L. (2010) 'The benefits of attachment parenting for infants and children: a behavioral developmental view', *Behavioral Development Bulletin*, 10(1): 1–14.

Mills, D. S., Dubé, M. B. and Zulch, H. (2012) *Stress and Pheromonatherapy in Small Animal Clinical Behaviour*. Hoboken, NJ: John Wiley & Sons.

Mitts-Smith, D. (2010) *Picturing the Wolf in Children's Literature*. Abingdon and New York: Routledge.

Montague, R. (2019) 'Puppy helps boy from Eastleigh cope with autism', *BBC News* (29 August). Available at: https://www.bbc.com/news/av/uk-england-hampshire-49497247/puppy-helps-boy-from-eastleigh-cope-with-autism.

Morell, V. (2015) 'Do animals teach?', *National Wildlife Federation* (28 September). Available at: https://www.nwf.org/Magazines/National-Wildlife/2015/OctNov/Animals/Animal-Teaching.

Morgan, P. L. and Fuchs, D. (2007) 'Is there a bidirectional relationship between children's reading skills and reading motivation?', *Exceptional Children*, 73(2): 165–183.

Morrison, M. L. (2007) 'Health benefits of animal-assisted interventions', *Journal of Evidence-Based Integrative Medicine*, 12(1): 51–62.

Muffitt, E. (2015) 'Children with pets are healthier than those without, study finds', *The Telegraph*, (29 October). Available at: https://www.telegraph.co.uk/pets/owning-a-pet-improves-childrens-health.

Muldoon, J. C., Williams, J. M. and Lawrence, A. B. (2016) 'Exploring children's perspectives on the welfare needs of pet animals', *Anthrozoös*, 29(3): 357–375.

Mulvahill, E. (2019) 'Dogs in the classroom improve SEL, cognitive, and even reading skills', *We Are Teachers* (25 October). Available at: https://www.weareteachers.com/dogs-in-the-classroom.

Muñoz Lasa, S., Máximo Bocanegra, R., Valero Alcaide, R., Atín Arratibel, M. A., Varela Donoso, E. and Ferriero, G. (2015) 'Animal-assisted interventions in neuro-rehabilitation: a review of the most recent literature', *Neurologica*, 30: 1–7.

Muris, P., Merckelbach, H. and Collaris, R. (1997) 'Common childhood fears and their origins', *Behaviour Research and Therapy*, 35: 929–937.

Murry, F. and Todd Allen, M. (2012) 'Positive behavioral impact of reptile-assisted support on the internalizing and externalizing behaviors of female children with emotional disturbance', *Anthrozoös*, 25(4): 415–425.

Myers, G. (1998) *Children and Animals: Social Development and Our Connection to Other Species*. Boulder, CO: Westview Press.

Myers, O. E. (1996) 'Child–animal interaction: nonverbal dimensions', *Society and Animals*, 4(1): 19–35.

Nesse, R. M. and Williams, G. C. (1996) *Why We Get Sick: The New Science of Darwinian Medicine*. New York: Vintage Books.

New, J. J. and German, T. C. (2014) 'Spiders at the cocktail party: an ancestral threat that surmounts inattentional blindness', *Evolution and Human Behavior*, 36(3): 165–173.

Newmyer, S. T. (2011) *Animals in Greek and Roman Thought: A Sourcebook*. Abingdon and New York: Routledge.

Ng, P. T. (2017) *Learning from Singapore: The Power of Paradoxes*. Abingdon and New York: Routledge.

Nicholas, C. E., Wegienka, G. R., Havstad, S. L., Zoratti, E. M., Ownby, D. R. and Johnson, C. C. (2011) 'Dog allergen levels in homes with hypoallergenic compared with nonhypoallergenic dogs', *American Journal of Rhinology & Allergy*, 25(4): 252–256.

Nimer, J. and Lundahl, B. (2007) 'Animal-assisted therapy: a metaanalysis', *Anthrozoös*, 20(3): 225–238.

Nittono, H., Fukushima, M., Yano, A. and Moriya, H. (2012) 'The power of *kawaii*: viewing cute images promotes a careful behavior and narrows attentional focus', *PloS ONE*, 7(9): e46362. DOI: 10.1371/journal.pone.0046362.

Noble, O. and Holt, N. (2018) 'A study into the impact of the Reading Education Assistance Dogs scheme on reading engagement and motivation to read among early years foundation-stage children', *Education 3-13*, 46(3): 270–290.

Nordgreen, J., Garner, J. P., Janczak, A. M., Ranheima, B., Muir, W. M. and Horsberg, T. E. (2009) 'Thermonociception in fish: effects of two different doses of morphine on thermal threshold and post-test behaviour in goldfish (*Carassius auratus*)', *Applied Animal Behaviour Science*, 119(1–2): 101–107. Available at: https://doi.org/10.1016/j.applanim.2009.03.015.

Nussbaum, M. (2004) 'Beyond "compassion and humanity": justice for nonhuman animals'. In C. R. Sunstein and M. C. Nussbaum (eds), *Animal Rights: Current Debates and New Directions*. Oxford: Oxford University Press, pp. 299–320.

O'Haire, M. E. (2013) 'Animal-assisted intervention for autism spectrum disorder: a systematic literature review', *Journal of Autism Developmental Disorder*, 43(7): 1606–1622.

O'Haire, M. E., McKenzie, S. J., Beck, A. M. and Slaughter, V. (2013a) 'Social behaviors increase in children with autism in the presence of animals compared to toys', *PloS ONE*, 8(2): 1–10.

O'Haire, M. E., McKenzie, S. J., McCune, S. and Slaughter, V. (2013b) 'Effects of animal-assisted activities with guinea pigs in the primary school classroom', *Anthrozoös*, 26(3): 445–458.

Ofsted (2014) *Below the Radar: Low-Level Disruption in the Country's Classrooms*. London: Ofsted. Available at: https://www.gov.uk/government/publications/below-the-radar-low-level-disruption-in-the-countrys-classrooms.

Organisation for Economic Co-operation and Development (OECD) (2018) *Children & Young People's Mental Health in the Digital Age: Shaping the Future*. Paris: OECD.

Pagel, M. (2012) *Wired for Culture: Origins of the Human Social Mind*. New York: W.W. Norton.

Panksepp, J. (1998) *Affective Neuroscience: The Foundations of Human and Animal Emotions*. New York: Oxford University Press.

Parfitt, T. (2011) 'Lambs to the slaughter: sheep sacrificed by Kyrgyzstan parliament', *The Guardian* (21 April). Available at: https://www.theguardian.com/world/2011/apr/21/sheep-scarificed-kyrgyzstan-parliament.

Patwardhan, I., Archbell, K., Rudasill, K. and Coplan, R. (2015) 'Shy children in the classroom: from research to educational practice', *Translational Issues in Psychological Science*, 1: 149–157.

Pavlides, M. (2008) *Animal-Assisted Interventions for Individuals with Autism*. London: Jessica Kingsley.

Payne, E., Bennett, P. C. and McGreevy, P. D. (2015) 'Current perspectives on attachment and bonding in the dog–human dyad', *Psychology Research and Behavior Management*, 8: 71–79.

Pederson, H. (2009) *Animals in Schools: Processes and Strategies in Human-Animal Education* (New Directions in the Human–Animal Bond). West Lafayette, IN: Purdue University Press.

People's Dispensary for Sick Animals (PDSA) (2018) *PAW Report 2018: The Essential Insight into the Wellbeing of UK Pets*. Available at: https://www.pdsa.org.uk/media/4372/paw-2018-full-web-ready-a4-printable.pdf.

Pepperberg, I. M. (1987a) 'Evidence for conceptual quantitative abilities in the African grey parrot: labeling of cardinal sets', *Ethology*, 75(1): 37–61.

Pepperberg, I. M. (1987b) 'Acquisition of the same/different concept by an African grey parrot (*Psittacus erithacus*): learning with respect to categories of color, shape, and material', *Animal Learning & Behavior*, 15(4): 423–432.

Pepperberg, I. M. (2013) *Alex and Me: How A Scientist and a Parrot Discovered a Hidden World of Animal Intelligence – and Formed a Deep Bond in the Process*. New York: HarperCollins.

Pets at Home (2015) *The Pet Report 2015*. Available at: http://petreport.petsathome.com.

Pfungst, O. (1911) *Clever Hans (The Horse of Mr. von Osten): A Contribution to Experimental Animal and Human Psychology*, tr. C. L. Rahn. New York: Henry Holt. (Originally published in German, 1907.)

Piaget, J. (1929) *The Child's Conception of the World*. New York: Harcourt.

Piaget, J. (1972) *Psychology of the Child*. New York: Basic Books.

Pimlott, B. (2012) *The Queen: Elizabeth II and the Monarchy*. London: HarperPress.

Pinker, S. (1997) 'Foreword'. In D. McGuinness (ed.), *Why Our Children Can't Read and What We Can Do About It: A Scientific Revolution in Reading*. New York: Free Press, pp. ix–x.

Piper, R. (2017) 'Drugs from bugs: the next blockbuster medicine could be lurking inside an insect', *The Conversation* (27 January). Available at: http://theconversation.com/drugs-from-bugs-the-next-blockbuster-medicine-could-be-lurking-inside-an-insect-71831.

Pollock, C. and Arbona, N. (2017) 'Behavior essentials: the guinea pig', *LafeberVet* (7 November). Available at: https://lafeber.com/vet/behavior-basics-guinea-pig/#12.

Pop, D., Rusu, A., Pop-Vancia, V., Papuc, I., Constantinescu, R. and Vioara, M. (2014)

'Physiological effects of human–animal positive interaction in dogs: review of the literature', *Bulletin of University of Agricultural Sciences and Veterinary Medicine Cluj-Napoca. Animal Science and Biotechnologies*, 71(2): 102-110.

Poresky, R. H. (1990) 'The young children's empathy measure: reliability, validity and effects of companion animal bonding', *Psychological Reports*, 66(3): 931-936.

Porter, J. (2013) 'Back home, little boy mauled in schoolyard by teacher's dog', *Belfast Telegraph* (1 July). Available at: https://www.belfasttelegraph.co.uk/news/northern-ireland/back-home-little-boy-mauled-in-schoolyard-by-teachers-dog-29384602.html.

Premack, D. and Premack, A. J. (2002) 'Why animals have neither culture nor history'. In T. Ingold (ed.), *Companion Encyclopedia of Anthropology*. Abingdon and New York: Routledge, pp. 350-365.

Pressley, M. and Harris, K. R. (2006) 'Cognitive strategies instruction: from basic research to classroom instruction'. In P. A. Alexander and P. H. Winne (eds), *Handbook of Educational Psychology*. Mahwah, NJ: Erlbaum, pp. 265-286.

Price, E. (2004) 'They served and suffered for us', *The Telegraph* (1 November). Available at: https://www.telegraph.co.uk/culture/3626468/They-served-and-suffered-for-us.html.

Prokop, P. and Dale Tunnicliffe, S. (2010) 'Effects of having pets at home on children's attitudes toward popular and unpopular animals', *Anthrozoös*, 23(1): 21-35.

Purewal, R., Christley, R., Kordas, K., Joinson, C., Meints, K., Gee, N. and Westgarth, C. (2017) 'Companion animals and child/adolescent development: a systematic review of the evidence', *International Journal of Environmental Research and Public Health*, 14(3): 234.

Rafferty, R., Breslin, G., Brennan, D. and Hassan, D. (2016) 'A systematic review of school-based physical activity interventions on children's wellbeing', *International Review of Sport and Exercise Psychology*, 9(1): 215-230.

Raidhan, I. (2018) 'Why do cats meow at humans?', *Psychology Today* (5 September). Available at: https://www.psychologytoday.com/gb/blog/all-dogs-go-heaven/201809/why-do-cats-meow-humans.

Rector, M. (2016) 'The effects of canine therapy on academics, behavior, and motivation of students'. *Education Dissertations and Projects*, 153. Available at: https://digitalcommons.gardner-webb.edu/education_etd/153/.

Rees, G., Bradshaw, J., Goswami, H. and Keung, A. (2008) *Understanding Children's Well-being: A National Survey of Young People's Well-being*. York: Children's Society.

Regan, T. (1983) *The Case for Animal Rights*. Berkeley, CA: University of California Press.

Ries, A. E. (2013) 'The effect of animal-assisted therapy on children with disabilities'. Research paper, St Catherine University. Available at: https://sophia.stkate.edu/msw_papers/254.

Ritchhart, R., Church, M. and Morrison, K. (2011) *Making Thinking Visible: How to Promote Engagement, Understanding, and Independence for All Learners*. San Francisco, CA: Jossey-Bass.

Rockett, B. and Carr, S. (2014) 'Animals and attachment theory', *Society and Animals*, 22(4): 415-433.

Ross, S. (2011) *The Extraordinary Spirit of Green Chimneys: Connecting Children and Animals to Create Hope*. West Lafayette, IN: Purdue University Press.

Rossman, Z. T., Padfield, C., Young, D. and Hart, L. A. (2017) 'Elephant-initiated interactions with humans: individual differences and specific preferences in captive African elephants', *Frontiers in Veterinary Science*, 28(4): 60.

Ryff, C. D., Singer, B. H. and Love, G. D. (2004) 'Positive health: connecting wellbeing with biology', *Philosophical Transactions of the Royal Society*, 359: 1383-1394.

Rynearson, E. K. (1978) 'Humans and pets and attachment', *British Journal of Psychiatry*, 133(6): 550-555.

Safina, C. (2018) *Beyond Words: How Animals Think and Feel*. London: Souvenir.

Sanchez, M., Delpont, M., Bachy, M., Kabbaj, R., Annequin, D. and Vialle, R. R. (2015) 'How can surgeonfish help pediatric surgeons? A pilot study investigating the antinociceptive effects of fish aquariums in adult volunteers', *Pain Research and Management*, 20(1): 28-32.

Sandler, I., Gersten, J., Reynolds, K., Kallgren, C. and Ramirez, R. (1988) 'Using theory and data to plan support interventions: design of a program for bereaved children'. In B. H. Gottlieb (ed.), *Marshaling Social Support: Formats, Processes, and Effects*. Thousand Oaks, CA: Sage, pp. 53-83.

Saunders J., Parast, L., Babey, S. H. and Miles, J. V. (2017) 'Exploring the differences between pet and non-pet owners: implications for human–animal interaction research and policy, *PLoS ONE*, 12(6): e0179494. Available at: https://journals.plos.org/plosone/article?id=10.1371/journal.pone.0179494.

Saxton, J. (2009) *Snail Trail: In Search of a Modern Masterpiece*. London: Frances Lincoln.

Schaefer, A. (2015) 'The most common behavior disorders in children', *Healthline* (31 August). Available at: https://www.healthline.com/health/parenting/behavioral-disorders-in-children#1.

Schiffman, R. (2019) 'I had finally found the right place for my son', *New York Times* (5 March). Available at: https://www.nytimes.com/2019/03/01/nyregion/special-needs-school-green-chimney.html.

Schuck, S. E. B., Emmerson, N. A., Abdullah, M. M., Fine, A. H., Stehli, A. and Lakes, K. D. (2018) 'A randomized controlled trial of traditional psychosocial and canine-assisted

intervention for children with ADHD', *Human–Animal Interaction Bulletin*, 6: 64-80.

Seldon, A. (2019) Speech delivered at the University of Buckingham's 5th Ultimate Wellbeing in Education Conference, London, 17 October.

Serpell, J. A. (2010) 'Animal-assisted interventions in historical perspective'. In A. H. Fine (ed.), *Handbook on Animal-Assisted Therapy: Theoretical Foundations and Guidelines for Practice*, 3rd edn. San Diego, CA: Academic Press, pp. 3-20.

Serpell, J. A., Coppinger, R., Fine, A. H. and Peralta, J. M. (2010) 'Welfare considerations in therapy and assistance animals.' In A. H. Fine (ed.), *Handbook on Animal-Assisted Therapy: Theoretical Foundations and Guidelines for Practice*, 3rd edn. San Diego, CA: Academic Press, pp. 481-503.

Sewell, A. (1877) *Black Beauty: The Autobiography of a Horse*. London: Jarrold and Sons. Available at: http://www.gutenberg.org/files/271/271-h/271-h.htm.

Shaver, P. R. and Tancredy, C. (2001) 'Emotion, attachment and bereavement: a conceptual commentary'. In M. S. Stroebe, R. O. Hansson, W. Stroebr and H. Schut (eds), *Handbook of Bereavement Research: Consequences, Coping, and Care*. Washington, DC: American Psychological Association, pp. 63-88.

Shaw, M. (2015) 'Children's animal tales', *British Library* (10 November). Available at: https://www.bl.uk/animal-tales/articles/childrens-animal-tales.

Sheldrake, R. (2011) *Dogs That Know When Their Owners Are Coming Home: And Other Unexplained Powers of Animals*. London: Arrow Books.

Shepherd, K. (2010) 'Ladder of aggression'. In D. F. Horwitz and D. S. Mills (eds), *BSAVA Manual of Canine and Feline Behaviour*, 2nd edn. Gloucester: British Small Animal Veterinary Association, pp. 13-16.

Sherwin, S. (2016) 'Albrecht Dürer's *The Rhinoceros*: the most influential animal picture ever?', *The Guardian* (11 November). Available at: https://www.theguardian.com/artanddesign/2016/nov/11/albrecht-durer-the-rhinoceros-1515.

Shropshire Star (2019) 'Polar bear led to overhaul in way zoos care for such animals, experts say' (7 October). Available at: https://www.shropshirestar.com/news/uk-news/2019/10/07/polar-bear-led-to-overhaul-in-way-zoos-care-for-such-animals-experts-say.

Siejka, A. (2016) 'Tail Waggin' Tutors: a doggone fun way to read', *Children & Libraries*, 14(2): 32–33.

Simpson, C. (2016) 'Effects of standardized testing on students' well-being', Harvard Graduate School of Education (May). Available at: https://projects.iq.harvard.edu/files/eap/files/c._simpson_effects_of_testing_on_well_being_5_16.pdf.

Singer, P. (1990) *Animal Liberation*. New York: Avon Books.

Siraj, I. and Taggart, B. (2014) *Exploring Effective Pedagogy in Primary Schools: Evidence from Research*. London: Pearson.

Skinner, B. F. (1965) *Science and Human Behaviour*. New York: Free Press.

Smith, K. A. (2010) *Impact of Animal Assisted Therapy Reading Instruction on Reading Performance of Homeschooled Students*. EdD dissertation, Northcentral University.

Snaith, E. (2019) 'Native bears and wolves to live side by side in Britain for the first time in 1,000 years', *The Independent* (16 July). Available at: https://www.independent.co.uk/news/uk/home-news/bears-wolves-lynx-wolverine-ancient-woodland-woods-forest-bristol-a9007386.html.

Snider, L., Korner-Bitensky, N., Kammann, C., Warner, S. and Saleh, M. (2007) 'Horseback riding as therapy for children with cerebral palsy: is there evidence of its effectiveness?', *Physical and Occupational Therapy in Paediatrics*, 27(2): 5–23.

Souter, M. A. and Miller, M. D. (2007) 'Do animal-assisted activities effectively treat depression? A meta-analysis', *Anthrozoös*, 20(2): 167–180.

Spadafori, G. (2005) 'Therapy dogs touch those in need', *Boston Globe* (25 August), p. H5.

Sprinkle, J. E. (2008) 'Animals, empathy, and violence: can animals be used to convey principles of prosocial behavior to children?', *Youth Violence and Juvenile Justice*, 6(1): 47–58.

Sroufe, G. E. (2017) 'Foreword: Familiar yet different: human–animal interaction'. In N. R. Gee, A. H. Fine and P. McCardle (eds), *How Animals Help Students Learn: Research and Practice for Educators and Mental Health Professionals*. Abingdon and New York: Routledge, pp. ix–xiv.

Stasi, M. F., Amati, D., Costa, C., Resta, D., Senepa, G., Scarafioiti, C., et al. (2004) 'Pet therapy: a trial for institutionalized frail elderly patients', *Archives of Gerontology and Geriatrics*, 9: 407–412.

Steinberg, M. (2005) *Fiction of a Thinkable World: Body, Meaning, and the Culture of Capitalism*. New York: New York University Press.

Steinmetz, K. (2011) 'Top 10 heroic animals', *Time* (21 March). Available at: http://content.time.com/time/specials/packages/article/0,28804,2059858_2059863_2060458,00.html.

Sterba, J. A., Rogers, B. T., France, A. P. and Vokes, D. A. (2002) 'Horseback riding in children with cerebral palsy: effect on gross motor function', *Developmental Medicine and Child Neurology*, 44: 301–308.

Stock, M. (2016) 'Dogs can read human emotions', *Reuters* (16 February). Available at: https://www.reuters.com/article/us-dogs-emotions/dogs-can-read-human-emotions-idUSKCN0VP1DH.

Svartberg, K. and Forkman, B. (2002) 'Personality traits in the domestic dog (*Canis familiaris*)', *Applied Animal Behaviour Science*, 79(2): 133–155.

Takaloo, N. M. and Ahmadi, M. R. (2017) 'The effect of learners' motivation on their reading comprehension skill: a literature review', *International Journal of Research in English Education*, 2(3): 10-21.

Tardif, T., Fletcher, P., Liang, W., Zhang, Z., Kaciroti, N. and Marchman, V. (2008) 'Baby's first 10 words', *Developmental Psychology*, 44(4): 929-938.

Taylor, N. and Signal, T. D. (2005) 'Empathy and attitudes to animals', *Anthrozoös*, 18(1): 18-27.

Telegraph, The (2018) 'Queen's last corgi dies, ending her 74 year connection with the breed' (26 October). Available at: https://www.telegraph.co.uk/news/2018/10/26/queens-last-corgi-dies-ending-74-year-connection-breed.

Tepfer, A., Ross, S., MacDonald, M., Udell, M., Ruaux, C. and Baltzer, W. (2017) 'Family dog-assisted adapted physical activity: a case study', *Animals*, 7(5): 35. Available at: https://www.ncbi.nlm.nih.gov/pmc/articles/PMC5447917/pdf/animals-07-00035.pdf.

Thagard, P. (2017) 'Do animals have emotions? A debate', *Psychology Today* (14 November). Available at: https://www.psychologytoday.com/us/blog/hot-thought/201711/do-animals-have-emotions-debate.

Thomas, S., Lynch, J., Friedmann, E., Suginohara, M., Hall, P. and Peterson, C. (1984) 'Blood pressure and heart rate changes in children when they read aloud in school', *Public Health Reports*, 99(1): 77-84.

Topolski, R., Weaver, J. N., Martin, Z. and McCoy, J. (2013) 'Choosing between the emotional dog and the rational pal: a moral dilemma with a tail', *Anthrozoös*, 26(2): 253-263.

Treat, W. A. (2013) *Animal-Assisted Literacy Instruction for Students with Identified Learning Disabilities: Examining the Effects of Incorporating a Therapy Dog into Guided Oral Reading Sessions*. Unpublished PhD thesis, University of California, Santa Cruz.

Trujillo, K., Tedeschi, P. and Williams, J. H. (2011) 'Research meets practice: issues for evidence-based training in human–animal interaction'. In P. McCardle, S. McCune, J. A. Griffin, L. Esposito and L. S. Freund (eds), *Animals in Our Lives: Human–Animal Interaction in Family, Community, and Therapeutic Settings*. Baltimore, MD: Paul H. Brookes Publishing, pp. 199-215.

Tuke, S. (1996 [1813]) *Description of the Retreat*. London: Process Press.

Twenge, J. M., Cooper, A. B., Joiner, T. E., Duffy, M. E. and Binau, S. G. (2019a) 'Age, period, and cohort trends in mood disorder indicators and suicide-related outcomes in a nationally representative dataset, 2005-2017', *Journal of Abnormal Psychology*, 128(3): 185-199.

Twenge, J. M., Spitzberg, B. H. and Campbell, W. K. (2019b) 'Less in-person social interaction with peers among U.S. adolescents in the 21st century and links to loneliness', *Journal of Social and Personal Relationships*, 36(6): 1896-1913.

UNESCO (2017) *Literacy Rates Continue to Rise from One Generation to the Next*. Fact Sheet No. 45 (September). FS/2017/LIT/45. Available at: http://uis.unesco.org/sites/default/files/documents/fs45-literacy-rates-continue-rise-generation-to-next-en-2017_0.pdf.

UNICEF (2018) *Learning Through Play: Strengthening Learning Through Play in Early Childhood Education Programmes*. New York: UNICEF. Available at: https://www.unicef.org/sites/default/files/2018-12/UNICEF-Lego-Foundation-Learning-through-Play.pdf.

Usher, A. (2012) *What Is Motivation and Why Does It Matter?* Washington, DC: Center on Education Policy.

van Bree, F. P. J., Bokken, G. C. A. M., Mineur, R., Franssen, F., Opsteegh, M., van der Glessen, J. W. B. et al., (2019) 'Zoonotic bacteria and parasites found in raw meat-based diets for cats and dogs',

Veterinary Record, 182(2): 50. DOI: 10.1136/vr.104535.

Verdet, A. (1952) *Prestiges de Matisse*. Paris: Éditions Emile-Paul.

Viau, R., Arsenault-Lapierre, G., Fecteau, S., Champagne, N., Walker, C. D. and Lupien, S. (2010) 'Effect of service dogs on salivary cortisol secretion in autistic children', *Psychoneuroendocrinology*, 35(8): 1187–1193.

Walsh, M. (1999) 'It was 5 years ago today: when Damien Hirst put a sheep in his tank', *The Independent* (25 April). Available at: https://www.independent.co.uk/arts-entertainment/it-was-5-years-ago-today-when-damien-hirst-put-a-sheep-in-his-tank-1089375.html.

Walton, N. (2013) *Partners: Everyday Working Dogs Being Heroes Every Day*. Dorchester: Veloce Publishing.

Watson, J. B. (1930) *Behaviorism*, rev. edn. Chicago, IL: Chicago University Press.

Weymouth, A. (2014) 'Was this the last wild wolf of Britain?', *The Guardian* (21 July). Available at: https://www.theguardian.com/science/animal-magic/2014/jul/21/last-wolf.

Wells, D. L. (2009) 'The effects of animals on human health and well-being', *Journal of Social Issues*, 65(3): 523–543.

Wells, I. M. (2018) 'Guinea pig costs: how much does it cost to keep a guinea pig?', *Exotic Direct* (30 October). Available at: https://www.exoticdirect.co.uk/news/guinea-pig-costs-how-much-does-it-cost-keep-guinea-pig.

Westgarth, C., Brooke, M. and Christley, R. M. (2018) 'How many people have been bitten by dogs? A cross-sectional survey of prevalence, incidence and factors associated with dog bites in a UK community', *Journal of Epidemiology and Community Health*, 72(4): 331–336.

Westgarth, C., Christley, R. M., Jewell, C., German, A .J., Boddy, L. M. and Christian, H. E. (2019) 'Dog owners are more likely to meet physical activity guidelines than people without a dog: an investigation of the association between dog ownership and physical activity levels in a UK community', *Scientific Reports*, 9: 1–10.

Whitehead, J. (2020) 'Coronavirus: How pets are supporting people through the loneliness of lockdown' (31 March) *The Independent*. Available at: https://www.independent.co.uk/life-style/coronavirus-pets-lockdown-emotional-mental-support-wellbeing-a9435651.html.

Wice, M., Goyal, N., Forsyth, N., Noel, K. and Castano, E. (2020) 'The relationship between humane interactions with animals, empathy, and prosocial behavior among children', *Human–Animal Interaction Bulletin*, 8(1): 38–49.

Wigfield, A. and Guthrie, J. T. (1995) 'Dimensions of children's motivations for reading: an initial study'. Reading Research Report No. 34. College Park, MD: National Reading Research Center.

Wilson, B. (2012) '*War Horse*: the real story – adding some historical heft to the fable', *The Telegraph* (2 March). Available at: https://www.telegraph.co.uk/culture/tvandradio/9114272/War-Horse-the-Real-Story-adding-some-historical-heft-to-the-fable.html.

Wilson, E. O. (1990) *Biophilia*. Cambridge, MA: Harvard University Press.

Wingersky, J., Boerner, J. and Holguin-Balogh, D. (2009) *Writing Paragraphs and Essays: Integrating Reading, Writing, and Grammar Skills*. Boston, MA: Wadsworth Cengage Learning.

Wohlfarth, R., Mutschler, B., Beetz, A., Kreuser, F. and Korsten-Reck, U. (2013) 'Dogs motivate obese children for physical activity: key elements of a motivational theory of animal-assisted interventions', *Frontiers in Psychology*, 4(796): 1–7.

Wohlleben, P. (2016) *The Inner Life of Animals*. London: Vintage.

Wolf, M. (2008) *Proust and the Squid: The Story and Science of the Reading Brain*. New York: HarperCollins.

Wolf, M. (2018) *Reader, Come Home: The Reading Brain in a Digital World*. New York: Harper.

World Animal Net (n.d.) Religion (Chapter 4). In *Animal Welfare in Context*. Available at: http://worldanimal.net/documents/4_Religion.pdf.

Wright, J. and Hensley, C. (2003) 'From animal cruelty to serial murder: applying the graduation hypothesis', *International Journal of Offender Therapy and Comparative Criminology*, 47(1): 71–88.

Yueh-Feng Tsai, L. (2008) *The Effects of Interacting with a Computer-Simulated Virtual Pet Dog on Children's Empathy and Humane Attitudes*. Unpublished PhD thesis, Simon Fraser University. Available at: https://core.ac.uk/download/pdf/56373366.pdf.

Zilcha-Mano, S., Mikulincer, M. and Shaver, P. R. (2011a) 'Pet in the therapy room: an attachment perspective on animal-assisted therapy', *Attachment and Human Development*, 13(6): 541–561.

Zilcha-Mano, S., Mikulincer, M. and Shaver, P. R. (2011b) 'An attachment perspective on human–pet relationships: conceptualization and assessment of pet attachment orientations', *Journal of Research in Personality*, 45(4): 345–357.

Children's books

Allen, J. (2003) *Are You a Snail?* London: Kingfisher.

Browne, A. (1983) *Gorilla*. London: Walker Books.

Browne, E. (1993) *No Problem*. London: Walker Books.

Browne, E. (2006) *Handa's Surprise*. London: Walker Books.

Dahl, R. (1974) *Fantastic Mr Fox*. New York and London: Puffin.

de Saint-Exupéry, A. (1943) *The Little Prince*. New York: Reynal & Hitchcock.

Donaldson, J. (2003) *The Snail and the Whale*. London: Macmillan.

Dubuc, M. (2015) *The Lion and the Bird*, tr. S. Ardizzone. Bristol: Book Island.

Field, J. (2018) *The Way Home for Wolf*. London: Orchard Books.

Forward, T. (2005) *The Wolf's Story: What Really Happened to Little Red Riding Hood*. Somerville, MA: Candlewick Press.

Gaiman, N. (2003) *The Wolves in the Walls*. London: Bloomsbury.

Gravett, E. (2006) *Orange Pear Apple Bear*. London: Macmillan Children's Books.

Gravett, E. (2009) *The Rabbit Problem*. London: Macmillan Children's Book.

Grill, W. (2016) *The Wolves of Currumpaw*. London and New York: Flying Eye Books.

King-Smith, D. (1983) *The Sheep-Pig*. New York and London: Puffin.

King-Smith, D. (1986) *Harry's Mad*. New York and London: Puffin.

King-Smith, D. (1987) *The Hodgeheg*. New York and London: Puffin.

King-Smith, D. (1996) *Harriet's Hare*. New York: Yearling.

Mannix, D. (1967) *The Fox and the Hound*. New York: E.P. Dutton.

Morpurgo, M. (1982) *War Horse*. London: Kaye & Ward.

Murphy, J. (1980) *Peace at Last*. London: Macmillan Children's Books.

Murphy, M. (2013) *Slow Snail*. Somerville, MA: Candlewick Press.

Raschka, C. (2000) *Snaily Snail*. New York: Hyperion.

Rosen, M. (1993) *We're Going on a Bear Hunt*. London: Walker Books.

Rundell, K. (2015) *The Wolf Wilder*. London: Bloomsbury.

Scieszka, J. (1991) *The True Story of the Three Little Pigs*. New York and London: Puffin.

Seuss, Dr (1965) *Fox in Socks*. New York: Random House.

Sidman, J. (2011) *Swirl by Swirl: Spirals in Nature*. Boston, MA: HMH Books.

Soanes, Z. (2018) *Gaspard the Fox*. Llanelli: Graffeg.

Trivizas, E. (1993) *The Three Little Wolves and the Big Bad Pig*. London: Heinemann.

Waddell, M. (1992) *Owl Babies*. London: Walker Books.

Index